THE COLOR OF HOMESCHOOLING

The Color of Homeschooling

How Inequality Shapes School Choice

Mahala Dyer Stewart

NEW YORK UNIVERSITY PRESS

New York

NEW YORK UNIVERSITY PRESS
New York
www.nyupress.org

© 2023 by New York University

Please contact the Library of Congress for Cataloging-in-Publication data.
ISBN: 9781479807819 (hardback)
ISBN: 9781479807833 (paperback)
ISBN: 9781479807864 (library ebook)
ISBN: 9781479807857 (consumer ebook)

New York University Press books are printed on acid-free paper, and their binding materials are chosen for strength and durability. We strive to use environmentally responsible suppliers and materials to the greatest extent possible in publishing our books.

Manufactured in the United States of America

10 9 8 7 6 5 4 3 2 1

Also available as an ebook

For my mother, Pammy, and my grandmothers, Hilda and Jeanne, and for all the mothers who shared their stories.

CONTENTS

Introduction

The Push and Pull to Homeschool

When Lynette's son, Trevor, was seven, his teachers began profiling him as "violent." He had no history of acting violently in school, though he was one of the only Black kids in his class. Lynette attributes the accusation of violence to school administrators' racial fear. Over a steaming cup of coffee, she discusses her decision to homeschool with palpable exasperation: "I just didn't want to have to *keep* going to the principal's office. I'm like, 'You're really targeting my kid for no reason, because he's the second biggest kid in the school.'" Lynette is a middle-class Black woman with two kids: Trevor, and her daughter, Arielle, who is not yet school-age. Before having children, Lynette had worked full-time in the service sector and as an accountant on the side. She pulled back to part-time employment upon becoming a mother, as her husband's career as an executive chef has kept him out from late morning until after their children are in bed five days a week. Now, in addition to picking up occasional shifts on her husband's days off, Lynette is also her son's primary educator. To her, it's worth it: Lynette explains she was pushed into homeschooling by Trevor's discriminatory encounters and the school administration's failure to respond. The result is that Trevor went from being one of the only Black kids in a primarily white classroom to being one of the only Black kids among white homeschoolers.

Maureen is a middle-class white mother who tells me, "Traditional education doesn't work for my kid." Maureen's decision to homeschool stems not from a push out of traditional schools but from a pull toward *intensive mothering* (a term Sharon Hays coined to describe the idea that childcare should be the primary responsibility of mothers, emotionally consuming, labor-intensive, and financially costly).[1] Although she was satisfied with the academic rigor of the charter school her daughter,

Amelia, attended, she worried over the academic and social pressure bearing down on her only child.[2] Further, because she had already pulled out of her career to care for her elderly mother and Amelia after school, it was relatively simple to expand her responsibilities to home-schooling. Like Lynette's husband, Maureen's husband has seen little change to his full-time software engineering career since becoming a father, and he is able to provide for the family financially. In contrast to Trevor, homeschooling has meant another difference in Amelia's educa-tion: she is now in a whiter academic setting than in her charter school since the homeschool group they've joined is primarily white. This, Maureen explains, is only an unintended consequence of a schooling choice made for other reasons—a line of reasoning I heard from other white mothers and one that saturates a great deal of research on whites in nonhomeschools.

In interview after interview with class-advantaged Black and white homeschooling mothers and their nonhomeschooling counterparts, it became clear that popular images of religious fundamentalist or countercultural-type homeschoolers fail to capture the range of ex-periences that structure school choice. Black and white middle-class moms alike described receding from (or even pulling out of) their careers to absorb family responsibilities, while their male spouses "leaned in" to their careers when they became fathers. Notably, while mothers arrived at different schooling choices—homeschools or nonhomeschools—their explanations aligned by race. Black moth-ers point to racial profiling as an unavoidable factor in their decision. Schools operate as racialized institutions,[3] and in the face of racism in public schools, homeschooling or transferring to a different school was one of the few viable options for Black mothers working to provide their child with an anti-racist education. By comparison, white moth-ers explain their choice in nonracial terms as an effort to individualize their child's learning program through homeschooling or transferring schools, despite it contributing to racial segregation in schools. Not "seeing" themselves as part of a racial group or not seeing the influence of race in such a deeply race-inflected context like schooling exposes the privilege of whiteness. Race and racial privilege are invisible to those who have it.

Why Study Homeschooling?

This book will not, and cannot, argue *for* or *against* homeschooling. Whether homeschooling is an adequate form of education must be addressed by educators and philosophers.[4] As a sociologist, I examine homeschooling as an underresearched social phenomenon at the nexus of two of our most prominent social institutions: school and family. I seek to understand why homeschooling continues to rise, how this growth is explained by families' regional context, and what the ramifications are from the merging of these two institutions. Specifically, I've set out to address three questions. First, what are the schooling strategies described by Black homeschooling and nonhomeschooling mothers? Second, how does this compare with the schooling strategies described by white homeschooling and nonhomeschooling mothers? Finally, how do social, legal, cultural, and economic forces shape these families' schooling strategies?

Homeschoolers are misconstrued through two popular images of white marginality: countercultural hippies or fundamentalist Christians. Both types seek to homeschool for ideological reasons that lead to the rejection of the institution of school. The former are politically liberal families who follow less structured schedules and often believe that when children are allowed to lead in their educational trajectories, their natural curiosity will take hold. The countercultural homeschool movement emerged in the 1960s and 1970s, sparked by educators such as Paulo Freire, Jonathan Kozol, and John Holt, who challenged traditional schools' focus on conformity and intellectual orthodoxy.[5] Today, such antiestablishment homeschool families persist in the popular imagination, yet they fail to account for the significant changes that have shaped K-12 schooling and the context within which homeschooling occurs.

The second popular image is that of white fundamentalist Christian homeschool families who are politically conservative and believe a more structured parent-led approach that incorporates religious teachings into daily lessons is the best method for raising good Christian citizens. The Christian homeschool movement also arose during the civil rights era as a response to government intervention in family life, influenced in large part by the research and teachings of a Christian homeschool couple, Raymond and Dorothy Moore.[6] This type of homeschooling was recently the focus of a controversial piece in the *Harvard Gazette* based on research by Elizabeth Bartholet, a professor of law at Harvard. Bartholet, focusing primarily on a perceived boom in Christian homeschooling, argues that the lack of government oversight of homeschooling in the United States "poses a threat to children and society."[7] The post's concerns regarding potential child maltreatment and the assumed inadequacy of homeschools to impart basic academic skills brought a firestorm of critical responses from proponents of homeschooling.

These oversimplified images persist just like other stereotypes. There *are* some homeschooling families who fit the description of Christian fundamentalists or countercultural hippies. And, like other stereotypes, these images hide a lot. They obscure the relevance of twenty-first-century educational inequities, they sidestep the current cultural-political context of homeschooling, and they influence public opinion without nearly enough scrutiny.

Homeschooling has also been misconstrued because the national data on homeschooling trends are so limited. No one actually knows how many families in the United States homeschool their children because collecting data on homeschool families requires household-based rather than school-based surveying. Unlike the annual data collected on children who attend public, charter, and private schools, we can only present estimates. For instance, the most extensive national homeschool data suggest these parents tend to be highly educated and reside in nonpoor households.[8] Only about 16 percent of homeschooling parents identify religious instruction as the most important reason for their decision, suggesting the majority of families homeschool for secular, nonreligious, reasons—such as the 34 percent of parents who said their primary motivation was concern about their child's school environment (safety, drugs, peer pressure).[9] In a society organized by race, class, and gender, it seems shortsighted to assume that family-level decisions regarding education are unaffected by these factors. Considering the context of families' local school environments and the comparative decisions made by families who keep their kids in traditional schools allows for a more nuanced understanding of educational choice. We come to see families as engaged in what I call *strategic schooling*: active work done by middle-class mothers to navigate the race and class context of schools to ensure learning stability for their child.

For the purposes of this study, homeschoolers are families who educate their children at home for more than twenty-five hours per week, not due to temporary illness or other temporary circumstances.[10] This definition excludes the many families who currently oversee their children's at-home learning due to concern of exposure to SARS-COV2/COVID-19 in school. There are two important distinctions between crisis-driven at-home learning and committed homeschoolers. First, parents overseeing at-home learning due to the coronavirus pandemic are likely doing so temporarily and will send their children back to school once outbreaks diminish or when their child is fully vaccinated. Additionally, most of these parents are not constructing their children's primary curricula but are supporting curricula provided by paid teachers.

It is unclear how the pandemic will impact the growth of traditional homeschooling. Families who had previously decided to homeschool may feel vindicated in their decision as they see schools struggling with the pandemic and distance learning. In addition, some families forced into remote learning may come to find at-home learning more desirable than sending their child to school, prompting them to register with their school district and become full-fledged homeschoolers. Other families may conclude that at-home learning is highly *undesirable* and so lean into nonhomeschool options. Another factor that may contribute to the growth of homeschooling in the coming months and years is political polarization. Schools have become a central battleground for these tensions, with many conservative families opposing, and many liberal families supporting, public schools' teaching of the deep legacy of racism and LGBTQ rights.[11] From this vantage point, it seems homeschooling is poised to become an even more prominent feature of American primary education.

The Color of Homeschooling

From the spring of 2014 through the fall of 2016, I interviewed a total of ninety-six Black and white homeschooling and nonhomeschooling mothers. Most respondents lived in or near the city of Elmford, in the US Northeast.[12] These middle-class parents helped me see how race, class, and gender operate within their families' school choices.

My first major finding signals how race shapes school choice. Among Black families, both homeschooling and nonhomeschooling parents frequently made schooling choices to avoid racial hostility, or what I refer to as *Black strategic schooling*. Black nonhomeschoolers dealt with dissatisfaction in their public school by transferring their child to a different school, hoping the new school would be more welcoming, while homeschoolers withdrew from the system entirely. Engaging what Patricia Hill Collins refers to as "motherwork," Black mothers' accounts highlight how race, class, and gender shape their navigation of school choice, while disrupting stereotypes that assume Black parents, particularly mothers, are uninvolved in their children's education.[13] Indeed, I found Black mothers work to resist historic and contemporary racist practices that limit Black children's academic success, through mobilizing school choice as education advocates to improve their children's lives. My choice of the term "Black strategic schooling" is purposeful, building on this research, along with Riché Barnes's concept of "strategic mothering," in which Black professional women privilege marital stability over work stability as they try to counter the racism their families experience.[14] Framing mothers' choices as *strategic* underscores the active work done by Black middle-class women to protect their children from racism in school—and how they privilege their child's schooling stability over other responsibilities.

The primary difference between these families came down to what they saw as feasible based on what their peers were doing. Homeschoolers reported that their relationships with successful homeschooling families led them to see it as a viable option. Those with few examples of successful home education were more likely to transfer their child to another traditional school. Regardless, these findings demonstrate the constraints put on Black families under school choice. They are *pushed* out of schools due to racial discrimination; for these Black mothers, addressing racism is clearly their burden, not the institution's. Race colors the homeschool choice.

Similarly, many of the white homeschooling mothers I spoke with described their choice as a response to the traditional school. Yet, across these respondents, *white strategic schooling* was described not as a consequence of a "push" but as white mothers' *pull* toward providing a more individualized learning experience for their child. Whether they transferred schools or brought their children home, the move often led

TABLE I.1. Strategic Schooling

| School type | Homeschool: Mother provides education |
	Public school: Mother oversees education
Racial identity	Black: Mothers use their class privilege to protect children from racism
	White: Mothers use their race and class privilege to secure advantage

to whiter academic settings—despite many of the white mothers expressing value in racial diversity. Some mothers addressed this tension through enrolling their children in racially diverse, low-stakes settings like extracurricular activities. This demonstrates the privilege of whiteness: white mothers pick and choose when to consider race, making schooling decisions appear nonracial despite their contributing to racial segregation.[15]

A second notable finding in this book is that Black and white class-advantaged women absorb the responsibility of school choice into their motherwork through what I refer to as *protective mothering*.[16] Other scholars have extensively considered how class-advantaged mothers' relationships to family and work are influenced by race.[17] My study builds on their work by adding schooling decisions as a significant site for women's racialized labor. It also builds from research on "security projects," or middle-class mothers' often invisible management of their families' sense of insecurity in politically and economically insecure times.[18] Security projects can involve intensive efforts to prepare children for later success by building flexibility under uncertainty so that parents can secure their own and their children's advantage.[19] I find that highly educated mothers come home from work and in some cases bring their children home too when institutions like schools fail to meet their expectations. Yet these protective strategies are racialized. Black mothers, like Lynette, seek to cultivate self-sufficiency in their children, while white mothers, like Maureen, focus on self-actualization, reflecting how race shapes mothers' approach to preparing children for insecure futures.

Important sociological research has documented homeschooling as labor done by mothers.[20] My research not only confirms this finding but also illuminates the merging of racialized mothering and schooling with class resources. The middle-class Black mothers in my study had a measure of financial flexibility—the ability to capitalize on their class privilege—that they could leverage to seek protection for their children from the racialized institution of schools. Their middle-class white counterparts capitalized on their racial and class privilege in hopes of securing their child's future (see table 1.1). The schooling decisions of these class-advantaged mothers begin to reveal the social processes through which inequities remain intact under school choice. Even when class resources are available, other status markers—race and gender—are implicated.

Motherhood Constructed

Like gender, mothering is socially constructed, not biologically inscribed. A wealth of family scholarship has looked at how gender—socially constructed categories based in perceived sex differences and the practices normative to those categories—is implicated in middle-class mothering. Mothering gets broadly defined as one individual nurturing and caring for another,[21] though it is gendered by expectations about divisions of labor surrounding reproduction. Because of this, mothering is misconceived through essentialist understandings that accept it as a natural, universal, and unchanging aspect of womanhood. All this is upended when we consider the variation in how women experience mothering across historical and cultural contexts. Mothering, that is, varies due to differences in time, political contexts, social policies, and cultural understandings of reproductive labor.[22]

In the United States, the cultural tension between work and family in mothers' lives arose with late nineteenth-century industrialization. As historian Stephanie Coontz explains, the economic and technological shifts of industrialization caused major changes in the meanings of work and family.[23] This included an ideological split between publicly organized production and privately organized consumption, coupled with the social reconception of childhood as emotionally priceless and marked by innocence.[24] The twin conception of intensive mothering— someone must protect and guide all those innocents, after all—emerged, requiring women to center self-sacrifice and moral purity for the family.[25]

Throughout the nineteenth and twentieth centuries most women engaged in mothering guided by the influence of these cultural ideals coupled with the parenting strategies employed within their communities. Their practices were shaped by and judged against their social circumstances (including their intersecting race, class, and gender locations). White class-advantaged mothers have historically been valued, protected, and relied on as ideal mothers (particularly full-time, stay-at-home mothers), while struggling for control over their reproductive capacity. Black mothers, on the other hand, have been deeply contoured by slavery and continuing racial injustice, such that many Black families rely on Black women's participation in the labor market as an aspect of their mothering. That is, Black women's labor was central to colonial expansion, white wealth-building, and the literal reproduction of low-wage workers.[26] Throughout the twentieth century, most Black women held the most devalued jobs. Still, due to the repercussions of their families' generations-long exclusion from living wages, higher education, homeownership, and legal rights, they had little choice but to remain in the paid labor force.[27] Since the civil rights era, many Black women have gained legal rights. However, persistent discrimination in nearly every social sphere shapes their lives, and discrimination cannot be disentangled from their choices about parenting and work—including schooling choices for their children.

The variation in mothering can also be seen in contemporary society. For example, comparing today's Russia and the United States, Jennifer Utrata finds single motherhood is problematized in the United States, whereas in Russia it is normalized.[28] In the United States, which has been shaped by a history of capitalism, cultural narratives normalize the two-parent, heteronormative nuclear family while emphasizing individualism and blaming single mothers for their failure to achieve this ideal family. In contrast, in Russia, which transitioned from socialism to capitalism relatively recently, single motherhood is seen as a by-product of structural problems. For example, there is a lack of eligible men due to a host of social problems and a weak state that no longer provides adequate support to families, particularly single-headed households. These examples show how political and cultural context construct very different notions of mothering (though in both, single motherhood is pathologized).

Thus, despite being popularly conceived as universal and unchanging, mothering is far from either. Theorizing on the social basis of mothering,

Evelyn Nakano Glenn and colleagues ask us to pay attention to variation inherent in mothering rather than drawing a universal and monolithic definition.[29] Nonetheless, politicians and pundits often assume an intensive mothering ideal in which there exists a tension between work and family due to the exorbitant amount of time and emotional, physical, and financial resources mothers are expected to invest in their children.[30] Much research finds evidence that this ideal is pervasive in American families. For example, Pamela Stone found that the rhetoric of choice and the reality of constraint leave white class-advantaged career women anxious in their decisions around work and family.[31] When workplaces fail to accommodate childcare responsibilities—including the perception of achieving a *certain standard* of mothering—these mothers are pushed out of their careers to more zealously care for children and family. Because men are encouraged to lean into their careers and embrace the breadwinner role upon becoming fathers, white class-advantaged women's careers and family paths are not individual choices but instead are structurally constrained, often agonizing decisions between career and family.[32] Intensive mothering, of course, moderates women's conceptualization of themselves as "good" mothers and women, which can lead mothers to view work and family decisions as something they do "for the family." Regardless of whether women remain in the workforce, pull back to work part-time, or leave the workforce altogether, mothers fulfill gendered expectations even in how they explain their choices— they are eager to be seen as putting family needs above their own.[33]

The ubiquity of the cultural contradiction between work and family as seen through intensive mothering is documented through privileged women's navigation of work and family life.[34] Yet as Glenn and colleagues posit, mothering is social, not universal, and while intensive mothering may capture the pressures faced by dominant groups, it does not necessarily capture the reality of mothering for everyone, particularly for women of color, immigrant women, and low-income women.[35] Less research has focused on mothering ideals among Black middle-class mothers or those who experience the privilege of class, yet face racial discrimination.[36] Those scholars who have examined Black middle-class mothering carefully render these mothers' historical context for navigating work and family. For example, Dawn Dow has found that Black middle-class women practice an integrative approach in which work outside of the home, financial independence, and involvement of kin and community are all assumed in mothering.[37] In contrast to intensive mothering, work and family are expected to be integrated rather than in competition. This difference can be attributed to Black women's qualitatively different social context as compared with whites and to their keen awareness of the racial biases their children will experience in relation to schooling, employment, and law enforcement. Class status does not offer the same material resources and security to middle-class Blacks that it does to middle-class whites, and so choosing career *or* family has never been an option. Black Americans will face racism and discrimination in their daily lives, regardless of socioeconomic status.

Educating Our Young

A large body of research considers how social class and race shape children's schooling experiences. Notably, scholarship has thoroughly documented racial bias in education, from children's earliest contact with school systems. Many school administrators and teachers are biased against Black children. For instance, research on the "school-to-prison" pipeline has consistently found that Black children's classroom behavior often is criminalized while the same behavior from white children is normalized as innocent child's play.[38] The racial gap in suspension rates makes this unequal treatment highly visible. Indeed, during the 2013–2014 school year, when I was conducting interviews for this project, Black students were four times more likely to receive an out-of-school suspension than their white peers.[39] As a result, parents plan for this discrimination through their child-rearing. For example, Dow has found that some mothers "border cross," teaching children to traverse lower-income Black spaces and middle-class white spaces. Other mothers "border police," enrolling children in middle-class Black social contexts as a way to build a positive racial identity, while distancing them from the economic struggle of low-income Black families. Finally, some mothers apply a hopefully color-blind approach of "border transcending," encouraging children to embark on lives that are not defined principally by racial identity.[40]

Race is intertwined with class resources, such that Black families experience a particular set of challenges in navigating school choice.[41]

While less research considers Black middle-class families, we can infer that such families seek to balance primarily middle-class white schools, which have a greater concentration of resources, with concerns about their child being the only Black student in the classroom, while curricula may not reflect the lived experiences of their child. We might also infer that those seeking more racially diverse schools are, at the same time, concerned that those schools have fewer material resources, and their children may be learning from out-of-date textbooks in overcrowded classrooms in crumbling buildings. Here race and class work in tandem to produce different expectations through which schooling decisions are made.

Much of the scholarship on middle-class white families' relationship to schools builds from the typology Annette Lareau has found in her research on class-based child-rearing.[42] In particular, "concerted cultivation" involves middle-class parents fostering in their children the skills that map onto success within the middle-class setting of public schools, such as learning to verbally reason with authority figures. Working-class and poor parents also foster valuable skills in their children, including independence, creativity, and maintaining strong bonds with family and with kids in their neighborhood, through the "accomplishment of natural growth." Yet the skills these children develop do not earn them the same benefits in school settings as their middle-class peers. For example, teachers may respond to these child-rearing differences by perceiving working-class children as less engaged should they fail to complete a classroom task, rather than considering that a child may not have entirely understood the assignment and has been taught by their parents not to interrupt a teacher with questions. By contrast, middle-class kids may be seen as engaged because they have learned from their parents to insist on receiving individual accommodations from teachers.[43] Schools' deficit response to the lived experiences that children from less advantaged families bring to the classroom results in the reproduction of social class inequalities.[44]

Middle-class white families' schooling decisions have been well documented and demonstrate the privilege of not having to consider racial discrimination in the process. These families purchase homes in school districts perceived as high-quality based on opinions and information gained through their (white) social networks.[45] They see their residential and schooling choices as reflecting individual concerns about their child's academic, behavioral, and social needs, and they are less likely to note that their ultimate choices are generally whiter and wealthier schools. Even among white class-advantaged parents who decide to keep their children in districts with fewer resources, families may draw on their financial, human, and cultural capital to engage in supplemental education work to ensure their child's ongoing advantage.[46] Thus, school choice results in a struggle for status and distinction as white class-advantaged parents endeavor to pin down their children's material and social advantage, unaware of or inattentive to the ways these choices reinforce race- and class-based school segregation and its associated and lasting inequalities.

Global economic restructuring, particularly in the 1990s, changed American education, situating schools not as a public good and a government responsibility but as education vendors within a quasi-marketplace propelled by neoliberal ideals seen through school choice.[47] *School choice* is a blanket term for a set of policies and rhetoric that emphasizes parents choosing the best school for their child (whether public, charter, private, or home), emphasizing personal responsibility, individual choice, and market solutions.[48] Since this restructuring, schools have been incentivized to focus on accountability, standardization, and central control, which would increase their rankings, enrollment, and funding. Parental choice is linked to competition between schools.[49] High-ranking officials, including our most recent US education secretaries, continue to support school choice, primarily disregarding the ways it has resulted in the isolation of Black and low-income students in underfunded schools and the concentration of white and high-income students in well-funded schools. This additional layer of segregation, atop residential segregation, exacerbates schooling disparities.[50]

Race, Class, and Gender in Schooling Decisions

How does this history of mothering and schooling influence the schooling decisions of Black and white middle-class families? Drawing on Patricia Hill Collins's theory of Black feminist thought, which centers the experience and knowledge of Black women as a way to grapple with questions of power and oppression, *The Color of Homeschooling* starts with Black mothers' narratives to consider how race, class, and gender interact in both Black and white middle-class families' navigation of school choice.[51] The intersectional framework of this book underscores the unequal power between oppressor and oppressed and the variations within each group in how that oppression is experienced.[52] The privilege of the former is not "free-floating" but is directly linked to the disadvantage of the latter.[53] In this way, inequalities are relational. They require that we study those with privilege to better understand how others with fewer resources are denied access to that privilege. Within the context of this book, the opportunities that white middle-class families experience through school choice (mobilized by white mothers) are contributing to Black middle-class families' disadvantage within the traditional school system (despite Black mothers' protective efforts).

Black middle-class women's approach to mothering is different from white mothers' in that they engage in the labor of mothering to protect their children from racism. Yet among Black mothers, protection can look different. They have "the talk," sitting down to discuss race and racism with their young children, in response to their own and their children's experiences in the world as well as anti-Black racism in general. These conversations are made more urgent by national headlines, especially law enforcement's excessive use of force with (and ongoing murder of) Black people, including Eric Garner, George Floyd, Breonna Taylor, Freddie Gray, and Jacob Blake, among countless others. White mothers can choose to avoid these difficult conversations because their children experience the privilege of whiteness. In other words, for white mothers, teaching their children about racial injustice is an exercise in their social awareness, not personal survival.[54]

Class-advantaged mothering varies, but the cultural narratives around what constitutes good mothering and the superiority of prioritizing children and family over careers persist.[55] My research starts with the tension between work and family, as well as another marker of parental success: schooling. I draw on the family-school relationship that education scholar Joyce Epstein theorizes,[56] yet consider the additional sphere of paid work that also shapes relationships across the first two. I build from Dow's theorizing of a market-family matrix, which highlights both dominant ideologies and alternative ideals of mothering that reflect the lived experiences of subordinate groups of women, specifically

Black women.[57] In particular, in this book I consider the market-family matrix in relation to Black and white women's navigation of their child's schooling.

I find homeschooling is the result of school choice and protective mothering logics. Combined, they encourage mothers to be responsible for selecting the best schooling option for their child to compete in an uncertain economic and political world. This is the context that leads some mothers to homeschool. Under school choice, parents (although I find it is invariably mothers) are positioned as active consumers who should seek out the "right" school for their child—whether homeschool or traditional—as part of their child-rearing work. School choice policies effectively hide the extensive labor these class-advantaged women— across school type—do to carefully weigh such options for their children. The work is undeniably racialized, since women's available approaches to managing the particular uncertainties of schooling are shaped by their location in the US racial hierarchy. While surfacing in different contexts, most of the Black and white mothers I interviewed face conflict when they work outside of the home and engage in protective mothering under school choice, encouraging part-time work, or pulling out of the labor force entirely to oversee children's schooling (figure 1.1). This highlights the societal pushes and pulls mothers confront based on racialized gender expectations and available resources.

As family scholars have highlighted, the public and private spheres merge through the blending of school (public) and family (private). Public schools are also based on the relationship between the paid teacher and the student, whereas homeschooling sets up a blending of private life with the unpaid work of class-advantaged mothers. Drawing comparisons to their nonhomeschooling counterparts, I will show that mothers utilize their class resources to protect their children from the racialized institution of schools (Black mothers) or capitalize on their class and race privilege in hopes of securing their child's future advantage (white mothers). This results in both groups experiencing a conflict between school, family, and work.

These findings are sociologically significant because they help us better understand how issues of power and inequality are experienced through the US education system. Black middle-class mothers experience social and economic advantages due to their class status, as

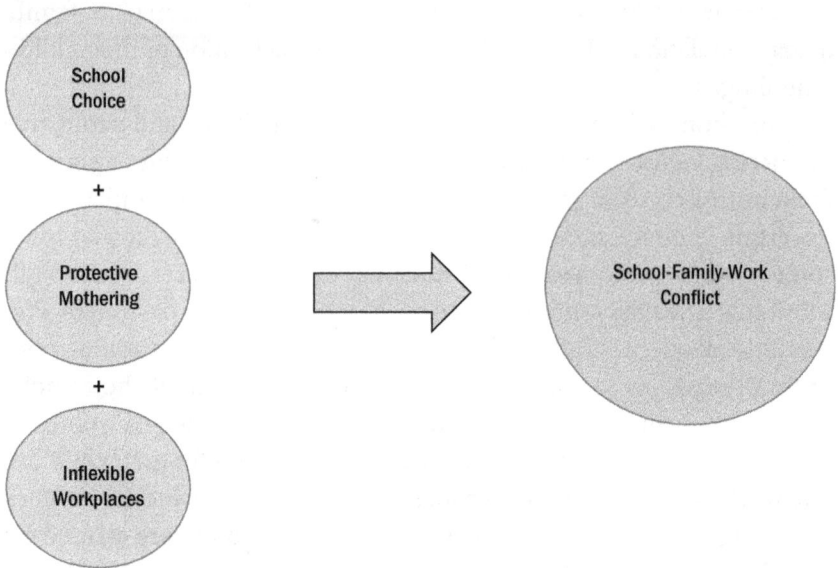

Figure 1.1. School-family-work conflict

well as simultaneous social and economic disadvantages due to their gender and race. Their experiences are qualitatively different from those of white middle-class mothers, who are socially and economically advantaged by both class and racial status and disadvantaged by their gender. Using the analytical lens of intersectionality, *The Color of Homeschooling* provides a window into the operation of race and gender in class-advantaged families.

Study Setting and Sample

Rather than observing families' practices or analyzing survey or textual data available on school choice opinions and policies, I collected in-depth, qualitative interviews. These purposefully center women's stories, so that I can unpack the meaning respondents hold around their schooling decisions. My two years of interviews with ninety-six Black and white families in and around Elmford, a midsize city in the northeastern United States, allow me to detail the regional context, including the politics of school choice and homeschooling in Elmford. For now, I will set the stage by describing the families' demographics.

Social scientists find mothers are more likely than fathers to volunteer to be interviewed about parenting.[58] Despite my intentional use of gender-neutral language in my study recruitment materials, this truism was reinforced: ninety-five of the ninety-six parents who volunteered for this study were mothers (the outlier was a white homeschooling father).[59] I located respondents by contacting homeschool organizations in the region, using respondent-driven sampling to contact other homeschoolers and nonhomeschoolers through the initial sample. I collected additional interviews and observational data in 2014 when I attended an annual, state-run, multiday homeschool conference, observing sessions, milling around the homeschool textbook exhibit hall, and introducing myself to parents between events.

Because I found locating Black homeschoolers to be more challenging, I contacted national Black homeschool groups as well as regional cultural and religious organizations to aid in recruitment. In the end, my interview sample comprised seventeen interviews with Black homeschoolers and twenty-one with white homeschoolers. I conducted interviews with nonhomeschoolers (primarily attending public schools) who were part of homeschool respondents' social networks in the region, making the comparison particularly effective. This led to interviews with fifteen Black and fourteen white middle-class nonhomeschooling mothers. The remaining twenty-nine interviews were conducted with interracial and non-Black mothers of color and those homeschooling outside of Elmford (see appendix B for details about the study).

All respondents had at least one child between the ages of five and eighteen at the time of the interview, and most respondents were partnered in primarily heterosexual relationships. The class advantage and regional focus control for differences, making the homeschool and nonhomeschool comparison meaningful. Together, these data situate each group in relation to the others, allowing me to examine how regional school choice politics are understood and navigated by class-advantaged families.[60]

The majority of respondents are middle-class. All homeschool respondents have at least a college degree, as do nearly half of the nonhomeschool respondents. Only three of thirty-eight homeschool mothers work full-time; seventeen are not in the paid labor force and eighteen work part-time. Most respondents fall within this country's two middle-income brackets (with household incomes over $30,000 and below $200,000); four Black and five white respondents earn above or below this range. Across the forty-six respondents who identified as religious, religiosity varied; most describe attending weekly worship, but a few homeschool families employ religious curricula and daily prayer.

Organization of the Book

The Color of Homeschooling provides a new framework for understanding the relational features of schooling inequalities by studying the other side of the story: schooling decisions of those who are class advantaged, including homeschoolers. This focus allows for a better understanding of how systems work to benefit those who are already advantaged. By applying an intersectional lens,[61] I explore the relational experiences of privilege, magnifying how even when class resources are available, race and gender inequalities are reflected in families' navigation of school choice. While lower-income families may be less able to navigate school choice through relying on mothers' unpaid labor, class-advantaged mothers describe picking up the slack for schools that fail to meet their expectations by seeking alternative options. This continues to lead Black and white women to opt out of paid employment and into unpaid caregiving positions. We begin to see the social processes through which school segregation and unequal gender divisions of labor remain intact under school choice.

Chapter 1 begins with the story of homeschooling's emergence and impact on Black and white families in the United States, primarily in the years since the Supreme Court ruling in *Brown v. Board of Education* (1954) determined educational segregation by race unconstitutional. This period saw legislative changes and social movements around race and gender that shaped integration and spurred homeschooling, followed by a dramatic rise in charter schools and homeschools organized by those social statuses in the 1990s and early 2000s.

Chapter 2 lays the groundwork for the empirical data presented in the subsequent chapters by providing a picture of women's daily routines around paid and unpaid labor. Through examining their explanation of employment before and after becoming mothers, along with their negotiation of these decisions with their spouses, this chapter highlights how, across race and school type, women find themselves opting out of paid employment to care for and navigate schooling their children. Chapter 3 examines how women understand their mothering within the context of their race and social class location. I found that women's conceptualization of mothering is deeply shaped by the material resources available to them, while also intricately linked to their place within the racial hierarchy.

Chapter 4 focuses on women's negotiations of schooling through an examination of how Black mothers understand their schooling decisions. Chapter 5 builds on the prior one but focuses on the white mothers' schooling decisions. Combined, these two chapters consider the strategies these mothers employ to navigate school choice—what I call *strategic schooling*—and how these strategies are influenced by race. Both chapters explicate the relationship between schooling decisions and placemaking, or the places where these families reside, including where they live and where they find community. Chapter 6 uncovers the range of benefits, challenges, and sources of support that homeschooling mothers report. This chapter shows how race, gender, and homeschooling shape women's relationships with nuclear and extended family. The concluding chapter rearticulates the book's central argument and considers broader implications of the research for race, class, gender, motherhood, and school choice. For now, it's time to consider how we got here, from court-ordered school integration to the rise of school choice.

1

Elmford Homeschooling

Regional and National Context

Homeschooling does not happen in a vacuum. Like all education efforts, it reflects social trends and movements, legislative decisions and compromises, and local context along with household particulars. Consider how the following four mothers, all homeschoolers, frame their decisions with respect to race and place.

Jackie and Divinah, both of whom are Black, chose to homeschool to prevent racism from holding their children back. Jackie shared that she had seen the school system's flaccid response to an incident in which a group of schoolgirls excluded a friend's child from play by declaring, "You can't play with us because you're not white." Jackie began homeschooling because she did not want her son to "be encompassed in all that kind of stuff in Elmford." Divinah, who made a similar choice, told me the Elmford public schools "don't care about Black families, they care about the white families." She said it's a "feeling that [her] family has," and described the difficulty in getting the education department to register them as homeschoolers. "My sister, who homeschooled her grandson, tried to get these forms filled out," Divinah recounts, and her sister got no response when she inquired, "'I'm homeschooling him. What should I do?'" With an air of resignation, Divinah sighed, "This is Elmford."

The white homeschooling mothers I interviewed framed their choices in terms of the Elmford schools' curricula and focus, as well as the high cost of local alternatives. They chose to homeschool to provide an education that better fit with their vision for their children. Though Tina echoed Divinah's sense that the Elmford public schools were dismissive, she seemed to attribute that fact to an overburdened school system: "We thought maybe we wanted to put [our son] in Elmford public school, so we made the Elmford public school system aware of him. . . . [But] nobody cares because they have ten thousand truancies a day in Elmford!

They don't have time to track down [my son]." Sarah bluntly reported, "I can't foresee ever going into [the Elmford] public school system." She wanted the more "child-centered" curriculum of the Montessori education model for her son, as well as the teacher stability across school years, but the cost was "extraordinary."

Most research on homeschooling has overlooked the influence of regional school context in parents' decision-making. For example, Mitchell Stevens's work situates homeschooling within the context of social movements, particularly the alternative school movement of the 1960s and 1970s and the Christian day school movement, arguing that families educate their children at home to avoid the mainstream institution of public schools.[1] Jennifer Lois looks to family life, finding that modern homeschooling mothers engage in emotional labor as they try to absorb home education into their ideal mothering duties.[2] Cheryl Fields-Smith, Ama Mazama, and their colleagues provide a crucial scholarly exception, reporting that Black families homeschool in response to the local schooling context—in effect, these families homeschool to avoid racial discrimination.[3] Kate Averett's research is a second exception, finding that a subset of the primarily white Texan families she studied homeschool in response to specific negative experiences in the local public school, while another set are motivated by ideology.[4] These outlier accounts led me to wonder how regional schooling context intertwines with race to shape both Black and white families' educational choices. I build on these scholars' work as I make direct comparisons of how mothers in and around Elmford chose a homeschool or traditional school path for their families.

Before I dive into the mothers' individual decisions, sociology demands that I set the local context in which those decisions are made. In this chapter, I trace important developments in US education policy to provide a sociohistorical context for the decisions parents make around schooling. I begin with the emergence of American compulsory schooling in the second half of the nineteenth century, then move to the racial integration debates that raged from the 1950s through the 1980s (and beyond) and their influence on the reemergence of homeschooling. I consider the emphasis on school choice emerging in the 1990s through 2010s, then close with the history of homeschooling specific to the study site of Elmford.

In the end, I argue that homeschooling in Elmford is not a countercultural protest but, paradoxically, a key feature of the neoliberal, market-based logic that has come to dominate contemporary US schooling. Just as neoliberal logics devolve responsibility to the individual (rather than the state), they put the onus on individual families to determine—and provide—what schooling is appropriate for their child: public, private, charter, or home.

While critics or those unfamiliar with homeschooling may question whether it harms children either academically or socially, the research suggests that children who have been homeschooled experience relative success not only academically and socially but also in gaining access to college. Overall, national and regional studies have found that homeschooled children score at or above their public school peers on standardized tests.[5] For example, a 2010 study found that homeschool students score between the 80th to 90th percentile on reading, language, math, science, and social studies, meaning that 80 to 90 percent of *non*homeschooled children score lower than homeschooled children.[6] When asked, college admission officers report homeschoolers are as academically and socially prepared for college life as public school students.[7] Once enrolled, the research suggests, homeschool students perform at least as well as public high school graduates.[8] This is not necessarily a surprise, as it aligns with nonhomeschool research that finds those who are class privileged are better able to secure academic success for their children, as compared with those who are less class privileged. Thus these results are likely due to the class resources available to those who see homeschooling as a viable option.[9]

In terms of social success, based on a variety of measures, homeschool students are found to be as socially adept as their public school peers. For example, evidence suggests homeschoolers are not socially isolated, as critics fear, but interact with people outside of their family on a daily basis through a range of activities.[10] Confidence, maturity, and positive notions of self are also found to be as strong or stronger among homeschool students as among their nonhomeschool peers.[11] Scant research has examined postcollege adults who were homeschooled, but given what we know about the rigidity of social mobility, we can speculate that those who are homeschooled are able to maintain the class status into which they were born. All this research must be assessed cautiously, since few studies have examined homeschooling families.

Emergence of Compulsory Schooling (Before *Brown*)

Homeschooling in the United States dates back to European settlement. Early colonizers educated their white children at home,[12] teaching them to read, write, and ply the family trade. The brutal system of chattel slavery, which relied on the physical work and agricultural knowledge of enslaved Africans and their descendants, meant that white slave masters prohibited the same education for Black men, women, and children. Still, in secret places and clandestine meetings, enslaved peoples educated themselves. Literacy allowed them to stay abreast of abolitionist activity, and it became an important means for their resistance and resilience throughout slavery and its aftermath.[13]

An educational shift was already underway in the mid-nineteenth century, prior to the Civil War. Reformers would spread their message throughout the United States over the next seventy years, urging states to assume responsibility for the provision of common education.[14] They envisioned school as both a child safety measure and a great equalizer. Up until this point, many children worked long days on farms, in textile mills, or in coal mines; going to school not only would reduce children's dangerous working hours but also would offer poor children access to economic mobility. By the end of the nineteenth century, officials across the nation supported school outside of the home. The city of Elmford was among the first to pass compulsory school attendance laws.

With industrialization, both the meaning of childhood and the purpose of schooling began to change. This shift was in part the result of the birth rate decline, which for married women dropped from 7 births in 1800 to 3.5 by 1900.[15] By the early twentieth century, childhood was reimagined; no longer were children expected to be contributors to the family, although this narrative remained out of reach for poorer families who relied on children's wages to ensure the family was housed and fed. Yet this reimagining of childhood as a learning period in one's life in which one is free from the responsibility of paid work was pervasive, an ideal against which all families contended. Mothers were expected to groom children to become moral adults, in part through overseeing the primary education of their offspring.[16]

The mothering ideals of the time suggested that women devote all their time and energy to raising children and keeping their households running. But this was always out of reach for marginalized women, whose labor was required for paid work to help ensure their families' survival. Black women, poor white women, and immigrant women alike came home from working in the fields or factories alongside their husbands and brothers to complete domestic tasks.[17] Ideal motherhood (indeed, ideal womanhood) was reserved for relatively affluent white women.[18]

Despite wide disparities in women's ability to provide the ideal of childhood learning, education in particular gained recognition as a means for overcoming social disadvantage. As educated adults, adult children would support their families and move up in society. Among Black families, even the poorest placed a particularly high value on education during childhood,[19] and Black children's enrollment in the common school was one of the major wins of the post–Civil War Reconstruction era.[20] Yet systemic racial segregation meant vast disparities in children's educational opportunities. Without reparations in other areas of their lives, such as employment and housing, Black families remained excluded from the economic and political mobility poor whites accessed through public education.

The struggle to earn a living wage during Reconstruction led some Black families to separate. Many Black men moved to northern cities seeking factory jobs, while Black women managed households by themselves.[21] The jobs available to their husbands up north were closed off to Black women, whose only opportunities came in undertaking tasks deemed unsuitable for white women and paid just 50 to 90 percent of white women's wages.[22] In short, accompanying their spouses would not have been worth the trip. Meanwhile, Black women remained essential to education efforts within their communities. Many founded, headed, and taught in Black schools, extending their maternal labors into out-of-home schooling.[23]

Compulsory schooling and the shift from home to school, parent to teacher, never removed parents (at least mothers) from education;

it simply put them in the back seat as supporters and overseers of their children's schooling. In 1897, Alice McLellan Birney and Phoebe Apperson Hearst founded the National Congress of Mothers to seek the betterment of white children's lives through education, health, and safety.[24] In 1926, Selena Sloan Butler founded the equivalent organization for families of color, the National Congress of Colored Parents and Teachers. It was not until 1970 that these two mother-led organizations merged, becoming the national Parent-Teacher Association.[25] Over the intervening years, racial segregation and motherhood were written into the compulsory school equation, while fathers were written out.

For the first several decades of the twentieth century, compulsory schooling was the primary form of education for Black and white children in the United States. Mothers were charged with supporting, but not teaching, their children. Of course, there were still exceptions. For example, in 1906 the Baltimore Calvert School began offering families materials for at-home learning when a whooping cough outbreak took nearly half of its students out of school.[26] The headmaster continued to offer this correspondence education well after the outbreak was contained, providing an option eagerly adopted by families across the country. Military families, traveling entertainers, lighthouse keepers, diplomats, and missionaries all found schooling from home desirable (if rather exceptional). In another example, Frederick Griggs, a Seventh-Day Adventist educator, founded the Fireside Correspondence School in 1909. This religiously oriented homeschool program served thousands of K-12 students throughout the twentieth century.[27] Other families seeking correspondence schooling included those with hospitalized children or children with disabilities, since schools did not offer accommodations to meet their needs; in these cases, mothers provided the home learning, and the children's work was evaluated by outside teachers. Homeschooling had become an option, but at this point an option pursued only as a last resort.

Brown v. Board and the Aftermath (1950s–1990s)

As C. Wright Mills so famously wrote in 1959, "Neither the life of an individual nor the history of a society can be understood without understanding both."[28] Likewise, to understand contemporary homeschooling requires considering individual cases as well as the history of American homeschooling. The reemergence of homeschooling coincided with the end of World War II, civil rights era school reforms, and the emergence of Christian day schools. Homeschooling's continued growth in the 1970s was fueled by white leftists who, generally disillusioned by the government and its handling of the Vietnam War, turned to homeschooling as a form of institutional avoidance.[29]

Some Black intellectuals and activists questioned the power of integrated schools to produce equality for Black students; yet others fought for integration through the work of the National Association for the Advancement of Colored People, which led to the Supreme Court's landmark 1954 ruling in *Brown v. Board of Education*. The *Brown* decision determined that segregated public schools were unconstitutional, given the Reconstruction era "equal protections" of the Fourteenth Amendment. Even so, American schools remained highly segregated and unequal. Desegregation efforts would not be funded and mandated until the passage of the Civil Rights Act of 1964 and the Elementary and Secondary Education Act of 1965. These interventions were focused on urban regions and, in the South, were compelled by courts and overseen by the federal Department of Health, Education, and Welfare.[30] In the North, considered more racially progressive than the former slave states of the South, there were few legal interventions, and education remained highly segregated.

In the years following the *Brown* decision, a variety of schooling alternatives were created by people like those in the Black Power movement, who were skeptical that school integration would actually challenge white power and help liberate Black America.[31] These options included community-controlled public schools, African American independent schools, and Black Panther schools, formed by educators and activists who believed in the purpose of African American–controlled institutions for building Black children's self-respect and knowledge of African American history and culture.[32] For example, in Harlem in 1966, Black Power activists founded the Arthur Schomburg Intermediate School to explicitly foreground Black community control of public schooling.[33] Black organizers advocated for providing high-quality, Black-led schools to promote racial equality.

Although *Brown v. Board of Education* declared "separate but equal" education unconstitutional, it took the passage of the Civil Rights Act and the Elementary and Secondary Education Act to spur formal integration efforts—and, even then, only in the American South. National efforts to integrate schools expanded with another set of Supreme Court rulings, in *Green v. New Kent County* (1968) and *Alexander v. Holmes* (1969), which ruled that freedom-of-choice plans were constitutional only if they supported integrating schools. The rulings did not dissuade Black and white parents who wanted to avoid sending their children to integrated public schools.[34]

In a nine-year period, 1967 to 1976, the typical US city lost roughly 33 percent of its white public school students, though national enrollment of white students dropped by only 6 percent.[35] What happened to the white city kids? A confluence of shifts in urban centers, including racial integration efforts by public schools, prompted many white urbanites to head for the suburbs, while many wealthier white families, especially in the North, pulled their children from public schools in favor of majority white private and parochial schools. That is, some families who did not move still engaged in white flight by seeking segregated educational alternatives, particularly private Catholic day schools.[36] Estimates suggest a 200 percent increase in Christian school enrollment between 1965 and 1975.[37] Together, the trends resulted in a steep decline in white public school enrollment.

Regardless of their intent, homeschool's American resurgence was primarily a white one. Their choice to opt out slowed public school integration. In 1968, 77 percent of Black students attended majority Black schools, with over half of these Black students enrolled in schools where 90 percent or more of their peers were Black.[38] But, with hundreds of school districts around the country made subject to court-ordered desegregation efforts, that changed. By 1980, only 33 percent of Black students attended schools in which 90 percent or more of their classmates were Black, still a substantial proportion but greatly declined from the 1960s.[39]

The Supreme Court's 1974 decision in *Milliken v. Bradley* blocked efforts for interdistrict desegregation, allowing de facto school segregation (usually matching patterns of residential segregation) in cities such as Detroit, Michigan, to continue for decades. Any progress gained in racially integrating school districts in the 1960s was undermined by imbalances between districts,[40] such that white schools continued to have far better resources than Black schools.

At the same time, white Christian parents sought—and were granted—a Supreme Court determination that protected parents' religious practices from state interference in *Wisconsin v. Yoder* (1972).[41] The following year, *Roe v. Wade* (1973) brought the state into the intimate aspects of families lives by giving women the right to choose an abortion. While neither case deals directly with homeschooling, scholars point to both decisions as contributing to the reemergence of religious homeschooling because they raise questions regarding state involvement in family life, the former limiting state involvement, the latter raising the question of the state's role in families' reproductive choices.[42] Together, these cases spurred white Christian parents to pursue homeschooling to keep government out of their lives.

After the *Yoder* decision, homeschool leaders and organizations began to crop up throughout the country, advocating for and modeling the practice. One, the educator John Holt, was an early booster who believed homeschooling was a liberatory endeavor. In his many popular books, including *How Children Fail* (1964), *Teach Your Own* (1967), and *Learning All the Time* (1968), Holt encouraged parents to reject traditional schools. His approach, commonly referred to as *unschooling*, urged parent-educators to follow the child's natural curiosity. Among the religious homeschoolers, Christian couple Raymond and Dorothy Moore were notable influencers. Their book *Home Grown Kids* (1981) rallied parents to take their child's schooling into their own hands. By being the primary educators, parents could instill the traditional family values and spiritual teachings they felt had been stripped from now-secular public schools.

Situated at opposite ends of the political spectrum, both white Christian fundamentalists and white countercultural families populated the modern homeschooling movement as a response to mainstream society and the government's handling of public schools.[43] They did so for starkly different reasons. For Christians, it was the secularization of society; for those engaged with countercultural ideologies, it was the cultural revolution of the 1960s that in contrast to prior generations held a deep mistrust in the US government. This mistrust was likely sparked by a variety of culminating factors, including the government's lack of response to years of anti-war protests, environmental catastrophes,[44] rapid growth in suburbanization, and increased questioning of the underlying function of public schools, which were perceived as instilling conformity and intellectual orthodoxy in children while allowing little room for critical thinking and individuality.[45] For both movements, educating children into an alternative society was a primary solution. This led many countercultural types to go "back to the land," forming communes and isolated societies in often rural regions where they engaged in home-based activities from home birthing to homeschooling. Again, regardless of their intent, the decision to homeschool countered public schools' integration efforts through variants of white flight.

As becomes apparent in the accounts of these early modern homeschoolers, white women's unpaid labor was the engine behind the movement. In her autobiographical piece in the *New York Times*, Margaret Heidenry describes her countercultural mother as assuming full responsibility for homeschooling. After six years, Heidenry's mother sent all four kids to public school: "Mom would only realize it afterward, she wanted a break from being a mother and teacher 24 hours a day, seven days a week."[46]

By the 1980s, homeschooling was common enough that state-enacted homeschool laws were emerging across the country to ensure parents had legal protection should the state challenge their decision to homeschool. Wisconsin was among the earliest states to pass homeschool legislation, in 1983, while Delaware was among the latest, in 1997.[47] The laws and requirements varied significantly by state. For instance, Oklahoma, a state with very little oversight of homeschooling, has legalized the practice as a public school alternative but does not require parents to notify their local school district of homeschooling if their child has never attended traditional school. While parents are expected to teach 180 days during each school year, no reporting of educational progress is required, and there are no subject or curriculum requirements. Some of the most highly regulated states are in the Northeast. For example, in New York, Pennsylvania, Massachusetts, and Rhode Island, parents are subject to teacher qualification requirements, are expected to instruct children in specific subjects, and must provide a yearly, and in some cases a quarterly, assessment of coursework to the state.

State-based homeschool legalization throughout the 1980s and 1990s correlated with rates of school segregation.[48] Regardless of the factors that "pushed" them out of traditional schools, homeschooling families were primarily white. Thus, similar to whites moving their children to suburban public schools or private schools, homeschoolers participated in another form of white flight.

School Choice (1990s–2010s)

One of the most influential organizations that sprang up after *Yoder* was the Homeschool Legal Defense Association, founded in 1983, which provides expertise to homeschooling families navigating state and federal regulations. In more recent years, it has been influential in shaping federal education mandates, including the No Child Left Behind Act (NCLB) and school choice initiatives.[49]

The early period of the reemergence of homeschooling, up until 2000, was marked as a legislatively supported and largely white response to the introduction and development of federal racial integration efforts. More recent trends in homeschooling have instead been shaped by the rollback of government intervention in all realms of family life, including schooling. This, too, is part of the neoliberal shift initiated by the Reagan administration and evidenced by the shifting educational debates from integration (a social goal) to academic achievement (an individual goal). The *Nation at Risk* report of 1983, published during the Reagan administration, focused on a variety of educational reforms that shifted the focus from equity to accountability, including an emphasis on standardized testing.[50]

With standardization and accountability through high-stakes testing, schools were placed in a quasi-marketplace in which the consumers (parents) must choose among products (schools), often by consulting ratings (school and district test scores).[51] In the 1990s, school reforms coalesced around two government-sanctioned approaches to education: (1) publicly financed but privately provided education programs, including vouchers and charters, and (2) a business model of public schooling that emphasized local responsibility under the national regulation of school outcomes. In the new century, NCLB solidified accountability-based school reform by imposing sanctions on schools that failed to meet federal proficiency standards. It also included a provision on school choice, ostensibly giving all students more options by allowing them to transfer out of low-performing schools. Subsequent research has found that NCLB had, at best, a very modest impact on Black students' rates of academic improvement.[52] Absent incentives for higher-performing schools to accept students from lower-performing schools, many students technically have "choice" but are stuck in low-performing schools. Those with more resources are able to leave. Meanwhile, the introduction of Race to the Top in 2008, an initiative that sought to reward states for successful education reform implementation,[53] only exacerbated the federal effort to sanction individual schools for failing to meet benchmarks.

Changes in educational policy, the legalization of homeschooling in the 1980s and 1990s, and the growth of the movement and resources available for homeschoolers have all made home education mainstream. The homeschool population has grown and become more heterogeneous: from 1999 to 2016, the share of the school-age population educated at home nearly doubled (from 1.7 percent to 3.3 percent),[54] and families of color have increased from 25 percent to 41 percent of homeschoolers.[55] Just as when white families took up modern homeschooling, the uptake among families of color led to the emergence of national and local organizations to support them. Notable for this study is the National Black Home Educators resource network, founded by homeschool veterans Eric and Joyce Burges in 2000. Their motto is "empowering parents to educate children for excellence" by providing African American parents with a range of resources, including trainings and consultations, to educate their children at home.[56]

With the emphasis on choice and changes in technology, homeschooling has become part of education reforms for rectifying "failing" public schools. Indeed, the secretary of education at the time of this study, Betsy DeVos, praised state-run programs that funnel tax dollars to homeschoolers (like Florida's, which if awarded provides a onetime $10,000 for homeschools serving children with special needs; recipients can reapply in following years).[57] DeVos was the first education secretary to meet with the Homeschool Legal Defense Association to discuss supporting that organization's efforts.[58] As part of the US government response to the COVID-19 pandemic, DeVos made relief funds available to homeschooling families.[59] More recently, the Education Freedom Scholarships and Opportunity Act has introduced federal tax credits to support voucher programs that can be used for private schools, vocational schools, and homeschools. Together, the past thirty years of school reform efforts demonstrate the mainstreaming of homeschooling as a viable option under school choice.

Homeschooling in Elmford

Like other cities in the Northeast, Elmford and its greater metropolitan region have a contested history of race and schooling.[60] Between 1940 and 1970, Elmford's Black population tripled, yet the city remained highly segregated, and its families grappled with institutionalized racial inequality.[61] Housing and banking authorities had long since divided the geography of the city by race. Elmford has been praised as one of the country's first cities to legally integrate public schools through busing, yet those programs were highly contested throughout the Northeast. Elmford's Black families continued to send their children to increasingly segregated and vastly underfunded schools.

Decades of organizing by Black city residents coupled with a series of national and local shifts laid the groundwork for instituting Elmford's school busing program. For example, in 1967 a group of Black mothers staged a racial justice sit-in at the city welfare office, presenting a list of concrete demands, including an end to unequal education for their children. Protesters gathered outside in solidarity, and the police responded with violence. The city would be roiled throughout that year and in the aftermath of the assassination of Dr. Martin Luther King Jr. the next.

Through the 1970s, members of Elmford's Black community organized to address the public schools' failures regarding Black students. They fought for culturally appropriate curricula that would celebrate Black people and their communities. They fought for Black educators to teach and mentor Black students. And they fought for revisions to schools' disciplinary codes to stop the disproportionate penalizing of Black students. Concurrent demographic shifts, including the decline in birth rates among white women, white out-migration from the region, and an increase in the number of Black immigrant arrivals to Elmford converged with Black residents' ardent organizing in a citywide busing program to support integration efforts. Strong, often violent resistance came from whites in the affected neighborhoods.

Elmford's court-imposed desegregation orders were lifted by the late 1980s. A 1987 ruling rescinded the district order to include racial guidelines in school assignment as a means for desegregation, and in 1988 the city put in place a "controlled choice" system for school assignment. This model divided the city into three geographic zones structured to incorporate students from Black and white neighborhoods within the same schools. Parents rank order their school preference from those within their zone, as well as any school within a one-mile radius of their home. If more parents choose a school for their child than there are seats available, a lottery system decides who gets the desired seat. In 2012, city officials modified the system in attempts to balance school quality with proximity, though this model remains heavily reliant on busing. Several Elmford schools offer citywide access to families who apply, meaning there are multiple options from which families can choose. This is an intradistrict integration plan, and like similar plans in other districts, it has largely failed to affect the metro area's race and class school segregation; this suggests families of color and low-income families still face barriers to full participation in school choice.[62] Similar to other large cities, Elmford is "majority-minority" within city limits, where just under half of the population is white and nearly one-quarter is Black. This contrasts with the state population, which is three-quarters white and less than 10 percent Black. The students living in the city limits are 56 percent low-income, as evidenced by eligibility for free or reduced-price lunch. This means that, to compare middle-class homeschool and nonhomeschool families in my study, I had to expand my fieldwork to include respondents living in the surrounding suburbs.

A broad range of resources are available to homeschooling families in Elmford. For example, no fewer than eighteen homeschool groups are listed on the state's homeschool website. There are also two regional homeschool organizations, well known to the mothers I interviewed. One is a Christian-based organization that I call Homeschool Faith, and the other is a secular group I call Homeschool Advocates.

Homeschool Faith defines its purpose as "promoting and safeguarding home education to the glory of God." Its annual, two-day conference features keynote speakers, homeschool workshops, and support sessions for Christian homeschooling families. The year I attended, 2014, there were two keynote speakers. The first was Mike Donnelly, a white Christian homeschool veteran and representative of the Homeschool Legal Defense Association. His talk, "Rotten to the (Common) Core," was delivered to a packed lecture hall and excoriated the problems he saw with federal and state adoption of standardization through the Common Core curriculum (a set of national math and English standards that states were incentivized to adopt by the Obama administration's 2009 "Race to the Top" grant competition).[63] Donnelly described the Common Core as "one of the most comprehensive overreaches of the federal government" and suggested it "may be unconstitutional." The second keynote speaker was Voddie Bauchman, who describes himself on his website as a "husband, father, former pastor, author, professor, conference speaker, and church planter." Dr. Bauchman, who is Black, spoke on "education and worldview," elaborating on the importance of homeschooling for instilling a biblical worldview in children. This time, the lecture hall was beyond packed. Families stood along the back wall or made do with the available floor space when the seats were filled. At both events, based on a quick scan of the room, I estimated the audience to be about 10 percent people of color and 90 percent white.

Unlike Homeschool Faith, the secular organization Homeschool Advocates does not offer an annual conference for its members. However, according to its website and confirmed by several respondents, Homeschool Advocates does offer a range of local events including how-to meetings that bring together new and veteran homeschoolers. The group also has a well-developed website that provides a range of state-based homeschool information and resources for the "nuts and bolts" of home education. While the meetups offer extensive question-and-answer sessions for new homeschoolers, other events include informational sessions on homeschooling without "breaking the bank," navigating the region's homeschool policy and homeschooler rights, and engaging a homeschool child in the local public schools. Homeschool Advocates self-identifies as welcoming to "anyone interested in homeschooling" and being against all discrimination on the basis of race, religion, gender, gender expression, age, national origin, disability, marital status, sexual orientation, or military status.

Conclusion

The distinctions between Elmford's two homeschool organizations harken back to the reemergence era of homeschooling, primarily defined by Christian fundamentalist or countercultural families. Had I studied homeschooling in Elmford by focusing on Homeschool Faith and Homeschool Advocates, I would have missed the broader educational context I gained in conversation with the city's Black and white homeschooling mothers. For them, homeschooling was not about a religious-secular divide. Instead, Black mothers sought to protect their children from racial discrimination in Elmford public schools, while white mothers sought to create a more individualized learning plan. Both groups were responding to their area schools—indeed, many had enrolled their children in the greater Elmford public school district or surrounding districts before bringing them home for school—and their own explanations of the choice were nearly identical within their racial groups.

Considering again the four mothers, Divinah, Jackie, Sarah, and Tina, from the beginning of the chapter, their reasoning is reflective of what I learned from Black and white mothers throughout my research. While existing research has explored homeschooling within the context of social movements and family life,[64] only Cheryl Fields-Smith, Ama Mazama, and their colleagues have discussed the fact that Black families homeschool to avoid racial discrimination.[65] Elmford and its surrounding area's school system hold a complex history of race, class, and gender politics, some very local, and some filtered down from nationwide fights, that shape the decisions of these homeschooling mothers. Through focusing on this specific northeastern region, I was able to hold context relatively constant while providing an extensive comparison of Black and white, homeschool and nonhomeschool families.

2

The Shape of Women's Work

Why Black and White Mothers Come Home

It was a sunny spring morning when I met Jamie, a Black homeschooling mother, at a Starbucks six blocks from her home. Setting the scene, she tells me that she and her husband both worked full-time before they had their three daughters. When Jaime became pregnant with their first child, Alana, she left her position in the registrar's office at a local college, then worked as a part-time administrative assistant at the family's church while Alana was still quite young. About two years later, she was pregnant again. "It became too much," she remembers, and she left that job, too. A third daughter arrived shortly after the second, and now Jaime describes a packed day-to-day schedule of homeschool child-rearing:

> It's just been me working with [the kids] 24/7 . . . at least four days of school, sometimes we'll take a Friday off and do errands or go on a field trip. . . . We usually only do school three hours for the younger one and typically four to five [for the older ones per day]. . . . We're usually done by midafternoon. I give them a lot of free time [in the afternoon for] reading, sports, and dance. . . . [One daughter] does basketball . . . [the other daughter] plays soccer . . . [my youngest] was also doing soccer this year. . . . We go to the library a lot and parks, museums.

Jamie is the primary caregiver and teacher of her three children, an especially demanding role because her husband's job often takes him out of town for weeks on end. To shore up support for Jaime in his absence, the family moved closer to Jaime's parents.

For families with kids in traditional school, the school provides not only the child's primary education but also serves as day care. Thus, by choosing to homeschool, mothers like Jaime are taking on the role not just of primary educator but also of day care provider. For many of the Black homeschoolers I met—and many class-advantaged Black families regardless of their educational choice—extended kin are an important part of the logistics when it comes to fulfilling education and care responsibilities. In Jaime's case, her children's grandfather is now involved in their homeschooling. For instance, Jaime says, "My dad is very into math, so just recently he's been sitting down with Alana and working with her on her math." Tapping into extended kin networks can also provide Black mothers and their kids with a way to avoid racial discrimination in dominant institutions like day care centers.[1] In this case, it also provides support for homeschooling, which, as we saw in chapter 1, is itself a racism-avoidance strategy for Black families.

Historically and still today, women remain responsible for the task of caring for children, sick, and elderly while being curtailed in various ways from building their careers. Competitive markets have shifted this form of patriarchal power, allowing more privileged women to outsource this care rather than provide it themselves. Yet the cost of such care is high, excluding many families from participating, while state subsidies are always at risk of being cut, often leading to reductions in quality of care. The economist Nancy Folbre highlights how this caring labor, which tends to rely on love, obligation, and reciprocity, has a direct emotional impact on well-being yet is hard to measure.[2] Within the competitive marketplace, such work gets devalued, which leads to a conflict of interest between family members; one spouse benefits when the other leaves the workforce to provide care work. In the United States, a persistent cultural narrative around intensive mothering and the righteousness of women placing children and family above all else results in pressures that both Black and white class-advantaged women must navigate. Albeit gendered, racism results in this narrative holding different meanings based on race, since unlike whites, Black mothers have historically been excluded from this patriarchal discourse.[3] Regardless, across race many class-advantaged women experience work and family as in conflict, as some women are pushed out of their careers.[4] Economic reasoning, a result of the gender wage gap, is particularly likely to push women to take on this care work at the expense of their careers.[5] In some other countries, this tension is eased by generous paid maternal and paternal leave, state-subsidized quality childcare, and K-12

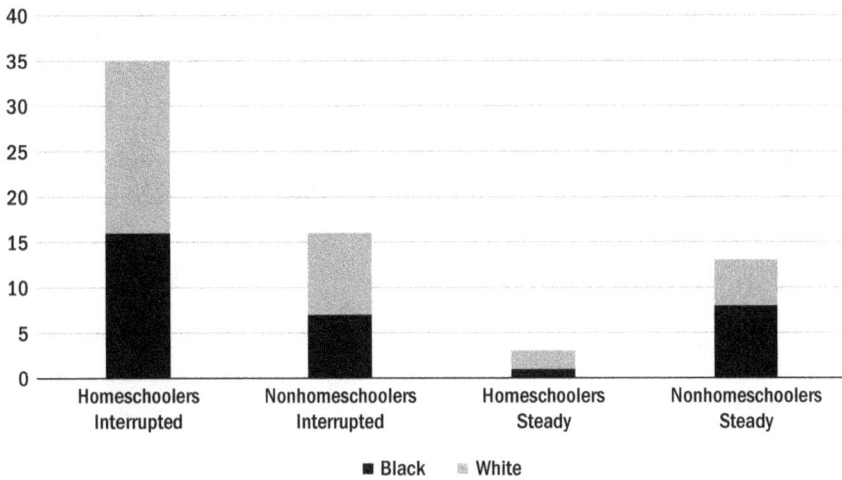

Figure 2.1. Career paths by school type and race

schooling. Yet in the United States, sharing responsibilities for the care of others is overshadowed by a cultural emphasis on intensive mothering and individualism, or each family for themselves.[6]

Across race, most respondents described similar work trajectories: established in careers with clear paths for advancement, these women opted out of full-time paid work to fulfill their families' various caregiving needs, while their spouses leaned into careers upon becoming a parent. Those women whose families chose to homeschool shouldered the task of educating as an extension of their caregiving duties. Those women whose families did not homeschool came home to provide care, manage the families' hectic schedules, and in some cases *oversee* their children's education, all as an extension of their caregiving duties. By considering mothers' career trajectories and daily schedules, this chapter reveals the various tensions between work and family obligation that these women face.

More than two-thirds of the Black women I interviewed (23 of 32, as presented in figure 2.1) and 28 of 35 white women had disrupted their careers upon becoming mothers, despite having invested many years in their educations and jobs. In my sample, 42 of 51 interviewees whose careers were interrupted held a bachelor's degree (several also had graduate degrees). Notably, only 5 (3 Black and 2 white) of these 51 were unmarried, meaning that most respondents were able to rely on their spouse for their household's financial support.[7]

Some of those who interrupted their careers continued to work part-time, while others, including over a third of Black and white women opted out entirely after having children. Broken down by school type, 16 (of 17) Black homeschoolers interrupted their careers, and 19 (of 21) white homeschoolers disrupted their careers. Just under half of Black nonhomeschoolers (7 of 15) and more than half of white nonhome-schoolers (9 of 14) interrupted their careers.

Homeschoolers Who Interrupted Careers

Both Black and white homeschooling mothers who had interrupted their careers expressed tensions that resembled what Pamela Stone calls a "choice gap": American women caught between the conditions of work and the lack of support for family obligations.[8] When those family responsibilities include the work of providing their children's primary education, a mother's career can be first on the chopping block—even though few of the women I interviewed identified homeschooling as the reason for leaving their career. Instead, most of these mothers retrospectively cited the failure of schools to meet their expectations as a reason they chose to *remain* out of the labor force.

Clara, a Black homeschooler, worked in the banking industry before she and her husband, a full-time church deacon, expanded their family. Now, with five kids, she is a full-time homeschooling mom. "We wanted someone to be home with the kids," Clara tells me, and though she "loved" her work, she knows working and raising a family at the same time would be "way too emotionally draining" for her. The couple initially started the kids in the local public school, but Clara's mothering responsibilities eventually expanded when they decided to homeschool. Her resulting daily schedule, like Jamie's, sounds rather hectic:

> I [lay out the kids'] daily and their weekly schedule of what they were expected to get done. . . . I work with a consultant to figure out what it is I'm doing. . . . Our local community college runs a program of classes during the day for homeschooled kids . . . so several of my kids actually [take] some classes there. . . . There was a secular homeschool group that

we belonged to . . . we did some writing classes there. . . . They've been involved in community sports . . . [and] theater.

While Clara is the primary caregiver and educator, her husband works long hours to provide for the family financially, which includes support- ing the children's supplementary writing classes, community college courses, extracurricular activities and paying a homeschool consultant. Despite "loving" her career, Clara does not believe that a two-earner household fits with what her family needs: a stay-at-home mom who can provide the children's care and education.

Julia is a Black mother with seven children, all being homeschooled. Her husband, the primary breadwinner, works full-time as a manager for a software product company. Julia works a few hours per week as a home-based customer service representative, and like Clara, her moth- ering responsibilities include being the primary caregiver and educator for their kids. To make Julia's part-time job feasible, her parents help out with the children's schooling. In particular, she notes: "I have a dad in the Chicago area who is a retired teacher . . . [he] is very good with the math and science . . . My daughter . . . she does her physics [with him]. She will scan her work, email it to granddad. He marks it and sends it back with comments. It's a huge help." When I inquire about her weekly schedule, Julia's response reveals the extent of her managerial skills:

> A typical week includes . . . driving [my two youngest] to lessons. Piano, ballet . . . they go to chorus . . . carving time for my part-time job, doing the errands. Then my time is mostly spent with the youngest one, who needs more of my hands-on interaction. . . . Some of their education has been parsed out to classes. . . . I have them going to a literature class that a homeschool mom teaches.

Julia's schedule as caregiver and educator for her kids is hectic. Now that her children are older, however, she spends less time on lessons and more time carting the children to and from activities, demonstrating how formal education extends beyond the traditional at-home class- room for homeschoolers. Yet Julia still provides the primary instruction for her youngest child. Somehow, she does all of this while keeping a part-time paid position.

Michelle holds a master's degree and used to work as a full-time communications specialist before her daughter, Emmy, arrived. Her husband remains a full-time software engineer, providing for the family financially. When these white parents decided to homeschool, Michelle stepped up to fulfill their childcare and educational needs. Today, Michelle has a relatively structured weekly schedule, as is apparent from her description:

> I do the primary schooling, except on weekends. If I don't feel like she's had enough science . . . it [is] something that she and her father could do. . . . By the end of the week I want to be certain that we've had her spelling, her grammar, her geography, history, it's pretty structured. . . . Video production [class] is two hours. . . . [My daughter] has been taking French, we have a French tutor now, and . . . piano lessons.

In addition to this schedule, Michelle explains that she is part of a homeschool group that hires an art teacher to run a class. This schedule keeps the new homeschooler busy. As she says, "I'm keeping track of everything, because this is also our first year. . . . I keep a ledger and I also use a spreadsheet." Along with overseeing homeschool, she maintains the home, which includes cooking meals, doing laundry, and cleaning.

Maureen is also a white homeschooling mother. She describes feeling squeezed out of her career upon becoming a parent. She earned her graduate degree and worked full-time as a manager at a health care consulting firm, returning part-time after welcoming to the world her only daughter, Amelia. She recalls being glad to get back to work, telling me, "Amelia would go to a day care provider part-time and part-time with my mother-in-law." But Maureen quickly found that her employer "basically created a different job for me . . . I didn't like it as much." Describing herself as "increasingly not satisfied with the job," which "changed to more bookkeeping," she ended up quitting to be home with Amelia full-time. Her experience maps neatly onto research that finds demotions or horizontal job changes imposed upon new mothers are one way that women are pushed out of careers upon having kids.[9] Still, it's interesting that Amelia, who was entering first grade when Maureen left paid employment, remained in school for another four years. Maureen's elderly mother needed care and had moved in with them, so Maureen's decision to leave her job had allowed her to provide that caregiving, while also overseeing Amelia's education. She did not become her child's primary educator until Amelia was in fifth grade, but now describes a busy schedule:

> We meet Sunday or Monday morning and agree on what [Amelia's learning] goals are for the week. . . . Mondays are open until two. . . . Tuesdays she has piano lessons and American Sign Language lessons, Wednesdays is ballroom dance. Thursdays . . . we go to a [homeschool] friend's house [for a philosophy class]. There's probably five or six or seven [other homeschool] kids, and we all watch [a philosophy lecture], and then we sit and have discussions. . . . Fridays are fairly open.

In addition to this full homeschool schedule, Maureen provides weekly assistance to her elderly mother, who now lives independently. As she explains, "My mom has her own apartment, but I still go take her grocery shopping. She doesn't drive. I still take her to doctor appointments." Now that Amelia is old enough, she can do some schoolwork on her own, and Maureen says the resulting schedule "works out pretty well," allowing her to feel that she's sufficiently managing the family's caregiving responsibilities.

Not all mothers who interrupted their careers to homeschool took on the bulk of this responsibility. For example, Kimberly describes a slightly more egalitarian "balance" of work and home duties with her spouse, partially owing to her husband's somewhat flexible work schedule as a full-time public school teacher. Like Julia and some other homeschooling mothers, Kimberly manages to be the primary home educator and caregiver while also working part-time; she teaches childbirth classes a couple of evenings a week at a nearby birthing center. Needless to say, her family's schedule is packed, as she describes:

> Monday in the morning [is] academic work, lunch, sometimes they'll work on making bread or some sort of tactile activity and then we alternate between houses with another family for geography. Then the kids just play. . . . Tuesday is like one of the only days that we're like really at home unless somebody comes over in the afternoon to play. . . . Wednesday is Audubon classes, there's a classroom of fifteen kids and

their teacher goes through [a] nature program with them. . . . Thursday there's an art teacher who's actually going to come teach twelve kids who will meet at my house. . . . Every three weeks also on Thursdays they have a book club, and then every Friday they have music class in the morning, then lunch and playing with their friends.

Kimberly's husband, who is home by 3:00 p.m. most days and sees his schedule freed up in the summer, cares for the children in the afternoons and evenings when she is teaching at the birthing center. She describes him as "part of the [homeschool] process," supplementing with topic lessons that she didn't get through with the kids during the day. Yet Kimberly's more egalitarian balance of work and home duties was an exception in my sample. Most mothers stayed out of the workforce to homeschool, and along with this responsibility they also found themselves doing the bulk of the housework, childcare, and in some cases eldercare. Their narratives expose the range of pushes—including educational ones—that can lead women out of their careers and into the home.

Nonhomeschoolers Who Interrupted Careers

Interrupting careers was not seen only among homeschoolers. Many nonhomeschooling mothers expressed tension around work and family obligations, leading them to come home. Among the Black respondents who had interrupted their employment, seven sent their children to traditional schools (see figure 2.1). They share stories of flexible schedules unhindered by full-time employment and explain how this allows them to fulfill their families' various caregiving needs. Now they can serve as their children's primary caregiver, ferry them to and from extracurricular activities, and keep up with the housework. Some of them describe this need as also including the oversight of schooling to ensure it is serving their child well.

Kyra is a Black stay-at-home mom to three children who attend public school. Her husband works full-time as a molecular engineer. Kyra describes a packed daily schedule filled with carting her kids to and from school and after-school activities, as well as keeping up with the housework:

My husband leaves at 6:30 . . . and then [the kids] leave the house typi-
cally by 7:30. . . . Most of the time we have a carpool. One of the other
parents picks [my daughters] up and then some days I do the picking up
and dropping off. . . . My youngest goes three times per week only for half
days [to preschool] . . . She has to be at school for 9:15 so when I get home
[from dropping the older ones off] I get her ready, and I drop her off by
9:15. If there's no school that day . . . we'll go for playgroup at the church
or . . . take her to the park, to the library, and then [run errands before]
getting dinner started.

Once the older kids are home from school, Kyra spends afternoons
transporting them to extracurricular activities. She tells me: "My oldest one does swimming, . . . the middle one likes acting so she's going
to [the local] performing arts center, . . . the little one is usually in the
car for all of this pickup and drop-off." Kyra's highly structured schedule reveals the concerted cultivation approach available to middle-class
Black and white US families.[10] The schedule is devoted to intensive
caregiving, which for her involves managing the family's busy schedule, including after-school enrichment activities—swimming, theater,
playgroup, library—that she has arranged for each child. In some ways
her schedule looks like those of the Black and white homeschoolers.
The notable difference is that Kyra arranges and oversees her children's
activities (educational and extracurricular) but does not serve as their
primary schoolteacher. Keeping up this schedule would be much more
challenging if Kyra was employed full-time like her husband.

Rose's daily schedule also is devoted to meeting her family's caregiving needs. As a white mother of two boys, she ended up coming home
when she became pregnant with her second child to ensure someone
was able to fill in the care gaps and manage the family's busy schedule.
Her husband works full-time in the pharmaceutical industry, as she did
before their first son arrived. "Somewhere along the line we had to decide whose career is going to take the lead," she explains. Because her
husband had moved for her career early in their marriage, Rose says,
"I thought this time it's his turn." His company ended up moving them
"all over the US," and though Rose kept up with her licensing exams to
work in each new state, when they moved to Elmford, she got pregnant
again. "I was supposed to go through all of the exams again to get the

licensing," she recalls, but having another child seemed like "a good excuse to stay home." Rose has been a stay-at-home mother ever since. Not that it's easy, as she explains:

> Monday, Tuesday, Thursday, [my younger child] goes to preschool [in the morning] that's three days in the morning. . . . My husband will take [our older child] to school around eight o'clock and then either come home to work . . . or if he goes into the office, he goes in very early so then I will be the one that drops [our older child] off. . . . Mondays and Thursdays I pick [my older child] up from school and a friend and then Tuesday, Wednesday, Friday the friend's mom, so we carpool. . . . When we come home the [kids] have some downtime. . . . [My husband] if he works from home [eats dinner with us]. If not, he comes home around seven thirty. . . . [My older child] has soccer practice, [Tuesday] and Thursday afternoons, and then Saturdays [are] games.

Rose's schedule, like Kyra's, revolves around fulfilling caregiving needs for the family—getting kids to and from school, as well as keeping up with the housework, grocery shopping, laundry, cleaning, and meals. If she had remained in her career, the family would have to hire someone to provide the care and then squeeze housework in at night and on the weekends. Her story highlights how the accumulation of small factors pushes class-advantaged women like herself and Kyra out of their careers and into the home.

Andrea, also a white mother of three, says she "felt fortunate" not to have to go back to work at a bank upon having kids. She explains: "Before the kids, I worked at a bank. . . . I got pregnant and then I ended up on bedrest." Once she was out of the paid labor force and caring for her first child, Andrea and her husband decided they could make it on his full-time finance income alone. Similar to Kyra and Rose, Andrea now focuses her energy on reproductive labor (childcare, housework, and managing her children's many activities). Their household schedule, which she describes, is as daunting and child-centered as the other families':

> Morning is chaos . . . just trying to get them up and dressed, fed some breakfast and then out the door to catch the bus at 7:40. . . . [My] husband

leaves to go to work, and [the little one] doesn't go [to day care] until 9:15, and so I clean up all of the breakfast stuff, get a load of laundry going and get her snack and her bag situated, get her dressed. . . . I drop her off [at day care three days a week] and I shoot to the gym. . . . I'll pick her up and then we'll either run more errands. . . . When [the older two] get home . . . I try to let them relax for a bit and then do homework . . . because then we have sports. . . . When we get home they eat again and then showers, get them dressed for bed.

Like Andrea, many of these stay-at-home mothers feel overwhelmed by managing their families' busy schedules. Just getting kids ready for school and out the door in the morning—dressed, fed, and with their lunches packed—is "chaos." Other mothers described similar intensity. For example, Heather, a white mother, told me that overseeing her two sons' schedules and schooling is "a full-time job." The decision to be a stay-at-home mom is a sacrifice. Indeed, as Kiara, a Black mother, tells me, deciding not to leave her kids alone after school "means I don't work full-time." At the same time, Kiara reflects: "I'm glad that I'm in a position to [be home]. Some families they just have to work more and the kids are left on their own." While many women express gratitude that the choice is available to them, being a stay-at-home mother is certainly a challenging, full-time job that involves career sacrifice.

For some of these women opting out of paid employment to fulfill their families' various caregiving needs also includes overseeing children's education. Whitney is an example of a Black stay-at-home mother who explicitly came home to oversee her kids' education. She remembers noticing her children were not receiving the accommodations she felt they needed in the public schools. It took an enormous investment of Whitney's time and energy to try to get them assigned to better public schools. First, the city lost her files, and she had to reapply. Then the family waited until September before getting the kids' new school assignments: "three different schools, and all three were failing." "After a whole lot of hooting and hollering," and after leaving her paid employment to focus on her plan to get her children into better schools, she decided to send the boys where they were assigned but enroll her daughter in the citywide busing program. It takes "inner-city kids into the suburbs to get a better education," Whitney explains. At least, she says gratefully, she doesn't have to "be stressed about" her daughter's education. However, catering to her children's educational needs has meant an "amplified" schedule: "Three different schools with three different staff. Three different parent council meetings . . . everything is amplified." Whitney's husband works full-time to provide for the family financially, while, as she explains, "most of the household, I keep up."

Among these nonhomeschooling mothers, coming home relieves the tension they feel between work and family by allowing them to fulfill their families' caregiving needs. While, for some, this means providing childcare and managing hectic schedules, for others like Whitney, it involves spending hours advocating for her children's education. Across school type, women describe a range of factors that push them out of their careers and into the home upon becoming mothers. As taken up in more depth in chapters 4 and 5, one of these pushes is the work involved in navigating school choice for their children.

Why Gender Divisions Persist

Looking closer, we see that inflexible workplaces, cultural child-rearing expectations, and families' various caregiving needs leave these accomplished middle-class mothers to follow traditional gender divisions of labor that they may not have envisioned for themselves. Fathers serve as breadwinners, while mothers provide unpaid reproductive labor (or the labor involved in sustaining life to grow the next generation through childcare, housework, and providing or overseeing children's education).[11] This aligns with what Nancy Folbre refers to as the problem in the United States of the "invisible hand" of the market being separated from the heart or family values of love, obligation, and reciprocity; market competition encourages workers to devote themselves to careers, while assuming they are free from care responsibilities.[12] This arrangement leaves these class-advantaged women to pick up the caregiving slack for children (and elderly or sick family members) when finding quality care or education through the marketplace proves too difficult. Fathers simultaneously lean into their careers to pick up the financial strain that results from their wives staying out of the paid workforce. The result is a push toward traditional gender divisions of labor.

Reproductive labor, or the caring and educating work these mothers do, is crucial for nurturing human life. From a market perspective, the work is also crucial for ensuring workers are healthy and happy (clothed, bathed, fed, educated) and that dependents are well cared for. In other words, women's unpaid reproductive labor is crucial for worker's productivity and capital gains. As many feminist scholars have argued, these patterns persist among middle-class two-partner households like those examined in this book by relying on women to perform unpaid childcare, housework, and general oversight of children's activities. While on average men contribute more to housework and care work than they did thirty years ago, women still spend substantially more time on these tasks than men.[13]

In the twenty-first century, the gender revolution has been uneven and stalled due to the continued devaluation of those activities associated with women. This is the result of structural and cultural patterns that are embedded in American workplaces, families, schools, and the very understandings of ourselves.[14] One of these patterns is that the market is involved in sectors of our lives that were formerly seen primarily as private and separate from the market. For example, many affluent families take advantage of the global care chain, hiring low-income women, often women of color, as nannies or domestic workers to relieve them from the second shift, or the care and household work done after a full day of paid work.[15] Second, workers face increasing insecurity in their jobs though it looks different depending on one's position within the social hierarchy: low-income workers, who are disproportionately people of color, face insecurity through low wages and underemployment, while high-income workers face insecurity through pressures of overwork (working fifty or more hours per week).[16] For those working in professional jobs, flexibility is often available through the introduction of workplace policies that are intended to balance personal and caregiving responsibilities (e.g., telework, flextime, compressed workweeks, reduced-hour arrangements). Yet these benefits and the gender-equalizing effect of such flexibility are overridden, pushing fathers to overwork and mothers to pull back from the labor force.[17]

In addition, occupational gender segregation has increased since the 1970s and 1980s. This not only prevents workers from moving into occupations they might find satisfying but also is a major cause of the persistent racialized gender wage gap: average earnings tend to be much lower in occupations with a higher percentage of women workers and to be stratified by race.[18] Finally, cultural expectations continue to normalize women with children as primary caregivers, and men with children as breadwinners, leading to work and family being experienced as what sociologist Mary Blair-Loy refers to as "competing devotions."[19] Even when women and men workers resist these expectations, they face harassment and discrimination in the workplace.[20]

How School Choice Contributes to Gender Divisions

Structural and cultural patterns embedded in our schools also shape family and work life. For example, over the past few decades there has been a hollowing out of the American public education system, the last of our public goods. This has occurred through changes made to tax codes and market expansion through school choice policies, emphasizing parents choosing the best school for their child, supporting voucher schemes, and the opening of nonpublic schools—homeschools, as well as private or quasi-private charter schools.[21] School choice programs have supported this dismantling of our public education system by encouraging options outside of traditional public schools, which has led to their defunding. These programs have been spurred by neoliberal policies that emphasize high-stakes testing as the way to measure success or failure of schools (an individual goal), rather than a focus on integration and equality (a social goal). Under NCLB, enacted in 2002, schools were sanctioned for failing to meet federal proficiency standards while allowing students to transfer out of low-performing schools. Yet because higher-performing schools have no incentive to accept students from lower-performing schools, many students technically have choice yet are stuck in low-performing schools, while those with more resources are able to leave but only because of their parents' resources and intervention, like those I examine in this book, including the homeschoolers and nonhomeschoolers such as Whitney.[22]

What is often obscured under school choice education reforms is the interaction between these neoliberal educational policies and their impact on women's careers.[23] Navigating these options is just another task that is part of families' caregiving needs and that ends up getting absorbed by women, while the ways in which this reliance reinforces racialized and classed notions of good and bad mothering is obfuscated. For example, mothers who invest in traversing school choice are idealized, while mothers who are unable to invest such time are demonized. As a result, one of our last sources of public good—so crucial to the reproduction of human life and our society—has been cut, putting this major responsibility onto individual mothers, which only exposes the vast disparities between women. The Black and white class-advantaged mothers in my study describe these high-stakes schooling decisions, as well as caring for children and elderly family members, as better taken out of the marketplace (schools, day cares, and eldercare facilities) and placed in their own hands. Thus, when push comes to shove, these mothers come home.

Steady Careers of Nonhomeschoolers

Of the thirty-two Black respondents in my study, nine women remained steadily employed after having children, with eight of them sending their children to nonhomeschools (see figure 2.1). The six women who were working-class had fewer resources than the bulk of my interviewees: none had completed college, all had lower household incomes, and four were single heads of household. This breakdown suggests that, as prior studies of nonhomeschooling families have found, social class matters in terms of what schooling options Black families view as feasible.[24] It also curtails their career choices: unlike their middle-class counterparts, the working-class mothers I spoke to did not consider leaving the labor force upon the birth of a child.

Caroline is a single mother who works full-time in medical billing for the city hospital. Having worked full-time in the hospital for most of her employment history, Caroline reports, "I make a pretty decent living. I can pay my rent. I can buy food and clothes for my kids." Her sons' father does not live with them, though the children see their dad when he's not working. "He works two jobs," Caroline tells me, "so his schedule is even more hectic than mine." That her former partner contributes financially helps Caroline make ends meet. Her two sons, Tyler and Nigel, attend the local public school. Caroline's schedule is structured around the boys' school schedule, their extracurricular activities, and her paid employment. Unlike the interrupted work pathways I described earlier, much of Caroline's day is spent at work. She explains how the rest of her time involves housework along with managing the oversight and care of her children:

> My alarm goes off at 5:11. . . . I try to get myself together before I wake my youngest son, Nigel, about 6:00. . . . Tyler takes him to the bus stop at 7:00, so he has a whole hour to get himself together, dressed, eat. . . . I'm out the door by 7:00, and at work by maybe 7:45 . . . [until] 4:30. . . . I just signed Nigel up for [the neighborhood] sports league. . . . They'll be meeting on Saturdays. . . . He goes to the community center after Tyler picks him up from [school].

Given her family's limited financial resources, Caroline has sought out fee-free extracurricular activities for Nigel and Tyler; the cost, in terms of both finances and travel time, of the activities middle-class parents reported curtails the options available to working-class families. The working-class Black moms I interviewed demonstrate aspects of the natural growth child-rearing approach, adopted by American working-class families. Their children spend more time in unstructured, child-directed activities than do middle-class kids, which provides many benefits, including the development of independence and strong relationships with family and neighborhood children.[25]

Another single working-class mother, Trinity, is a full-time resident services coordinator at a senior living facility. She co-parents but does not live with her daughter Kayla's father, sharing that "we're still very close, [especially] when it comes to Kayla's education . . . or in general, when it comes to involvement." He contributes financially, having earned a trade school degree; he now works in heating and ventilation, holding down a full-time technician job and taking on after-hours side jobs. Yet, as the head of her household, Trinity explains accommodating her work schedule to meet Kayla's transportation needs: "I'm at work an hour and a half early . . . on my way to work, I bring her to school." Trinity mentions leveraging kin and nonkin networks—"making arrangements with friends"—to cover the other end of the day, ensuring that Kayla is picked up from school and brought home while her mom finishes the workday.

Just seven of the thirty-five white respondents remained steady in their careers upon becoming mothers (see figure 2.1). Unlike their Black counterparts, these white steady respondents had high levels of income and education. All had earned a bachelor's degree, a few had completed graduate degrees, and all but one lived in two-parent households. Abby, a white mother of three, provides a ready example. She and her husband are both employed full-time, and their children are enrolled in public school. She is a professor at a local college, and he is a manager at a computer software company. The family, Abby tells me, moved to the district because of its high-quality public schools. She describes what a typical week looks like in their household:

> My sons are both involved with the middle school in the enrichment activities before and after school . . . so most of the time we get up very early and one or both boys will head off to middle school early for whatever their early [program] is. . . . There's a city bus they take with other buddies or they just walk the whole way. . . . At 7:20, I usually walk out the door with my daughter to walk her to school . . . it's actually on the way to the [subway] . . . to go to [my] work. After school a couple days a week, her daddy picks her up. . . . Three days a week . . . we have her enrolled in an after-school program . . . Chinese dance. . . . [The program coordinators] take her to this after school. . . . The boys do drums. . . . My husband . . . runs [our daughter's] Girl Scout troop Friday nights. . . . I go to church and drag kids with me, so that's Sunday. Saturdays I go [with my daughter] for her dance practice.

Abby and her husband have the flexible schedules of their white-collar jobs to thank for the ability to pick up and drop off kids at school and extracurricular activities, and for the disposable income to pay for these after-school programs. In addition, because Abby's husband works at home, her youngest can come home and play on her own but with the security of her working dad's presence in case of an emergency.

Like Abby, Janet, a mother of two, provides an example of a white woman who manages to stay steady in her career after having children. Janet went to graduate school and now works full-time in physical therapy. Her husband works full-time from home in software sales, and so, along with her flexible work schedule, that means someone is always able to be home when their daughters come home from school. Janet describes their typical schedule:

> School starts at 8:45. The playground opens at 8:15, and we live a block away so we get there at 8:15 so that they can play. . . . Two days a week they have before-school activities. . . . My older one plays flag football and then she does a math . . . program . . . the younger one is in a similar kind of a [math program]. They're in school until 2:45. This semester we are just doing one sport each, because we were overcommitted. . . . They each [have] one practice per week and a game on the weekend. . . . They get home [from school] and I have them play outside first and then do homework. . . . [My older daughter] has one after-school activity from the school, which is her newspaper club . . . just for an hour after school on Thursdays.

Though Janet and her husband both take responsibility for helping with the kids' supplemental education work and getting them to and from their sports activities, even this level of oversight hinges on their having the flexibility that comes with white-collar jobs.

Middle-class parents (especially those in two-parent households) can enroll their kids in often expensive extracurricular activities, which can incubate the skills and sense of entitlement that are linked to access to college and securing professional careers. Both parents and children come to understand these activities as necessary parts of the development project, regardless of the consequences: hectic schedules, emphasis on competition, and weakened family relationships.[26] Unlike Caroline, who described after-school time as managed by her older son looking after her younger one, Janet and her husband juggle before- and after-school *adult*-led activities, like the math program, newspaper club, and football. This juggle is possible, in part, because of their two-parent household but also because they have flexible work hours, something more common in middle-class careers. Again, these middle-class arrangements may result in transferring class privilege from one generation to the next, yet they also can result in negative consequences, like deterring strong relationships between siblings, while the hectic schedules can leave kids stressed out and dependent on highly structured routines.[27]

One of the highest-income households in my study is headed by Jill, a lawyer, and her electrical engineer husband, who send their two children to public schools (and, like Abby, moved to get into the district). Both have advanced degrees and work full-time, though Jill's steady career did change after having children. She tells me, "Before I had kids, I worked at a big law firm. Then I went to a small law firm, which is where I had my daughter, and then when I got pregnant with my son I left there and started my own law practice for the purpose of having flexibility." Opening her own law practice was a way to have greater flexibility for parenting, yet Jill and her husband also employ a nanny to help manage their busy schedules, which Jill describes as follows:

> Monday through Friday everybody's either in school or working. School doesn't start until 8:45, but I think four days every week at least one of my kids has to be at school at 8:00 to do math club or student council or computer club or whatever . . . either we'll drop them off or they'll take the bus. After school we have a nanny who either picks them up or gets them off the bus. . . . My husband and I are still at work usually, and she'll take them to their activities, help them with their homework. . . . One of us will get home usually by 5:30 and then . . . try to have dinner together a few nights a week anyway . . . and then go to bed.

When Jill and her husband get home from work, they enjoy a family dinner before bed, relying on their nanny to handle other aspects of cultivating their children.

It is important that, like Janet and Abby, most of the steadily employed white respondents see remaining in their careers while fulfilling middle-class child-rearing expectations as possible because they and their husbands have laid out more equitable divisions of household labor and care. Just as important, these respondents' ability to find more equitable divisions of labor is the result of their class status. For example, those in professional careers, like Jill and her husband, can afford to hire a nanny to provide what they see as the necessary oversight in their children's lives such as completing homework and engaging in a range of extracurricular activities that uphold their children's class status.[28] Thanks to the flexibility that comes with professional jobs, others lean in to the control they have over when and where they work to fulfill their middle-class child-rearing expectations.[29]

Conclusion

Across race and regardless of school type, the vast majority of mothers in my study decided to interrupt their careers to ensure their families' various caregiving needs were met. For some women this meant providing care and managing hectic schedules. For instance, both Rose and Whitney describe their careers as first on the chopping block when it became apparent that more caregiving support was needed in their families. For some women, interrupting careers to stay home eventually led to serving as their child's primary educator. Indeed, homeschoolers Clara and Michelle were the ones pushed out of their professions, not their husbands, even though they had invested many more years of education into their careers. Here the work involved in raising children, including educating them, is explained as part of women's motherwork.[30] Notably, these women did not suggest that they left work to homeschool. Rather, they retrospectively cited the labor involved in managing their children's education as a reason they chose to *remain* out of the labor force.

To the extent that mothers remained steady in their careers and kept their children in traditional schools, I saw differentiation primarily by race and class. These Black mothers were more likely to have fewer resources in terms of income, workplace flexibility, and task-sharing (for instance, if they were parenting in single-headed households), while white mothers had resource levels similar to those of their interrupted counterparts but also more equal divisions of labor with their husbands and flexible work schedules. For example, the highest-income household—Jill and her family—was able to outsource after-school care and oversight for the children by hiring a nanny and buying a home in a wealthy white school district to fulfill the parents' schooling expectations. However, it's important to note that such arrangements, while fulfilling middle-class work and family ideals, can come with real consequences—such as having less time to cultivate relationships with siblings, hectic schedules that leave children burned out, and a dependence on adult-led schedules.[31] These are consequences that the steadily employed Black women and their children were likely able to avoid.

Indeed, existing research suggests low-income families are more likely to develop strong relationships with family members, including siblings, while also cultivating in children independence and creativity.[32]

As always, there were some exceptions, in this case homeschool mothers whose narratives did not map onto the work pathways of the majority of women I interviewed. For example, three homeschoolers continued to work full-time in their careers. Among them, the two white mothers were in single-headed households and had children of high school age, a confluence that helps to explain working outside of the home while juggling homeschooling. Sharon, the Black homeschool respondent who is employed full-time, lives in a dual-earner household. Unlike the eight Black steadily employed nonhomeschooling mothers, Sharon is middle-class and has a doctorate in nursing. She works full-time as a professor of nursing, while her husband is a full-time teacher. She describes their decisions around employment in this way: "I chose to sacrifice [pay] to have more flexibility so that I could be with the kids, so I went into academia." She explains that her current schedule leaves her teaching nursing students four days per week, but because of her flexible hours she doesn't have to "be in the office at a specific time."

> Wednesdays [I go in to work] a twelve-hour day. That day [my kids] are with either of the grandparents. . . . Thursdays and Fridays [I'm working from home]. Sometimes in the afternoon [the kids] go off with their biological dad so I have the whole afternoon to [work]. . . . Saturday and Sunday we do stuff with [other] families.

Unlike the Black nonhomeschooling respondents who work full-time, Sharon has more resources—higher education, higher pay, a flexible schedule—but also a husband and extended kin who help make homeschooling her two children possible. Sharon's story is more similar to the white steadily employed mothers' experiences, like Janet and Jill, than to those of other Black families, except that she relies on family for support rather than paid caregivers.

School choice is powerful for tapping into core American values of individual freedom. It is also a result of a market economy in which schools compete with each other to appeal to parents as consumers of education for their children. While holding the potential for positive outcomes, the flip side of school choice is that it places the burden of navigating children's education on individual families, and, I find, particularly mothers. Those with fewer resources will inevitably have fewer schooling options, but despite such barriers these mothers are actively involved in their children's schooling.[33] However, the constraint of fewer resources under school choice is reflected in the narratives of Caroline, Trinity, and the other Black nonhomeschool mothers I interviewed. Thus, instead of schools serving as "the great equalizer," school choice hinges on gendered, raced, and classed components; middle-class families rely on mothers to use class resources to locate quality schools for their children, as in the case of Whitney and the homeschool respondents, reinforcing gendered work patterns and adding to the unpaid labor absorbed into women's culturally scripted motherwork.[34]

Overall, in comparing class-advantaged mothers' work pathways, I found much less variation than I expected. Most of the Black and white homeschoolers and many of the nonhomeschoolers interrupted their careers upon becoming mothers. Those who remained steadily employed were primarily Black lower-income mothers and white middle-class mothers with employment flexibility. Things begin to diverge more clearly by race when we take into account women's racialized understandings of what it means to *be a good mother*, the focus taken up in the next chapter.

3

Protective Mothering

Black and White Women's Mothering Narratives

"It's tough. I'm Black, and I'm a stay-at-home mom. This is rare. Black women work. That's the standard." It's a blustery day in late April, and Jazmine is describing her decision to leave her career as a product design manager. Jazmine had invested years into graduate school and building her career. Extended family members warned that she was "throwing away" her life when she left the labor market, but she had watched a coworker struggle to care for their children and keep up with the demands of their job. Thus, when she became a mother, Jazmine decided to stay home.

She describes stepping out of the labor market as the decision that allows her to best fulfill her mothering obligations for her two children, Jahmal and Jonelle. It's "keeping the team together," she smiles, adding that her husband was able to redouble his commitment to his work as a computer programmer after their kids arrived. Jazmine has big plans for her children, and so she wants them to be self-sufficient. Because she is sure that self-sufficiency is not taught to Black kids in Elmford public schools, the family homeschools.

"It may be because I'm Black. I plan for catastrophes. As a Black person, you got to plan for the worst," Jazmine explains of her mothering style. "I made a decision that, at nineteen, Jahmal . . . needs to be able to buy a house, feed his family." From there, she says, she worked backward, figuring out what she needed to do as a parent to realize that goal. Jazmine is convinced that the public school in Elmford would be a waste of time for Jahmal and Jonelle, but homeschooling fits with her vision for their future.

Jazmine's story diverges from research that finds Black middle-class mothers have been found to view mothering as an "integration" of work and family life, while their white counterparts see the two roles as conflicting under the ideals of "intensive" mothering.[1] Yet, in my study, the narrative of leaving the workforce upon having children to ensure their successful future—or what I refer to as *protective mothering*—was common across Black and white mothers. As described in the previous chapter, many women across race left behind their careers when they had children; in the process, they absorbed the work of managing their family's schedule, including their children's education (if not directly teaching them). At the same time, most of these women described their husbands' careers as unchanged by the transition to parenting. Yet what was left unexamined and what will be explored in this chapter is how the meaning behind this sacrifice—the mothering narrative—is shaped by race, gender, and class.[2]

Take Victoria, a white homeschooler with a college degree and several years' experience working in publishing. On a snowy February morning, Victoria enthuses, "I absolutely loved [my job]!" She was married and advancing in her career when her daughter, Harmony, was born, and Victoria had every intention of returning to work. During maternity leave, though, she changed her mind, realizing "this wasn't going to happen." And so, "I gave my official notice to my boss," she recounts, while her husband's career as a scientist hummed along. Victoria tells me her decision to leave her job was well worth the sacrifice and that this "situation is the best" for her family: "I love being with Harmony. [We] spend the day together, and I can see her interests." Stay-at-home homeschool mothering, Victoria adds, "is rewarding" and "I love it." Victoria is clear that coming home was worth the career sacrifice. The move allows her to fulfill her idea of "good" mothering by developing a strong bond with her daughter so that she stays attuned to Harmony's interests and can cater to them through homeschooling.

In this chapter, I consider women's own ideas of "good mothering" by tracing the historical context of racialized middle-class mothering before unpacking women's narratives of what I refer to as *protective mothering*. When institutions such as schools fail to meet their expectations, both homeschooling and nonhomeschooling working professional women turn inward, toward their families—by coming home from work and in some cases bringing their children home too. Yet these protective strategies are shaped by the families' place within the racial hierarchy, as well as their position as middle-class women. Black middle-class mothers, like Jazmine, use their class status (husband's financial stability and their own human capital) to cultivate self-sufficiency in their children, while white mothers, like Victoria, use their class status to focus on self-actualization. Across race, mothers' narratives reflect their insecurities about children's racialized futures and their sense of responsibility to counter this precarity through drawing on their class resources.

This protective mothering builds from recent scholarship on mothers' "security projects," or the work women do to prepare children for politically and economically insecure times.[3] For example, Allison Pugh finds among class-advantaged mothers a deep commitment to raising a *flexible* child who is able to adapt to change.[4] In my study, I found the "security project" is shaped by gender, class, *and* race; Jazmine, Victoria, and many of the other mothers I spoke with expose how the racial hierarchy and women's places within it shape the contours of the particular uncertainties from which these middle-class mothers seek to protect their children. By drawing homeschooling families into the debate, this chapter highlights how women's understandings of what constitutes "good mothering," even among those who are class privileged, are formed not only through labor insecurity, unresponsive husbands, and sociohistorical cultural scripts but also through school choice policies that in the end encourage mothers to take on the responsibility of securing quality education for their children.

Racial Herstories of Motherhood

Jazmine, Victoria, and the other mothers who are profiled in this chapter provide narratives that are embedded in constructions of Black and white motherhood and that date back to slavery. Racial slavery was premised on Europeans' attempt to prove their superiority and based on notions of a body's biological difference to grant relative value.[5] Along with phenotype, French, Dutch, and English elites and armchair cartographers developed fears of Black women's imagined fat bodies as a sign of immorality through gluttony, which contrasted with constructions of white women's imagined thinness, morality, and role as ideal mothers.[6] The obsession with Black women's bodies led to notions of Black women's hypersexuality and reproductive potential.[7] This thinking linked racial and religious ideas that denigrated Black women and justified racial slavery.[8]

Black feminism draws important connections between the state control of Black women's reproduction in contemporary society (i.e., state-sponsored birth control and sterilization) and that of Black women during the four centuries of chattel slavery in the Americas and the Caribbean.[9] As social and cultural scholar Jennifer Morgan argues, the institution of slavery rested on enslaved Black women's reproductive and productive capacities—both their toiling in the fields and their giving birth to children who were crucial for sustaining the slave trade.[10] While long in the past, slavery holds a "reproductive afterlife" in that it lives on as a thought system, as seen through parallels between forced sexual and reproductive labor of Black women during slavery and contemporary notions of Black motherhood as shaped by state-based control.[11]

The mothers in this study are primarily from class-advantaged families, which provides them with some buffer from state intervention. Yet, the reproductive afterlife of racial slavery and the contrasting meaning constructed around Black and white women's reproduction should not be underestimated. The forced reproduction and rendering of Black women's bodies and children as property of white sharecroppers are the backdrop that has shaped the American psyche. The twentieth-century eugenics movement and federally funded health programs that continue to push sterilization and birth control onto women of color and low-income women, while encouraging white class-advantaged women to reproduce, shape experiences of mothering today.[12] This is the backdrop that Jazmine and Victoria, from earlier in this chapter, as well as the other women in this study, must navigate.

Black Protective Mothering through Self-Sufficiency

Monique was working part-time at a bank when she and her husband, a full-time electrical engineer, decided it made more sense, and would be less frustrating, for her to stay home with their children. "I was missing my kids' [sports] games . . . we had to find carpooling, and it just didn't make sense anymore. I loved my job. But I said, 'I can come back to that.'" In this, she was like many other mothers I spoke with: they shared the sentiment that employment would still be there once their children were older. This reflects the emotion work that Jennifer Lois finds white homeschoolers use to manage the intensity of the work and the sacrifices they have made in their careers.[13] Thus, by reflecting on the temporary nature of mothering young children, Monique, a Black homeschooler, justifies her decision to come home.

Monique's decision to opt out of paid employment also fits with her understanding of good mothering, particularly an emphasis on raising self-sufficient children:

> I could definitely have a job in the financial industry if I wanted to, but I think while people might say it's a sacrifice . . . I wouldn't sacrifice that for doing what I do. . . . *I want to grow [my kids] to be independent learners*, thinkers, productive members of society. . . . I don't want to become a crutch for them. I want them to grow into being on their own [and] interested in learning. (emphasis added)

Ironically, to promote her children's self-sufficiency, she sacrifices some measure of her own, becoming economically dependent on her husband. This stands in contrast to Black mothers who seek to raise "community kids" who learn to rely on the larger community and extended kin instead of solely on the mother.[14] While extended kin are important, I find Black mothers, such as Jazmine, express facing scrutiny for opting out to try to secure a class advantage for their Black children and generations to come. This demonstrates how class advantage works in tandem with gendered racial disparities: only those who can afford to opt out of paid work can manage homeschooling. Black class-resourced families rely on Black women's labor to raise successful, middle-class children who are resilient and able to navigate the realities of racial discrimination.

Monique and Jazmine, deeply involved in every aspect of their children's lives, evoke aspects of white middle-class child-rearing, such as reliance on mothers to ensure enrollment in extracurricular activities and intervening in institutions,[15] yet they also shoulder the work of cultivating Black children's success in an anti-Black world. Regardless of individuals' education, occupation, and income, wealth is passed down from generation to generation, and in the United States the racial wealth gap is both wide and certain to raise Black mothers' sense of insecurity. At the time I spoke with Monique, the median wealth of white households was ten times higher than that of Black households.[16] Living in what sociologists call a risk society, characterized by concern about personal employability, safety, and economic security,[17] we can easily understand that class-advantaged families, buoyed by their individual safety nets, are better able to navigate risk (and the risk their children face); the difference results in what Marianne Cooper refers to as "inequalities of insecurity."[18] Certainly other spheres of risk, such as educational contexts and racial discrimination, also shape maternal responses to the security project. Indeed, Monique, Jazmine, and other Black mothers' narratives highlight the ways in which race, class, and gender shape how families navigate this risk society.

Grace traces her decision to opt out of paid employment and to homeschool her children to her own experiences as a child—and to her mother's responses:

> When I was young, . . . being African American, I came home and saw things differently than my mom. I didn't understand where she was coming [from]. So [with my own kids] I felt like being a minority . . . it's heartbreaking to have to try and explain things and for [my daughters] also to go through that. . . . [My mom] grew up in segregation times. [My siblings and I] went to a private school that was mostly white, mostly wealthy. For [my mom] it was just very difficult. Even just driving us out to our friends' houses it was just like trauma, flashback. So, if I put [my daughter] in an environment where she's surrounded by a viewpoint that I don't share, there's nothing else to expect than that she'll come home with that viewpoint because she's there all day. So why put our family through that stress if I don't have to?

While Grace's husband continues in his full-time professorship at an area college, Grace cut back her part-time public health coordinator work after the birth of her first child. She has a master's degree in public health and fully intended to return to full-time work, yet as the return date approached Grace realized that she really wanted to be home with her children and so she resigned from paid employment. "[A] lot of people only feel [like staying home with] babies, like, 'I want to be with my baby . . . I'm the one who can care for her best' and all that sort of stuff. But I guess I just never stopped feeling that way." For her, homeschooling was just "a natural extension of full-time parenting. . . . I already know how she learns, so why don't I just keep her home?"

Grace's story is complicated by the fact that she converted to Islam as an adult. In school, her daughters would face discrimination as both African American and Muslim girls, but at home she can protect them from disparagement and foster a positive racial and religious identity. Grace's recollections of her mother's approach to child-rearing influence her own approach, as do her own experiences with racism as a child. Grounded in the narratives of her family network, Grace understands that sacrificing her career relieves her children from some of the stress of racial and religious discrimination.

Sociologist Sarah Damaske argues that class- and race-diverse mothers "do" femininity through fulfilling narratives around self-sacrifice that put their family's needs ahead of her own.[19] Notably, Grace's performance of gender is framed by notions of Black middle-class womanhood as linked to mothering. She explains decisions made for the family, especially around homeschooling, that are available because of her husband's generous professor's salary that can support the whole family. In some ways, this reflects the characteristics of the dominant intensive mothering ideals—childcare should be the primary responsibility of mothers, labor-intensive, and financially costly, and should cultivate skills that map onto children's future success.[20] However, I see a distinct thread in the stories of Grace and other Black stay-at-home moms: their decisions to opt out of paid employment are undeniably shaped by their class resources but also their motivation to protect children from anti-Black views in school (and, sometimes, in other institutional contexts). Across school type, Black middle-class mothers evoked similar sentiments: they wanted to develop self-sufficiency in their children to combat racial discrimination and ensure their future success.

Upon having kids, Kyra became the stay-at-home mother of all three of her public schooling children, while her husband's career as a scientist did not change. Kyra emphasizes how her approach to mothering diverges from that of the primarily white parents with whom she interacts:

> I volunteer at the school, but that's pretty much where I'll stop. . . . There is an intensity [from other parents]—maybe it's just me coming from a

different culture, but I don't need to be that intensely involved. *I don't try to solve the problem for [my kids]; I encourage them to try to solve it for themselves.* I do not like to be involved in their lives too much. I just want them to be independent and be able to solve problems on their own . . . because I think if they start solving problems now, when they go to college, they are able to think for themselves. (emphasis added)

While homeschoolers like Jazmine, Monique, and Grace sought to secure their children's positive racial image and independence through teaching them at home, Kyra, also a middle-class Black mother, believes the distance that comes from sending them to public school is the best way to develop her children's independence and prepare them for the separation they will experience when they go to college. This, too, is part and parcel of a racialized security project. Among Black professional mothers who remain in the workforce in order to fulfill mothering expectations, sociologist Dawn Dow reports their use of an "integrated mothering" ideology that frames work and family as complementary, not opposing, spheres, and a mother's economic self-sufficiency as a positive model for raising resilient children.[21] I found a similar emphasis on self-sufficiency among the middle-class Black mothers I interviewed, but instead of ensuring *mothers'* self-sufficiency, they focused on *children's*. In other words, some Black mothers opted out of paid employment for the same reason others remained in their paid work: it was part of what they saw as good mothering.

Even among those Black mothers who did not turn inward by coming home but remained steadily employed (nine women) they still described a protective mothering approach. Of these, all but one sent their kids to nonhomeschools. This exception was Sharon, who homeschools her son, Jerome and her daughter, Emily. Her work pathway is exceptional and made possible through the childcare her own parents and husband provide when Sharon is at work. (Her husband's career as a public school teacher allows him to be home in the afternoons when she's at work.) However, Sharon's mothering narrative hewed closely to that of the other Black mothers in the study:

I really try to help [my kids] to realize . . . they need to be loving and kind to everybody and when someone's not kind to you, you can't control that, but all you can do is be kind back. . . . You're not gonna let someone hurt you. Your body is yours, but you don't need to use your fists. . . . I'm trying to find experiences for them that are real, everyday experiences, *because what advantage is it going to be to you if you know everything about mathematics but you don't know how to balance a checkbook?* (emphasis added)

Sharon speaks of equipping her children for survival in a harsh world, teaching them bodily autonomy and how to avoid using physical violence to resolve problems, as well as some practical skills, all of which build self-sufficiency. Despite having the class resources that might suggest a safety net for her children, Sharon believes good mothering requires acknowledging that her Black children will need to build their own secure futures. Indeed, other scholarship documents Black professional mothers' efforts to protect their Black sons from the controlling image of "the thug" from very young ages (or what Dow describes as mothers managing "baby racism").[22] For Sharon, these protective measures extend to her children's education: she homeschools to prepare her children for the real world, which includes the reality of racism.

The Black mothers in my sample who opted out of paid employment after becoming parents had more resources than two-thirds (eight) of the Black mothers who were steadily employed, yet they all expressed similar approaches to mothering. Emory and her husband both work full-time, she as an administrative assistant and he as a truck driver. In terms of oversight of their daughter's charter school experience, Emory describes her husband as "there but clueless," and so she views herself as primarily responsible:

> I try to advocate for what she wants, but at the same time, [she hasn't] had experiences in life to see how this may be beneficial. I think especially with a highly emotional teenage girl, you have to be careful. You don't want to be too pushy because then they'll express their frustration in other ways and then you don't want to be too soft because how are they going to learn how to work hard for what you want?

Like other Black respondents, Emory describes seeking a balance so that she listens to her daughter but also pushes her to develop the skills necessary to survive. For Emory, this means encouraging her daughter to work hard in school so that she can get into a good college.

Caroline, the Black single mother who works full-time in medical billing at the city hospital, sends her children to the local public school but speaks passionately of the same protective mothering as Emory and Sharon:

> If you're gonna have kids, take the job seriously. . . . [I am their] first teacher. They don't teach us about money in school. . . . I would rather that they taught about money before they taught about how to put a condom on. It's so essential, how you live, how you need it, how much you should probably have for your future. . . . Nobody discusses that until you're in debt and you realize, "I need to dig myself out of this."

In a world that limits Black individuals' access to economic security and bodily safety, Sharon, Kyra, Emory, and Caroline—despite the variation in their education and income levels—all feel that good mothers teach their Black children the skills to survive and thrive, handing down this currency as its own form of generational wealth.

It is notable that unlike the Black middle-class mothers who opted out to oversee their children's schooling while relying on their husband's breadwinning, the steadily employed Black respondents in this study were primarily working-class. Over one-third were also in single-headed households and thus relied on their own full-time employment to secure their families' survival. As countless scholars have documented, female-headed households are more common within working-class and poor Black communities. The 1965 publication of *The Negro Family: The Case for National Action* by Daniel Patrick Moynihan sparked narratives linking father absence with welfare dependency and pathologizing Black low-income men using the controlling image of the "deadbeat dad," meaning one who is irresponsible and neglectful.[23] However, much research documents the discriminatory opportunity structure in the United States. Black men born into low-income families have little access to reliable and stable employment; this, combined with discriminatory policing practices, contributes to the disproportionate incarceration rates of young Black men.[24] These factors make it nearly impossible for Black men to fulfill financial expectations of fatherhood. They also harm their marriageability, since financial precarity is seen as risky for a successful marriage.[25] While many steady working-class Black respondents were married and relied on both their own and their husband's income to get by, this context helps explain the challenges that Caroline and the other five steadily employed mothers faced as the sole providers for their families.

White Protective Mothering through Self-Actualization

White women also described a protective approach to mothering, but rather than preparing children to deal with discrimination, white mothers sought to really know their child so they can cater to their needs. Bringing children home for school allowed these mothers to foster their child's self-actualization through emotional connection and individualized learning. Take, for example, Maureen, who has a graduate degree and worked full-time as a manager at a health care consulting firm before becoming a stay-at-home mom and eventually a homeschooler for her daughter, Amelia. Maureen's husband has less formal education (a bachelor's degree), but his career as a software engineer has remained steady since having Amelia. Maureen says making "that conscious decision to step back" and leave work "was really hard." Still, she stresses that it was worth it: "It was a big deal, and it's changed everything." Now, she describes herself as "very close" with Amelia and suggests that wouldn't be as possible if she attended traditional school. Maureen sees homeschooling as what's best for her daughter. Amelia struggled with social anxiety when she attended traditional school, but homeschooling has dissipated that anxiety. Now, not only do mother and daughter spend more time together but the time is also "spent being relaxed in each other's company" rather than managing Amelia's anxiety.

Maureen placed her daughter's needs over her own career, but, like the other white mothers, she did so because she saw institutions as failing to meet the needs of her child. As fathers remain steady in their careers, regardless of their earning power or educational investment in their careers, mothers cite inflexible workplaces and schools as "pushes" toward opting out and cultivating children's individuality and the mother-child connection as "pulls." When she saw traditional schools as exacerbating Amelia's anxiety, Maureen was left to spend much time managing this with her daughter. Now, with the privilege of whiteness and class advantage, Maureen uses homeschooling to address Amelia's anxiety, bond with her child, and live up to her own mothering ideals.

Michelle is a stay-at-home mother and homeschooler seeking to provide individualized learning for her daughter, Emmy. Michelle earned a graduate degree and had worked as a communication specialist prior to having her daughter. Her husband, who did not complete college, has worked as a software engineer with no change to his career upon becoming a father. Michelle describes her surprise at the degree to which education figured into her mothering role:

> [Mothering is] a huge endeavor. It's humbling, and I take [it] extremely seriously and quite passionately. . . . I thought [homeschoolers] were crazy! [But] I didn't imagine having children. . . . Schooling was so far outside anything I thought I was gonna have to worry about. Not even on my radar that school would be anything that we'd talk about as a family. And it has been just about the *only* thing we talk about as a family.

Rather than Black mothers' emphasis on educating their children in self-sufficiency, I find that white mothers, like Michelle, emphasize developing their child's individuality. Michelle's resources allow her to follow this logic—catering to the individual child—by opting out of her career and into an individualized learning plan through homeschooling. This is paradigmatic intensive mothering, in which women are expected to direct their time and resources to their children rather than to paid employment.[26] Similar to the intensive mothering that Jennifer Lois found surfacing among her white homeschool respondents,[27] the white mothers I spoke with saw their role in ensuring self-actualization through school choice as part of what it means to be a good mother. By virtue of the racial hierarchy in which they live, they have the privilege to ignore race despite the racial hierarchy and their position in it being implicated in their mothering approach.

Scholars studying mother-child relationships identify white middle-class mothers' response to insecurity as a possible pathway to "out of control" oversight.[28] In particular, Marianne Cooper found that in contrast to lower-income families, white middle-class families tended to point to macroeconomic trends and describe feeling insecure despite their relative economic security.[29] The white mothers I spoke with took on this insecurity by trying to create an insurance policy through good education (along with the fathers' provision of economic stability) to secure their children's futures.

Ana Villalobos, in studying women's management of precarity in pregnancy and early motherhood, refers to the logic Michelle and Maureen use as the motherload, or valorizing the subjective importance of the mother-child relationship to counter real and constructed insecurity.[30] Though the women in my study have school-age children, I find that Villalobos's research bears out in the case of white class-advantaged mothers who see themselves as trading the economic security of their paid work for what they view as far more valuable: protecting their child's future security. But when we compare the narratives of similarly situated Black and white mothers, it is clear this security work is inescapably shaped by race. Notably absent from white middle-class mothers' narratives is the need to protect their children from racism, while concern for future security is conceivably less weighty relative to Black middle-class mothers' concern. The privilege of whiteness allows these mothers to instead focus on self-actualization through building the close relationship needed to develop the appropriate individualized learning program for their child.

Interrupting careers and coming home looks very similar for white middle-class mothers whether they sent their children to nonhomeschool or chose to homeschool. Rose, a white stay-at-home mother to Charlie and Evan, is not responsible for her sons' primary education, yet her mothering can be described as intensive. As she explains:

> It's pretty important for me as a mom . . . to be involved. . . . I chose to stay home with my children in order to *be there for them* in helping them through their academic afternoons. . . . I think that is crucial. . . . I will be there to try and work with [their teachers] to try and see what we can do that's the best for [my sons]. . . . I have a lot of phone calls with Charlie's teacher, and then we meet with her like every quarter. . . . I think we need to be as involved as we possibly can to help our kids' success for the future. My husband will work with [the kids] doing nighttime reading . . . that's his time with the kids, so he will spend that with them. (emphasis added)

The rhetoric of school choice and best-fit education comes through in Rose's description of good mothering; her family moved to a new town to access good schools, yet she is also involved in directing her sons' education by regularly conferring with their teachers, overseeing their homework, and generally managing their schooling. She describes her push out of paid employment and into stay-at-home mothering as circumstantial, with her husband's high-paying job and the time she needed to take off upon the birth of each child as contributing factors. This arrangement also ensures her availability for the oversight of public school to help foster her kids' future success.

Cindy, a white middle-class mother whose kids attend nonhome-schools, only interrupted her career as an attorney after the birth of her fourth child. She explains that "when push came to shove," the high cost of day care combined with her inflexible work hours led to her decision to come home and focus on reproductive labor (childcare, housework, and navigating her children's education). Her husband, who did not go to college, continued as the full-time family breadwinner through his work at a car dealership. Despite years of investment in her career, Cindy's choice to opt out meets her bar for good mothering. She explains:

> My role is to provide an expansive educational experience . . . and I don't just mean money. . . . Your time . . . I think your experiential education is probably as important as your formal classroom education. . . . It's my role to *track kids into a situation that gives them the skills* to . . . successfully perform at the next level, all the way along. . . . You just hope that you're offering the kids the best tools to be able to think. (emphasis added)

Cindy tells me she struggled to find an expansive educational experience that would give her children the tools she believes they need to succeed. The family started with the children in private school, became dissatisfied, and enrolled the younger two children in the local public school. It was costly—several thousand dollars a year per child—to send the children to the private school, but it was just as costly in terms of Cindy's time to have them in either public or private school. Her focus on mothering to ensure her children have the best education involves spending much of her time advocating within schools on their behalf. Still, by placing her kids into the experiences that she thinks will help them perform well, she has focused on catering to their individual strengths, which she argues involves *really* knowing your child; being a stay-at-home mother allows Cindy to fulfill her mothering expectations as her children's educational director, even without homeschooling them.

Other Approaches to White Mothering

Not all the white middle-class mothers describe good mothering as fostering their child's self-actualization through emotional connection and individualized learning. Although a small number, the four non-homeschool mothers who had remained steadily employed since having kids describe their mothering approach as involving more distance from their child, while receiving childcare support from paid caregivers or husbands. These respondents also have high levels of education: all have earned a bachelor's degree, and a few have graduate degrees (see table A.2, appendix A). Recall that, across employment status and school type, the Black mothers I spoke with express similar protective mothering strategies. By contrast, the white mothers who were steadily employed diverged from their white counterparts.

Jill and her husband both work full-time, and Jill describes her husband as equally involved in the parenting responsibilities. When I ask about her approach to mothering, her response hinges on a comparison to other mothers and trying to manage the tensions between work and family:

> Some moms who are stay-at-home moms are super-involved. . . . I just don't have the time. . . . I try to know what's going on with the kids' homework, but we're not the ones who oversee it [the nanny does]. . . . I don't talk about [parenting] for the most part with parents around here. . . . I don't want to feel judged. I already feel judged as a working mom . . . and I don't want to be further judged for not doing enough for my kids. I think *I'm doing the best for them by my approach.* . . . I talk to stay-at-home moms who feel judged for not working. . . . The grass is always greener.

Jill feels pressure to be more involved in her children's life, like the stay-at-home moms she knows, while recognizing that those moms are *also* feeling judged—in their cases, for not working. Her sentiments capture the anxiety of contemporary motherhood among class-privileged white women.[31] They also coexist with her privilege: her high-status career allows Jill to arrange a more flexible work schedule and to outsource some of the family's reproductive labor by hiring a nanny to be with the children after school and until she and her husband are home from work.

Abby, a professor, and her husband, a full-time computer software manager who primarily teleworks, have three children. All the kids are enrolled in the local public school—in fact, the quality of the schools is what drew them to buy a home in the district. Both parents' flexible work schedules help them juggle parenting and their continued full-time careers. When I ask about her mothering strategy and how she sees her role in their children's education, Abby emphasizes the ways she and her husband both work to supplement and support their schooling:

> My job is . . . to try to make sure [the kids] have spaces to do their work . . . pencils and pens and that we encourage them to set aside time for their homework. . . . We've advocated when we saw that there was something that needed advocacy. That hasn't happened very much. . . . As a parent, [I] write notes of thanks when [teachers] do things well . . . to reinforce all that is really good that is going on, which is a lot. . . . Anytime there is any parent-teacher meeting we both try and be there. . . . We do try to volunteer at the schools . . . we do show up for those things. . . . We try to make sure that at home, kids write thank-you notes, they write letters to their grandparents, they have a lot of books around. They have art supplies. They listen to a lot of music. They talk about interesting movies. . . . If the TV goes on, a parent has to give permission.

Abby's account includes a shared parenting strategy that none of the mothers who interrupted their careers express, regardless of race or other factors. She and her husband split responsibilities like attending parent-teacher meetings and providing after-school supervision. This equal—and exceptional—division of reproductive labor is likely possible because of Abby and her husband's exceptional class and race privilege; men with higher earnings, like Abby's husband, are more likely to share "feminine" responsibilities because their high income and racial privilege can make up for a perceived undermining of their masculinity.[32]

In addition, crucial to shared parenting are workplace policies, like the flexible work schedules of Abby and her husband, which are more common for those in professional careers.[33] Why she and her husband opted for equal divisions of labor while other white middle-class families did not is unclear.

When compared with Black men, white men have historically been more likely to perform traditional gendered labor because of their access to the breadwinner role. By contrast, in part due to the employment discrimination Black men face, but also to differing values, two-parent Black families across class often rely on co-breadwinning between husband and wife without it posing a threat to Black masculinity, while leading to more egalitarian divisions of reproductive labor.[34] Abby and her husband are an exception in that their division of labor is more equal, looking more similar to what has been found in research with Black families. Abby's circumstance is certainly influenced by class privilege (the flexibility in her and her husband's work hours) and accentuates the importance of taking into account how gender, race, *and* class interact in family life.

It is notable that the few white mothers who maintained full-time employment describe good mothering as involving an equitable division of household labor and care work in their families, but they also rely on class resources to achieve such a balance. Professional careers are more likely to allow for tag-team parenting because they are more likely to give employees control over when and where they work. Thus, Abby and her husband can take turns picking up and dropping off their kids. Jill and her husband, who also are solidly upper-middle-class, pay for a nanny who can provide the oversight they see as crucial to good child-rearing in the hours when they are still at work. Full-time employed white mothers differed in this way from their Black counterparts, most of whom were working-class and worked full-time in jobs with less autonomy to secure their families' survival.

Conclusion

This chapter builds from the sociological research on the vast political and economic insecurities we face today as well as the reproductive afterlife of slavery that is embedded within the American psyche.[35]

Scholarship suggests the rollback of the US welfare state, alongside the growth of precarious employment over the past several decades, has left all American families dealing with heightened insecurity,[36] but like other risks, this one is experienced unequally across families. Upper- and middle-class families are better able to navigate risk because they effectively provide their own individual safety nets, while lower-class families are much less successful at buffering their families against risk. As education becomes its own sort of commodity under school choice (rather than a publicly available good), the risk of a potentially inadequate education is also shaping approaches to child-rearing. Quality schools are not a given, and middle-class mothers expend great energy to secure their child's future. Part of this may involve shopping for the best school to fit each child.

We have seen how Black and white professional women navigate the demands of work and family through ideas of protective mothering. Both Jazmine and Victoria are "opting out" and describe their reason for doing so as "for the family."[37] This is not to suggest that these women are unhappy with their decisions; many respondents emphasized the sense of fulfillment they experience from engaging in protective mothering. Rather, their narratives illuminate how cultural values and structural arrangements affect professional women's decisions about work and family vis-à-vis their visions of good mothering. In particular, under school choice, child-rearing ideals emphasize not just the financial resources of two-parent families but also class-advantaged women's embrace of an underexplored aspect of mothering work, ensuring quality schooling through turning inward (coming home) to provide protective mothering.

When we dig into these women's mothering narratives, we can understand how approaches to mothering are linked to class resources but also reflect women's different positions within the racial hierarchy. In seeking to secure their children's future, Black mothers emphasize building children's economic and emotional self-sufficiency and resilience in a racist world. This points to the heightened sense of precarity shared by Black mothers (even those with class resources) who feel compelled to, but are unable to, entirely protect their children from racial discrimination. By contrast, white professional mothers need not explicitly consider their child's race in the process and instead emphasize building the child's self-actualization through cultivating connection and individualized learning. Here we see how the construction of good mothering is shaped by the intersection of racism, class relations, and gender inequalities that impact women's navigation of the tension around work and family life. This tension includes the push to navigate quality schooling for their child. The next two chapters focus on the factors that shape women's negotiations of school choice—in particular, how Black and white mothers understand their schooling decisions.

4

"They Made Me Feel Like He Was a Terrorist"

Schooling Decisions of Black Mothers

"They had [my son] in the principal's office. He was crying . . . they ostracized him. This is a good little boy. They made me feel like he was a terrorist and so after that experience . . . he said, 'I don't want to go to school next year, mom,' and I said, 'OK.'" Sharon recounts this emotional scene on a crisp October morning as we have coffee at a suburban café just minutes from her home. The location is convenient because by the time we finish our interview, Sharon's two children will be awake and ready for their home lessons.

Sharon, who was introduced in earlier chapters, is a Black homeschooling mother and a full-time professor of nursing. "I was a mainstreamer for the most part," she says of the years before her family switched to homeschooling their two children. "I never really question(ed) anything." It was the "bad experience" in which Jerome, then seven years old, was suspended for bringing matches to school because he wanted to "show my classmates and talk to them about it" that initiated her questioning. Sharon and her husband, a high school teacher, had had mostly positive interactions with the teachers and principal in Jerome's school prior to that day. She's exasperated as she recalls: "Jerome's crying. He's like 'I'm so sorry. I said I was sorry. . . . I wasn't going to do anything.'" It seemed that Jerome was being targeted as one of the only Black students in his classroom—in fact, the public school and the neighborhood in which it stands are primarily white and middle-class, with a population that's less than 2 percent Black.[1] When Jerome insisted he did not want to go back to school, the idea did not fit with Sharon's original plan, but because she and her husband had relatively flexible work schedules and extended kin who could provide support, they decided to try homeschooling.

Of the thirty-two Black mothers I interviewed, almost one-third (five homeschool and five nonhomeschool) explained their schooling decisions as shaped by racial experiences with public schools. Racial bias toward Black children in schools is not new. As I lay out in this chapter, existing research documents how navigating racial identity and racism puts Black boys and girls from all class backgrounds at elevated risk of experiencing the school-to-prison pipeline.[2] Black mothers are painfully aware of this reality and resist by serving as their child's education advocate.[3] What has been less examined, and what I address here, is how the carceral state's presence in schools shapes particularly middle-class Black mothers' navigation of school choice.

Development of the School-to-Prison Pipeline

The metaphor of the school-to-prison pipeline rose to prominence in the 1990s and was linked to three major developments. First, in the 1970s and 1980s, political leaders began introducing tough-on-crime initiatives that were framed in racial terms. For example, in 1986 the Reagan administration signed into law the Anti–Drug Abuse Act. While most commonly recognized as leading to mandatory sentencing that disproportionately targeted Black Americans because of the harsher sentences for possession of crack versus powder cocaine, this act also heralded in a tough-on-crime precedent in response to an array of social ills, including perceptions of violence in schools.[4] Second, political leaders sought to win the vote of white working-class Americans through framing Black Americans as the perpetrators of violence, despite the increase in white men aged fifteen to twenty-four being the main culprits of the increase in violence during this period.[5] By misconstruing the problem of increased violence as a Black one, political leaders tapped into white Americans' racial fears, buying support through a tough-on-crime response that targeted Black communities.[6]

Third, in the 1990s there was a rising fear of rampage shootings or of school shootings committed by current or former students against multiple random victims.[7] Within the cultural imagination, such school violence was constructed as an urban problem, one that plagued inner-city schools that were majority Black. On the contrary, school rampage shootings were and continue to be primarily an artifact of white suburban and rural schools, and perpetrators are overwhelmingly men and most often white.[8] Another misconception of school shootings that is fueled by this racial fear is the idea that these tragic events have been increasing over time, yet despite the media coverage, the actual numbers show variation that is directly linked to the loosening of gun restriction laws.[9] One study found that while the number of school-based violent deaths decreased from 44 to 15 between 1993 and 2001, news of school shootings more than doubled during this period, from 200 news stories on the topic to 450.[10] In 2014, when I started interviewing mothers for this project, the number of school-based violent deaths totaled 10 that year, the lowest annual count in the past decade, while the annual average for the decade (32 deaths) was lower than the average in 1993 (44 deaths).[11] Yet this fear has been a catalyst for federal and state funding of zero-tolerance policies and employment of school police officers (SPOs), which, despite the location of many of these tragic events, have been disproportionately implemented in urban majority-minority schools across the country.[12]

These three developments have solidified relationships for Black students between schools and prisons.[13] This relationship is conceptualized as the school-to-prison pipeline, defined by Bryan Sykes and colleagues as "a collection of education and public safety policies" that place a disproportionate number of Black and Latine youth at risk of "discontinuing their academic careers" and "increasing their likelihood of correctional contact" due to discriminatory education policies, practices, and laws.[14] These discriminatory practices surface in several ways. First, regardless of class location, Black students are more likely to attend urban majority-minority schools that are underfunded, while white students are more likely to attend suburban and rural schools.[15] In response to cultural fears of a superpredator, or youths of color constructed as predatory and threatening to public safety, the 1990s ushered in zero-tolerance school policies, or approaches that deter misbehavior through harsh consequences yet have disproportionately targeted students of color, particularly Black students.[16] Zero-tolerance policies are often paired with the employment of SPOs within primarily majority-minority schools. Indeed, in 2000 (the year after the Columbine school shooting), $68 million was spent on hiring 599 SPOs in 289 schools.

Since then, federal funding for SPOs has decreased, yet state and local governments have kicked in to cover the costs. Current estimates suggest that since 2000, $1 billion has been spent on SPOs and that there has been steady growth in the number of SPOs employed in schools.[17] At the time of this writing, 58 percent of schools in the United States have an SPO, with an estimated 67,000 employed in schools across the nation.[18]

Research shows that zero-tolerance policies and the presence of SPOs in schools result in harsher punishment for minor offenses than in schools without SPOs. Students in schools with SPOs are more likely to be arrested and referred to the criminal justice system. Given where SPOs are hired, the result is that some behaviors from Black students are more often disciplined through arrests, while for white students similar behaviors more often lead to visits to the principal's office.[19] This differential response is hugely impactful. For example, in 2015–2016, when I was in the middle of conducting interviews for this study, Black students accounted for 36 percent of school arrests, despite constituting only 15 percent of the student population; white students accounted for 33 percent of arrests, despite constituting 50 percent of the student population.[20] This is how Black students have come to be disproportionately represented within the school-to-prison pipeline, which is correlated with incarceration into adulthood.

Second, discriminatory treatment also surfaces in how teachers respond to students, as made visible through the Black-white student suspension and expulsion gap.[21] During the 2013–2014 school year, when I began conducting interviews for this project, the US Department of Education reported 2.6 million students (5.3 percent) received out-of-school suspensions, with a disproportionate percentage (41 percent) of Black students, despite their representing only 16 percent of the total student population that year. By contrast, white students accounted for only 33 percent of out-of-school suspensions, even though they represented 50 percent of the total student population.[22] This means that Black students are four times more likely than white students to receive an out-of-school suspension. Why does a disproportionate percentage of Black students get suspended from school? Rather than these students being more likely to engage in disruptive behavior that results in suspensions or expulsions, researchers consistently find that the primary culprit is racial bias in how school personnel interpret the behavior of Black students. School personnel hold perceptions of Black students as troublemakers, dangerous, and less innocent than white students who engage in the same behaviors.[23]

This discriminatory treatment is also shaped by the gender of the student, with those at greatest risk of suspension being Black boys (17.6 percent compared with 5 percent for white boys).[24] This means that Black boys are 3.5 times more likely than white boys to experience out-of-school suspension. The use of stereotypes that make social injustices like racism and sexism, and the power upheld through these arrangements, appear normal is an example of what Patricia Hill Collins refers to as *controlling images*.[25] Framing Black boys through the controlling image of the "thug" is not reserved for teens or young adults but extends to very young boys in what sociologist Dawn Dow terms "baby racism".[26] Within the classroom, these controlling images lead teachers and administrators to read the same behavior from white boys as normal child's play, and from Black boys as aggressive and violent.[27] For example, in her study of Black and white boys in a public school, Ann Ferguson finds that administrators and teachers perceive Black boys' cultural forms of blackness (seen through behavior, dress, language, and preferences) as indicators that they are troublemakers and "naughty by nature," assuming maturity beyond their age; on the other hand, although white boys are also construed as naughty by school personnel, their behavior is seen as childlike and innocent.[28]

Black girls also experience discriminatory treatment that frames their behavior as aggressive, defiant, and loud, resulting in disproportionate rates of suspension and expulsion as compared with their white counterparts.[29] While Black girls are less likely to get suspended than Black boys, at 9.6 percent as compared with 17.6 percent, they are more likely to get suspended than both white boys (5 percent) and white girls (1.7 percent). In other words, Black girls are 5.5 times more likely to get suspended than white girls.[30] In their analysis of school discipline data from the Denver public school system, Subini Annamma and colleagues found that Black girls are most likely to have their behavior labeled as disobedient, defiant, or detrimental, or to receive office referrals for third-degree assault. Yet these are subjective charges, since they are based on teachers' or administrators' judgment of what is harmful, willfully disobedient, or knowingly causing bodily injury of another.[31] How can one know whether an action was willfully versus unwillfully disobedient? How can one assess whether a student knew they would cause bodily harm? By contrast, non-Black girls were more likely to receive an office referral for an objective reason (drug or alcohol possession or distribution). This research confirms that the very way that behavior is interpreted by school personnel is imbued with racist and gendered stereotypes, resulting in disparities in schools' disciplinary practices.

This unequal treatment of Black students relative to their white peers results in the naturalization of power arrangements and the oppression faced by Black students. These discriminatory practices contribute to the school-to-prison pipeline, in which Black students' behavior is criminalized and results in early contact with law enforcement.[32] It is no wonder that among Black students there is lowered trust in schools, a lowered feeling of belonging, and a lowered sense of personal agency.[33]

Aligning with this existing research, the stories from Black mothers presented in this chapter show the extent of the racial biases that school personnel hold toward Black students. Like Sharon, mentioned earlier in the chapter, mothers describe how their Black sons and daughters are singled out in the classroom as violent and aggressive by teachers, peers, and other school personnel, which leads the children to spend more time in the principal's office or in detention—time they could have spent learning in the classroom.[34] For Sharon, experiences like these led her to choose homeschooling for her son. The situations of three other mothers, Juanita, Lynette, and Hilda, allow us to further examine how experiences of racial bias in schools impact how Black mothers navigate their child's schooling.

Pushed to Homeschool

Juanita is a Black, college-educated widow with two daughters, Amber and Jamilla. She tells me that she removed her daughters from their all-white public school after her older daughter, Amber, had a negative encounter there:

> When she moved to the school, she was doing well. . . . I remember the teachers saying that she was at the top of her class. . . . [But] there was an

issue where she was assaulted by a [white boy] student. . . . I got a lawyer, because they weren't handling [it] and it kept being an issue. . . . They weren't keeping the [student] away from her. . . . Things just continued to get worse. . . . It was to the point that I was so nervous about my kid being in school . . . I just had to take her out.

As the school "pushed it under the rug," Juanita tried numerous tactics to address her daughter's assault. She explains, "Being a professional, I handled it in a professional manner." As a teacher herself, Juanita discussed how to handle the situation with her fellow teachers and professors but eventually hired a lawyer (though she ended up not pressing charges). "Amber being Black . . . played an important role" in her primarily white school's failure to handle the situation, Juanita concludes. Despite the financial hardship she faced as a single mother, she decided to remove both daughters from the school partway through the year. At first, Juanita sent both girls to a Christian school, but because of the cost and distance (with no public transportation options, Juanita's drive to the school took more than an hour round trip), she eventually switched to homeschooling. She knew some homeschoolers yet was otherwise fairly unfamiliar with the arrangement. Still, with the public school unresponsive, and the religious school too expensive, homeschooling seemed like the most feasible option for Juanita's family.

In discussing how racial discrimination is upheld, scholars have traced how organizations operate through providing whites access to material and social resources that Blacks are denied.[35] The narratives of Sharon, Juanita, and other Black mothers highlight how under school choice policies, schools diminish the agency of Black families: rather than having access to a full range of educational choices, these mothers are *pushed* to handle schools that fail to address discriminatory practices and incidents. Black homeschooling mothers feel that the only way they can address nonhomeschools' institutional racism is to remove their children from those schools.[36]

The first chapter of this book began with a description of Lynette and her son, Trevor, whose teacher profiled her then-seven-year-old as "violent." The married Black mother of two spent a great deal of time intervening at the school on her son's behalf, talking with the principal and Trevor's teachers but eventually decided to homeschool him. She says, "I had known of a homeschooling family. That's how I heard that it existed and that it was legal." Like Juanita, Lynette recalls knowing very little about homeschooling other than that it appeared to be the only good option for her child.

Importantly, schools do not have to be located in white districts to exhibit institutional racism. Hilda, a Black homeschooling mother and now grandmother, recalls how dismayed she had been almost two decades prior as she watched these dynamics unfold in her neighborhood school, with its majority-minority student population. Hilda started homeschooling when her youngest son was in high school and she was worried he might be "falling into the wrong crowd." As she tells me:

> In my family, since slavery, the men have done really poorly. . . . It's almost like a curse in my family. I thought with my son, I'm going to do everything I can to keep him on the straight and narrow. Then when he wanted to go to public school, he went downhill; he's doing very well now, but that was my reason to homeschool.

Research on how the carceral state targets Black students supports Hilda's account: discrimination, coupled with a lack of resources in majority-minority schools, act as barriers to Black students success, particularly for boys.[37] How this discrimination materializes is different due to varied classroom compositions: here, rather than being targeted as the only Black student in a white classroom, Hilda's son was experiencing the dearth of resources and opportunities in a low-income majority Black and Latine classroom.

Existing research suggests that along with race, or being Black, a host of other factors including student poverty and school resources are correlated with higher risk of school suspension and entry into the school-to-prison pipeline. For example, Pedro Noguera's research makes clear that the school a child attends and the neighborhood in which they live greatly impact their life, both factors that are shaped by race and class.[38] Children growing up in poverty are more likely to attend schools with fewer resources and larger class sizes, making discipline a managing strategy for overextended teachers. Poverty is also correlated with a higher risk of school suspension due to added challenges students face outside of the classroom that can lead to disruptive behavior. In

addition, because of racial discrimination, Black children are dispro-
portionally represented in these lower-resourced schools. Even still,
race remains a persistent predictor of harsher punishment, regardless of
socioeconomic status.[39] Hilda's story shows how despite their class resources, Black middle-class families face a particular challenge that can
place their child in schools where discipline through the carceral state
can be inevitable. These families seek to have their child interact with
other Black students, yet given the racial wealth gap, this often means
enrolling their child in an underresourced school.

Pushed to Change Schools

"Claudia never had a fight in school until this time," Dejah points out
before describing intervening in her daughter's education. When Claudia
had an altercation with another student, Dejah, a married, working-class
mother of three, found herself dealing with much of the same language
deployed against Lynette's young son, Trevor. As Dejah tells me:

> A girl said . . . something negative about my daughter. . . . Claudia lunged
> past the teacher to get to the girl. . . . Because Claudia is a taller girl, and
> she didn't look like any of the other girls in her accelerated class what-
> soever; she is the only Black girl . . . all the other ones are Caucasian. . . .
> That's when the principal told me that the teacher does not feel safe
> around her; this is a white teacher. I said, "What do you mean, [not] feel
> safe? . . . If I have to go over your heads I will."

In Dejah's case, racial bias pushed her family out of the school.
Homeschooling was familiar but did not seem like a viable option for
their dual-earner household, so Dejah moved Claudia to another public
school in the region.

Like the Black homeschooling mothers, those who didn't choose to
homeschool, like Dejah, describe racial bias as affecting their school
choice. Because I sampled for nonhomeschoolers through homeschoolers' networks, these Black mothers knew other homeschooling families,
yet these relationships did not lead to their viewing homeschooling as an
appealing or viable option. Instead, mobilizing school choice, working-
class mothers like Dejah draw on what resources they have, to move

their child to a different school. Dejah's response to the racial discrimination that surfaced in her Black daughter's majority white classroom demonstrates how the school operates as a racialized organization, since it limits her ability to exercise school choice.[40] Dejah's agency is diminished because her "choice" involves being pushed out of the school due to racial discrimination, while she has fewer material resources than many of her Black homeschooling counterparts.

The targeting of Black students is not specific to public school classrooms. Married, middle-class Amelia has three children, all of whom began their education in a local private school. She and her husband paid the tuition out of pocket, yet Amelia soon realized she "wasn't happy" with the school and its treatment of her kids. The teachers were "very rude" and often "yelling at my son for no reason," Amelia recalls. She believed "if I was paying money," the teachers "should have some respect." Reasoning that the public schools were "just as good" and more "cost-effective," Amelia and her husband decided to go in that direction.

Amelia tells me that her kids didn't "say anything" about being the only students of color at their private school, but that it "probably had some effect" and that the kids "didn't have a lot of friends" there. Once they got to the "very diverse" local public school, her kids "met a lot of friends. People from Africa . . . a lot of people [who spoke] Spanish." The school has larger class sizes and fewer resources, but Amelia describes being much happier with it and says the teachers are far better. If they "know the parent is involved," she tells me, noting that she has "gone to all the parent-teacher meetings," she believes the teachers "will go out of their way to help the students." After advocating for her kids within and being pushed out of a racially discriminatory private school setting, Amelia had to do a great deal of research to assess the schooling options available to her kids. Now she stays involved in the new school to ensure her children receive the quality education she knows they deserve.

Not all Black mothers I spoke with framed their schooling strategies as a response to racial discrimination. Emory, a Black middle-class married mother to teenager Ruby, feels they were pushed out of their neighborhood's majority-minority public school because it failed to meet Ruby's academic needs. Under her Individualized Education Program, Ruby was supposed to receive special education services to help develop her math skills, but the school wasn't holding up its end of the bargain.

Indeed, existing research shows that responses to specialized learning plans are raced. Diagnosis and services are less likely to be provided to Black students than to white students (especially white boys).[41] Black students with disabilities are more likely than white students to attend schools that lack the support necessary for success. The result can be disciplinary responses to childlike behavior that some research finds is linked to undiagnosed disabilities. Instead of receiving the diagnosis and support necessary to manage disabilities such as attention deficit disorder, dyslexia, or anxiety, young Black students may be disciplined for disruptive behavior and funneled into the school-to-prison pipeline.[42] However, the results are not necessarily better for Black students from higher-income backgrounds who attend primarily white, well-resourced schools, since these districts are found to overenroll Black students in special education programs.[43]

The lack of response from schools to Ruby and other Black students with disabilities has long-term implications for education inequality. The failure of the neighborhood school to recognize Ruby's learning needs led Emory to invest her time and energy into advocating for her daughter and, when the needed accommodations failed to appear, send her to one of the region's charter schools. She has dreams of Ruby going to college, and the charter school seems like the best way to get her there. "My experience," she says, is that sending Ruby to the local school was "a harder journey." At the charter, Emory adds, "being a smaller school, I can still call and speak to a staff member or principal and because it's a new school hopefully their ears are open . . . they are trying to get this all right."

At the same time, Emory frets over the intensive schedule at Ruby's new school. With her daughter in school until 4:30 p.m. each day and attending an additional half day on Saturdays, Emory says she wonders whether it is good that her daughter is "working those extra hours." She continues:

> I think that sometimes [the school] is trying to take a certain group of kids. I notice that a lot of kids get sent to the summer school and to the Saturday school. . . . They are mostly Black and Puerto Rican. And so you throw them into this "study, study, study" . . . there's something with that. I'm sure they want everybody to be at a certain level, but why [does Ruby] have to do eight hours per week to get to the same level that other people are already at?

Emory's observation suggests that the Black and Puerto Rican students spend much more time in school than "other" (presumably white) students. Informal segregation of this sort is not surprising: recent trends show that charter schools tend to be segregated, with especially high proportions of Black and Latine students.[44] Yet instead of training teachers and administrators to be highly educated on issues of race and racism and to develop culturally relevant curricula, Ruby's school seems to engage a deficit model that holds whiteness as the standard and blackness as an educational liability. In other words, teachers assume that Black students just need to catch up to whites.

Despite her concerns with the charter school, Emory is hopeful that the rigor and attention to her daughter's special needs will pay off, particularly when Ruby transitions from high school to college. It is unclear, however, whether this will happen; current research remains inconclusive regarding the benefits of charter schools for student learning outcomes.[45]

As described in the next chapter, Emory's schooling strategy parallels, to an extent, the strategies of white nonhomeschool mothers who transfer schools: the mobilization of her school choice came in response to a lack of specialized attention for her daughter rather than to overt racism. Yet the type of school Emory is leaving is drastically different than the schools that white nonhomeschoolers are leaving. While Emory transferred Ruby from a low-income majority-minority school to gain specialized attention, white mothers tend to transfer their children from well-resourced primarily white schools to access *even more* specialized attention.

Scholars have carefully documented how the widespread pattern of racial discrimination shapes Black families' schooling experiences and decisions.[46] For example, Black mothers of children entering kindergarten are particularly concerned with the racial composition of the school and the perspectives and practices teachers describe. These mothers draw on close family relationships to bolster their child's Black identity, compensating for the anti-Black rhetoric children face in dominant institutions, including schools.[47] In her research, education scholar Camille Wilson Cooper found that, contrary to common stereotypes school personnel may hold, Black low-income and working-class mothers are actively involved in their children's education. They carefully research the best schooling options available to them and volunteer within the school to advocate for their own children, but also for other Black children.[48] These mothers fight tirelessly on behalf of their children, demanding quality education, respectful treatment, and culturally relevant curricula. Similarly, I found through the narratives of Black mothers such as Dejah, Amelia, and Emory that a lowered trust in schools results in Black families with the resources to do so using school choice to remove their children from these discriminatory spaces by transferring schools or homeschooling. Still left unexamined is why similarly situated families—Black, mostly middle-class families facing racism within educational settings—make such different choices.

Distinguishing Homeschoolers from Nonhomeschoolers

Black mothers' accounts highlight how neoliberal-era school choice policies and the prominent American value of individualism through relying on market mechanisms converge to maintain schooling inequalities. Note that, under school choice, Dejah was able to remain living in the same neighborhood yet transfer her daughter to another city school to remove her from a racially discriminatory environment. Under the guise of individual choice and market forces, school choice asks families, specifically mothers, to deal with the racial discrimination their children experience in schools by leveraging their freedom to "choose" the school that best fits their individual child and family. Those unable to mobilize school choice due to less flexible work schedules, transportation challenges, and fewer resources, especially single-headed households, are left behind—and their inability to make a different choice leaves the impression of satisfaction with their current option.

Like Dejah, Amelia, and Emory, many of the Black mothers I spoke with describe starting their children in traditional schools, drawing from dominant middle-class mothering approaches to intervene on their child's behalf after a negative in-school interaction,[49] and then transferring their child to a new school when they find the administrators noncompliant. This is the racialized toll of Black mothering under school choice. And while the intervening nonhomeschoolers did look very similar to that of their homeschooling counterparts, the differences in their final school decisions are based at least in part on the influence of a homeschooler and their family characteristics. For example, all of those who homeschooled described a homeschool family they knew as motivating their decision. For nonhomeschoolers, while all of them knew homeschoolers, the family did not persuade them to homeschool. In addition, it is notable that all but one of the Black homeschoolers are in married households and most are middle-class, suggesting the resources that come from this family form also shape their ability to see homeschooling as a viable alternative (see table A.1, appendix A). Resources also most likely shaped the neighborhood in which the family lived and therefore the schooling options seen as available to solve the problem of racial discrimination. Those living in white neighborhoods were more likely to bring their children home to solve the problem, while those living in neighborhoods of color were more likely to intervene in the school on their child's behalf or, if they had the resources, transfer their child to a different school.

For the Black mothers in my study, racial discrimination was the main driver in their school choices—even for Emory, it factored into the lack of special education attention her daughter received relative to white students—while for the white mothers it was individualized learning. These differences highlight how the racial hierarchy manifests among Black and white class-advantaged families through grade school education. As sociologists Melissa Wooten and Lucius Couloute posit, racialized organizations such as these schools "prevent certain organizational actors," such as Black students and their families, "from successfully laying claim to the rewards that they are due."[50] In school choice, the same context that constrains Black mothers' agency (pushing them out to avoid discrimination) enables white mothers' agency (they respond to the pull to cultivate individualized learning). This suggests that blackness serves as a barrier that limits school choice for Black families, while whiteness serves as a credential that mobilizes school choice for white families. At the same time, we should not assume Black mothers accept this injustice. Indeed, serving as their child's education advocate is a form of political resistance and an act of care through which these mothers seek to ensure their child's educational success and racial empowerment.[51]

Both homeschool and nonhomeschool mothers are making decisions that disrupt a common assumption that children attend the same school for years on end. Certainly, increased mobility among class-advantaged families due to precarity in employment has resulted in children changing schools more frequently than in decades past.[52] Still, these accounts suggest that some of this movement is driven by persistent racial discrimination in schools and is a strategy employed by middle- and working-class families alike.

Placemaking among the Black Middle Class

Black families are "strategic place makers and city makers who used the assets of size, concentration, and cultural production to create cultural and economic power that influenced the spatial organization of the American landscape," write sociologists Marcus Anthony Hunter and Zandria F. Robinson in *Chocolate Cities*.[53] The map of current Black life needs to address the legacies of inequality and the Great Migration of Black people out of the American South in the early and mid-twentieth century. Dreams were not fulfilled but deferred as receiving cities came to be marked by expanded poverty, mass incarceration, police violence, and diminished opportunities for Black Americans. Today, in what Hunter and Robinson refer to as "chocolate maps," we see striking similarities across Black communities in the United States that reflect the lived reality of Black Americans, yet chocolate cities are also geographic concentrations of Black life and crucial spaces where Black cultural, economic, and political power can flourish beyond the white gaze.[54]

These patterns of racialized migration, marginalization, and resistance surfaced within my research through many Black mothers' stories. Those who lived in predominantly Black communities spoke of being denied access to the material resources considered normal in white spaces, rather than overt discriminatory encounters. Those who lived in white communities, on the other hand, routinely framed their choices around their children's schooling in terms of racist incidents. These Black middle-class mothers face tough decisions around residence and schooling, given the realities of Black life in America.

Juanita, a Black homeschooling mom to Amber (discussed earlier in the chapter), describes her relatively rural town outside of Elmford as having "little diversity." Even though she brought her daughter home to provide an anti-racist learning environment, their family remains racially isolated, being part of the less than 1 percent Black population in their 86 percent white town. That the town's school is representative of these demographics helps to explain why Amber felt targeted: she was one of the few Black kids in a primarily white school.[55] A similar situation surfaces in Lynette and Trevor's suburban neighborhood, where 78 percent of the population are white and 5 percent are Black. At Trevor's neighborhood public school, fewer than 2 percent of students were Black, the same share as at Jerome's school at the time his mom, Sharon, brought him home (their neighborhood and public schools are 89 percent white).

There are many reasons these families live in the predominantly white communities they do, including the opportunity to access good housing, jobs, or schools. Indeed, existing research has found that Black middle-class families face an untenable situation: move to primarily white neighborhoods for schools or jobs but deal with being the only Black family, or move to neighborhoods composed primarily of families of color and have access to fewer resources.[56] Racial discrimination in the housing market circumscribes their choices, again influencing respondents' residential and schooling decisions.[57]

As we have seen in research with nonhomeschooling families, race is inextricably linked to parents' schooling concerns.[58] In her research with Black middle-class mothers, Dawn Dow found that it can be challenging to find communities composed of other Black middle-class families. When seeking to temper the societal reception of their children and their ability to survive and thrive as African Americans, these families' residential and schooling decisions carry extra weight.[59] Some families may decide to live in white neighborhoods for the equity that comes in their home value and living conditions, while others may find living in low-income Black neighborhoods, or the surrounding community, as more accessible, desirable, and fruitful for community and building a strong Black identity in their children.[60]

Those parents who choose to homeschool are unlikely to find a socially connected Black community to join. Now that she homeschools, Sharon mentions, "I'm usually the only Black person [at homeschool events]." Their children's nonhomeschool extracurricular activities tend to be very white, too. Sharon states, "Even [my daughter's] ballet class. She's the only Black student." Deciding to homeschool while living in a white residential neighborhood still means navigating a host of white spaces that reflect the demographics of their town.

Black respondents' ability to mobilize their agency under school choice is also inflected by the widening racial wealth gap in the United States. Although I did not ask respondents about their household wealth, at the time of my study, national data showed a white median net wealth of $142,000 compared with $11,000 for Black families—in other words, the median white American family had ten times the accumulated wealth of the median Black American family.[61] This racial wealth gap is the result of complex, overlapping, and racially motivated policies and practices. Thus, even though my middle-class respondents had equivalent household *incomes*, the Black families all but certainly held less wealth than their white counterparts. In those cases where mothers opted out of paid work to homeschool, we can surmise that it was a tougher shift for the Black families' home economies.

Unlike Sharon, Juanita, and Hilda, who first enrolled their children in nonhomeschools before bringing them home, the second set of homeschool respondents (ten Black mothers) were those who never sent their children to traditional schools at all. These families tended to be more religious and, like Sharon, to live in majority white neighborhoods and school districts. Monique, a Black middle-class and married homeschooling mother of six children, lives in an Elmford suburb that's just 2 percent Black. Even the homeschool community is predominantly white, with Monique musing, "I don't know too many Black families that homeschool." Her children play on sports teams in a neighboring town, "just because that's where their friends live, and it's more diverse." Monique prioritizes a religious education first but supplements it by making sure the kids socialize with other Black children (even if that means traveling to a neighboring town). Her story is almost paralleled by those of Sandy and Viola, both working-class married Black homeschoolers, who live in towns that are primarily white and attend churches that are also primarily white. As Sandy puts it, "We're the only chip in the cookie at church, so to speak," referencing how their blackness stands out in a primarily white church. Families like theirs can be isolated in white spaces, making their residential and schooling decisions particularly difficult.

Not all the Black homeschool mothers I interviewed lived in primarily white neighborhoods. I found that some Black middle-class mothers, like Hilda (the homeschooling mom and grandma mentioned earlier), were able to disrupt the material disadvantages accruing to their children in attending majority-minority schools by drawing on their material resources to homeschool. Hilda lives in a majority Black low-income neighborhood, where 11 percent of the population is white and 57 percent Black. Hilda and her husband both hold master's degrees and work in professional careers, and they leverage these class advantages to resist the institutional barriers that prevent Black students, particularly Black boys, from achieving success in the neighborhood public school.[62] Existing research finds that Black middle-class families who live in predominantly low-income Black neighborhoods demonstrate secondary marginalization; these findings reveal the limits of building solidarity across classes in Black communities because there are hierarchies at work even within racial enclaves.[63]

Black Strategic Schooling

I refer to the decisions that these mothers make as *Black strategic schooling*, which involves parents' weighing the various racial factors that will shape their Black children's schooling experiences and outcomes. Karyn Lacy's research, for instance, found that Black middle-class families use "strategic assimilation" to navigate white middle-class spaces while seeking Black middle-class neighborhoods or Black social and religious organizations outside of their neighborhood to provide additional spaces to build racial identity and solidarity.[64] Some mothers in my study, like Juanita, Lynette, and Sharon, made that decision, choosing to live in primarily white neighborhoods with better living conditions and well-resourced schools, even though their children may be racial outliers in their classrooms (opening the possibility that they will be targeted for their race within the classroom). After such encounters, these Black mothers made the *strategic* decision to turn to homeschooling to buffer their children from the racism of white-dominated spaces. Effectively, their decision allows Black middle-class mothers to develop children's racial identities through the family, gain access to the resources that come with middle-class white neighborhoods, and avoid a measure of overt racism in schools. Other mothers in my study, like Hilda, chose to live in Black communities at least partially to help their children cultivate a strong racial identity and sense of belonging, but they leveraged their material resources to homeschool and avoid sending kids to the underfunded majority-minority neighborhood school.

We have seen how some Black mothers, like Juanita, Lynette, Sharon, Monique, and Viola, practice Black strategic schooling by choosing to *live* in predominantly white middle-class neighborhoods, but homeschool to avoid the racial isolation their Black child could experience in those neighborhoods' white schools. The trade-off is racial isolation imposed by the composition of homeschooling families—after all, the homeschooling community's demographics will largely match those of the entire community. By contrast, Black strategic schooling plays out differently for lower-income families. Many of the Black non-homeschoolers in my study are financially constrained as they navigate their neighborhood and schooling decisions; several head single-parent households, few attended college, and most work full-time in low-wage jobs. This difference in class resources and location is notable given that I located nonhomeschooling Black families through the middle-class Black homeschoolers. Thus, these families are at least loosely part of the same social network but access very different neighborhood and schooling options. In the end, I found that, rather than living in primarily white and middle-class neighborhoods, the Black nonhomeschooling families tended to live in racially consonant neighborhoods and send their children to neighborhood schools (figure 4.1).

Working full-time in medical billing, Caroline sends her two boys to the Elmford public schools. A Black, working-class, single mother, Caroline lives in a neighborhood that is 47 percent white and 22 percent Black. Though her younger child, Nigel, was given the option of being bused to a suburban white school under a decades-old antisegregation program, "he knows everybody" at his neighborhood school and "didn't feel comfortable leaving" his classmates of many years. Caroline recalls it as a "tough decision," since she knew the suburban school would have provided better educational opportunities for Nigel, but the trade-offs in terms of hours of commuting and racial isolation made it an ultimately unappealing choice. Contrary to stereotypes that suggest lower-income Black mothers are uninvolved in their children's schooling, Caroline is clearly involved in overseeing her children's education, doing extensive research to assess her son's options under school choice, despite her

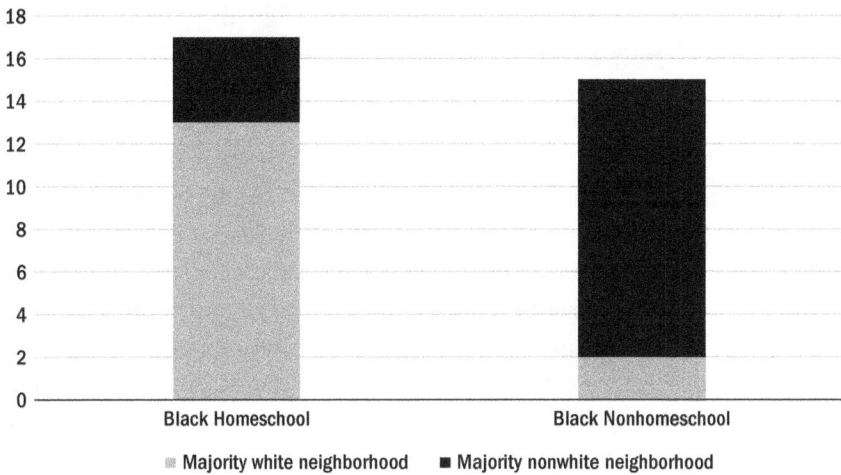

Figure 4.1. Black mothers' neighborhoods

full-time and inflexible work schedule. This is what Cooper refers to as "positioned school choices" and reflects decisions that are shaped by mothers' sociohistorical positionality and are based on how they define educational goals for their children.[65]

Sheila and Sarita are also Black working-class mothers who send their children to their local public school. Both mothers live in majority-minority neighborhoods (32 percent white, 45 percent Latine, and 21 percent Black). Sheila tells me the public school her children attend is "fine" and has not caused her "any problems." As a full-time student and part-time employee, she finds it convenient to drop her kids off at the bus stop on her way to work and let them take the bus home (that way, "I don't have to deal with the extra traffic"). Sarita is also fairly satisfied with her son Jonathan's neighborhood public school, though she says his current teacher is "not a good fit" for him. Before Jonathan entered school, Sarita interviewed the principal and kindergarten teacher, and she joined the Parent-Teacher Association so that she would be involved in what was going on in the school. Despite these efforts, Sarita's confidence in the school has dropped in the past year; Jonathan's teacher is "very strict" and structured, which she says doesn't fit with Jonathan's strengths as a "gifted" and "artistic" student. In addition, Sarita describes the school as rife with "behavioral problems" that disrupt Jonathan's learning. Her narrative mirrors some of the language used to describe schooling concerns by white mothers (discussed in the next chapter) and signals the influence of school choice—fostering the uniqueness of your child through finding the "right" school—as an ideology that is embedded in contemporary child-rearing.[66] Yet the meaning behind her choice demonstrates the significance of race; while not framed in racial terms as seen with many of their Black middle-class counterparts, the ability of Caroline, Sheila, Sarita, and other Black working-class mothers to "choose" an alternate school comes with the stumbling block of not just racial discrimination but also the limitations of having fewer material resources. Despite these obstacles, Black working-class mothers remain highly involved in their children's schooling and in navigating school choice.

Some of the working-class Black mothers did signal the racial undertones of their child's schooling experience. For example, Lulu, a single working-class mother lives in a multiracial neighborhood and school district. Lulu works full-time to support herself and her daughter, Esther, which limits the schooling options available to them. Thus, her daughter attends public school (where the student body is 56 percent white, 35 percent Latine, and 5 percent Black). Esther's experience at the local public school is, according to her mother, "challenging." When Esther was in kindergarten, for instance, one teacher repeatedly called Lulu and reported her daughter for misbehavior. It made Lulu wonder whether the teacher was "targeting my daughter" because the girl is African American. Though the teacher was "making it sound like my daughter is the biggest problem," Lulu remembers her gratitude that the principal was understanding and helped her deal with the teacher. As a result, she has no plans to transfer Esther to another school.

Homeschoolers or not, Black families face tough decisions when it comes to securing their child's education. Many of the Black homeschooling mothers in my study live in predominantly white and middle-class neighborhoods, and they homeschool to help their kids avoid the racial isolation or discrimination they could experience (or have already experienced) in those neighborhoods' primarily white schools. The downside, since the homeschool groups are also mostly white, is that the children and parents both contend with racial isolation as homeschoolers. By contrast, most of the Black nonhomeschoolers in the region live in neighborhoods composed of families of color and send their children to neighborhood schools where their children can build racial pride. Yet this often involves attending schools with fewer resources. Regardless of a Black mother's decision, school choice comes with trade-offs for Black families, including isolation, underresourced schools, or racial hostility. Whether homeschooling or not, mothers demonstrate Black strategic schooling by weighing the racial factors that will privilege their children's schooling stability over other responsibilities. While leading to different outcomes—homeschooling, transferring schools, or staying in the same traditional school—all three options highlight Black mothers' efforts to protect their children from the racial hostility present under school choice.

Conclusion: Choice, Constraint, or Resistance?

This chapter has examined how schools themselves shape Black mothers' schooling choices. One set of Black mothers chose to homeschool from the beginning, while a second set started their children in non-homeschools and ended up homeschooling rather than transferring schools when the school seemed to fail them.[67] Research on this second group looks very similar to that on Black homeschooling families in the Mid-Atlantic and southern United States, in that these families homeschool primarily to protect their children from racism within schools—a choice that can be seen as an act of resistance.[68] Yet, previous research does not provide direct comparisons to similarly located nonhomeschooling families living in the same region. By drawing on the social networks of these Black homeschooling families to interview their non-homeschooling counterparts, I found that both can be pushed out of traditional school due to racial discrimination. Yet, despite being embedded within overlapping social networks, these families live in different neighborhoods—which leads to finding different solutions to solve the problem of racial discrimination. Those living in white neighborhoods bring their children home, while those living in neighborhoods of color intervene in the school on their child's behalf or, if they have the resources, transfer their child to a different school. Another factor that may contribute to these decisions is having a personal role model of a homeschooling family in one's network; those who did not homeschool their children knew other homeschoolers but did not mention them as influential in their decision.

Through Black strategic schooling, Black mothers draw from their various class resources to navigate the racial constraints within their region's schooling landscape and mobilize school choice for their children. Plenty of research shows that Black boys and girls are targets of discriminatory treatment within traditional schools, framed as aggressive and violent,[69] and the stories I heard from Black mothers indicated that their children face similar stereotyping. Serving as education advocates by removing their children from this context is a form of resistance—mothers free their children from the racism embedded in schools, at least temporarily. Much like the middle-class families in Dawn Dow's research, who can afford to take their kids to childcare centers but choose to rely on extended kin to avoid racial discrimination,[70] the Black mothers highlighted in this chapter report seeking to avoid racial discrimination in schools by transferring out of majority white schools, starting their child in majority-minority schools, or relying on the racial solidarity of their extended family to homeschool (as discussed in chapter 6).

In sum, Black mothers' explanations for why and how they make the schooling choices that they do demonstrate respondents are deeply invested in their children's education and are particularly aware of the racial discrimination embedded in schools. They are also very aware of the future repercussions if they fail to ensure a successful schooling experience for their children. How respondents go about putting this quality schooling into place is shaped by the choices afforded them by their class resources and the constraints they face due to racism. School choice initiatives paradoxically leave these Black families to deal with school-based racial discrimination on their own. When school administrations are unresponsive, mothers are left on their own to find a less discriminatory schooling option for their child. For those who live in predominantly white neighborhoods and have positive homeschool role models, this may lead to homeschooling, while those who live in predominantly Black neighborhoods often transfer their child to a different school in the hope that it will be a better option.

Black middle-class mothers are making decisions that are shaped by their country's vast race and class segregation. Inequality is nothing out of the ordinary in Elmford and its surrounding area because it's nothing out of the ordinary in the United States. Racial discrimination in neighborhood policies and preferences is a contributing factor in respondents' residential and schooling decisions, because barriers to spatial and social mobility are linked.[71] As Hunter and Robinson state, "there is a power in movement," and so "restricting the movements of Black people is a central feature of anti-Black racism." This means that a Black family "leaving a place is an essential act of political agency."[72] As strategic schooling navigators, Black mothers are asserting their resistance to racism by leaving a place, in this case, a white school.

As W. E. B. Du Bois so famously wrote in 1903, "The problem of the twentieth century is the problem of the color-line—the relation of the darker to the lighter races."[73] We are well into the twenty-first century, and the color line remains powerful. We can see it calcifying in school choice policies, propelling Black families to wade into school choice in ways white families need not. Still, I find it is the interaction of the color line with the gender line that truly amplifies the extensive labor thrust upon Black mothers, who are charged with dealing with systematic discrimination, preparing their children for its effects, intervening in schools, and shouldering much of the supplemental schooling work that goes along with market-logic education.

Further, homeschooling and schooling transfers are unequally accessible, leaving those most marginalized to deal with the racial discrimination in nonhomeschools on their own. Homeschooling is among the least accessible, yet still crucial, options—and even that choice cannot undo racial isolation, given that the practice itself is highly white in the Elmford context. By comparing homeschoolers to their nonhomeschooling counterparts, this chapter has highlighted how Black schooling strategies, while similar, are significantly shaped by neighborhood, class resources, and social networks.

"I Wish It Was a Bit More Diverse"

Schooling Decisions of White Mothers

"I don't want to be in a very gentrified area where it's all white," Sarah told me, adding that racial homogeneity "really restricts" her son's "experiences and ability to connect with others." I sat across from this white homeschooling mom in a hip coffee shop—one sign of gentrification's creep toward Elm Park, the majority Black neighborhood where Sarah and her seven-year-old son, Caiden, lived. Speaking over the coffee shop's buzzing atmosphere, she conceded that homeschooling Caiden meant immersing him in a nearly all-white educational environment: their own home and their mostly white homeschool group. She sighed, "I wish it was a bit more diverse."

All of this diverged from Sarah's original plan. She had moved to Elm Park, where in 2010 more than 50 percent of the population was Black and some 30 percent Latine, specifically so that her white son would have a chance to "connect with others." Now, having decided to homeschool, Sarah enrolls Caiden in nonacademic activities in the neighborhood—he plays, for instance, on the Elm Park soccer team. The decisions haven't been easy, yet this mom felt the neighborhood school had not been able to provide individual attention for Caiden and that his teachers there seemed to aggravate his tendency for "testing boundaries" while making "all these excuses" for Caiden's behavior and reporting to her that he was "doing fine." To her mind, Sarah was plainly better equipped to manage Caiden's behavioral and learning needs, and so she brought him home.

Sarah is not alone in making schooling decisions that keep her child in a mostly white learning environment, while expressing the sentiment of valuing racial diversity. Again and again, the white mothers I interviewed described schooling decisions that place their child into primarily white spaces while lamenting the lack of racial diversity. This pattern is a troublesome workaround for dealing with systemic racism and left me wondering: Did Sarah and other white mothers really feel the best schooling option was a white one and not see the connection to systemic racism, or was this a performative measure that white mothers used to avoid appearing to contribute to racism? Interviews cannot disclose respondents' conscious and subconscious thoughts, but my interviews allowed me to explore white mothers' decisions and the harmful impact of these decisions for our education system, which are the focus of this chapter.

Notably, Sarah is the only white mother I spoke with who proactively decided to move her white family into a predominantly Black neighborhood. Most of the white mothers in this study lived in white neighborhoods, sometimes seeking out nonacademic activities for their children in neighboring, less-white districts. Certainly, this pattern is not new. Studies show that regardless of a public school's academic performance, it will lose white middle-class students if it is in a district with a higher racial minority composition, particularly of Black students.[1] This is to say, framing their decisions in nonracial and even color-blind terms, white middle-class families make schooling decisions that echo long-standing patterns of white flight from integrated neighborhoods and schools.[2] As Eduardo Bonilla-Silva puts it, their white privilege is wielded as if they wear "color-blind eyeglasses" that are "tinted with the myth that race is no longer relevant."[3]

Studying white mothers allows me to tell a different side of the racial segregation story: the white privilege to pick and choose when to acknowledge race in parenting decisions and the troubling impact of such decisions on schools and families. Whether or not they chose to homeschool, white mothers described making decisions to place their children in white learning environments, while many simultaneously sought out racially integrated nonacademic settings. The outcome is that these white mothers engage in a *partial* white flight. They mobilize their agency under school choice and within the racial and class hierarchies of the United States.

The negative outcomes of racial segregation in schooling for all students are well documented.[4] Racial segregation is linked to unequal distribution of material resources between majority white and predominantly Black schools. Further, whites' increased contact with students of color proves to be a significant indicator of the racial views they hold.[5] This is especially the case for whites' views of Blacks, suggesting that integrated schools can increase whites' awareness of existing racial injustices and disrupt their color blindness. For example, whites who express color-blind views are less likely to support diversity-driven affirmative action policies or to have awareness of how whiteness provides daily privileges in their lives, while making neighborhood and schooling choices that tend to support racial segregation.[6] In contrast, whites who choose integrated neighborhoods and schools tend to be more aware of contemporary racism and their own racial privilege.[7] Here I argue that white mothers in this study make decisions under school choice policies that (regardless of intention) rely on racial privilege by appearing to support racial diversity while simultaneously viewing schooling decisions as nonracial. Not "seeing" race in a deeply race-inflected context like schooling is how white privilege and power are maintained.

Pulled to Homeschool

As described earlier in this book, scholars have carefully documented racial disparities in classroom interactions, particularly how Black children's behavior often gets criminalized while the same behavior from white children gets normalized.[8] In fact, the book's opening story was about Trevor, a seven-year-old Black boy whom public school teachers and administrators portrayed as "violent" in their frequent meetings with his mother, Lynette. We know little, however, about how white families respond to their child's experience of normalization in school—or whether they notice the difference at all.

Mostly, I find that white mothers' responses to children's treatment in the classroom do not focus on racialized treatment but on whether their child is getting the individualized education they see as imperative. For instance, Joan, a white upper-middle-class married woman with two sons, explains how she and her husband prioritized "fit" in their decision to homeschool their son Matthias:

> We kept trying to work with the school to almost make it a forced fit. Third grade it was obvious, it wasn't a very good fit. At first, I thought,

"Oh, he's the youngest in the class." He just didn't feel very good about himself, so I thought, "Well, we'll just give him a year off the grid."

Matthias's low self-esteem led to his parents' pull toward other educational options. Their unfamiliarity with homeschooling meant Joan framed the switch as a sort of temporary information-gathering period: "We'll also take the year to get to know him a little better, in terms of his academic style, and then we can find a school that better fits." Homeschooling suited Matthias so well that his parents decided to continue past the first year, even though Joan and her husband chose to keep their younger son, Toby, in traditional school. Toby is "very social" and likes being in school, his mom says, "having his group of friends . . . teachers and rules . . . he just likes the whole thing about school." Thus, Joan's schooling strategy involves seeking the best fit for each child, even if it leads to increased responsibilities in managing her sons' education, since she has to navigate two different school types.

For Emily, a white married middle-class homeschooling mother, the same strategy of prioritizing individualized learning pulled her to homeschool all five of her children. She tells me: "That's one thing that's cool about homeschooling is that you learn that there is no one-size-fits all. . . . People are organic beings. . . . Every child deserves a special education . . . so that's where the schools fail." Emily's local school was primarily white and low-income, and she saw it as wholly unable to provide the "special education" she says each of her sons deserves.

Importantly, Joan's and Emily's ability to choose homeschooling relies on their husbands serving as primary financial providers so that these mothers can remain out of the workforce to serve as their children's primary educator and caregiver. This arrangement is certainly a sacrifice for the women's careers, since both had invested in college (and Joan in graduate school) and had worked full-time in professional careers before having kids, Joan as businesswoman and Emily as a preschool teacher. Yet we can speculate that this option is less accessible for single-headed households and lower-income families. In addition, these white families are able to prioritize individualized learning in their schooling decisions, contrasting with the Black mothers who were primarily motivated to homeschool to protect their children from racial discrimination in the classroom.[9] This pattern fits tidily with the idea of schools as sites of institutional racism; as defined by race scholars, organizations like schools are *racialized* when they enhance the agency of whites and diminish the agency of Black families.[10] When school choice policies fail to account for the ways in which schools and school enrollments are shaped by race, their enticement to parents to select the option that best fits their child effectively applies a wash of color blindness over an undeniably racialized mechanism of de facto school segregation.

Put differently, even Black families with similar material resources as whites are not given full agency under school choice due to the racial discrimination embedded within the schools and the staff who frequently racially profile Black children as aggressive and violent.[11] This leaves Black children more likely to be tracked into noncollege courses and more likely to receive detentions and expulsions, which hinders their learning.[12] While the topic is outside the scope of this study, early criminalization through labeling and punishment in schools is demonstrably tied to contacts with the criminal justice system—itself an exceedingly risky proposition for people of color in the United States.[13] Black mothers' choices are severely constrained when their children are being targeted, labeled, and pathologized in one or more of those "choices." By comparison, white mothers like Joan and Emily can focus on the available options for providing individualized learning programs for their children.

Victoria, a white middle-class married woman, and mother to Harmony, was more explicit than Joan and Emily as she described the process of school choice. She explains being pulled to find the most individualized learning program for her child:

> I clearly want the best for my daughter by way of her education, and I truly feel as though I'm giving her that [by homeschooling]. . . . As mothers, [we] want nothing but the best for our children. . . . I know many women who send their children to day care, preschool and that's fine if that's what works with their family. . . . I know for myself that [homeschooling] is what is true to me and my family.

Rather than advocating that all families could benefit from homeschooling, she suggests that mothers know what is best for their own kids. As like Joan and Emily, homeschooling also meant career sacrifice for

Victoria (as described in chapter 3). After college she spent several years developing her career in publishing and had planned on remaining employed after Harmony was born but ended up staying home to provide her daughter's primary care and education.

Prioritizing individualized learning as these moms do aligns with intensive mothering narratives. These highly gendered narratives assume women are *naturally* nurturing (despite scholarly consensus that gender is *not* biologically inscribed but socially constructed, contingent on history and cultural context).[14] At the expense of their careers, Victoria and other homeschooling women take on the primary work of educating children, while their husbands remain steadily employed. This, too, is unsurprising, given that intensive mothering narratives construct work and family as relative contradictions in women's lives, reinforcing the expectation that mothers (and not fathers) remain primarily responsible for child-rearing.[15] Intensive mothering also results in women's conceptualization of themselves as "good mothers" hinging on the sense that they make decisions "for the family" and put family needs above their own.[16]

Beyond the tension between work and family, I found that Victoria and other white homeschooling mothers demonstrate an added tension specific to school choice: that of work and education. Women, as this book makes clear, are vested with the responsibility to seek out and choose the best possible education option for their child, while the system is set up in ways that exacerbate the very real gender and race inequalities of this country. White class-advantaged mothers like Victoria, Joan, Emily, and Sarah have concluded that being a good mother means providing their children's primary education themselves, regardless of their own career aspirations, teaching acumen, and so on. These strategies match up with what Jennifer Lois found among white homeschooling moms in the Pacific Northwest, whose notions of good mothering are deeply embedded in their decisions to opt out of professional careers and teach their kids at home.[17]

Pulled to Change Schools

There are very few differences between white homeschooling mothers and their nonhomeschooling counterparts in terms of schooling strategy. For example, Janet, a white married middle-class mother with two children, Alexis and Madison, who attend public school, also evoked the idea of "fit": "I think everybody just wants what's best for their kid, and it's hard to find out what fits. We have friends in town, two of [their kids] are in private school and two of them are in public school; they are just figuring out what's the best fit for their kids." Janet's example—a family sending some kids to public school and some to private school—hearkens back to Joan's story and captures the way that class-advantaged white families rely on mothers to choose schools based on each child's particular learning and behavioral needs. These mothers talk about how their experiential knowledge about their kids makes them the best authority on the education style that will "work," despite very few of them being trained as professional educators or child psychologists. This intensive mothering expectation puts pressure on women to fulfill good mothering through being education experts who tailor lessons for each child.

The language of "best fit" does not come out of thin air. School choice policy and rhetoric emphasize parental choice in schooling, using the language of "best decision" to position parents as consumers in a free market in which competition is meant to improve the quality of education for each child.[18] For example, former US secretary of education Betsy DeVos (a controversial Trump appointee who retired in the last two weeks of the president's term) explained the varied forms of school choice policy as providing parents "the freedom" to make "the best decisions for their children."[19] Market logics like these have long since elided other powerful social forces in the United States: they hide inequalities by assuming that all options are equally accessible to all consumers. When school choice is treated as a commodity exchange, the discourse of "individual learning needs" results in white class-advantaged kids being sorted into whiter middle-class academic settings, where they miss out on other kinds of learning, such as peer learning from lower-income children and children of color who likely have very different life experiences from their own.[20]

Another nonhomeschool example comes from Rose, a white middle-class married woman with two sons, Charlie and Evan. She sends both boys to public school because, as she tells me, she believes their school currently meets the learning needs of each of her sons:

Teacher wise, I think [the school is] very solid. Charlie has had great teachers, and that's really good for what he needs. . . . Every year you fill in a form by the end of the year to say what your child's strengths and weaknesses [are], where he should be going the next year, what kind of teacher would fit well with him, and so forth. And then they match profiles up with the teachers that they have . . . they've been very accurate so far.

The local public school has a system for distributing students among different classrooms and teachers based on fit between teacher and student—the school itself works to cater to each child's individual learning style. It would seem that the decision Rose and her husband made to live in their town rather than elsewhere on the basis of the high-quality schools has paid off. The same is true for Jill and her husband, who moved to Waterville, a middle-class, white Elmford suburb, for their careers (she's an attorney; he's an electrical engineer) and the school district. Their school choice journey, however, included a detour. Jill tells me of her approach to school choice, "I think I'm doing the best for my kids." She notes that when her older child, Gianna, had "one bad teacher," they sent both Gianna and their son, Austin, to a private school. The commute became unbearable after a year, though, and Jill reconsidered the local public school. As she tells me:

I just sort of got my bearings, talked to a lot of other parents. Talked to the principal of the public school and talked to the superintendent of the Waterville public schools . . . about my concerns and hopes and expectations and things like that. . . . [I] got to a place where I felt comfortable.

Having gathered additional information, Jill decided to give the public school another chance and reports that she has been relatively happy with that choice. Her family's schooling journey demonstrates the extensive labor that Jill expended to navigate school choice for her children. Along with the time commitment, it has also involved her comfort (a sign of privilege in itself) with talking to school administrators (the public school's principal and superintendent) as a way to assess whether the school could meet her standards for educating her kids.

That a comparison between white homeschool mothers and non-homeschool mothers demonstrates very similar schooling strategies (reliant on notions of intensive mothering and concerted cultivation that assume good mothering is about intervening in schools to prioritize individualized learning) suggests that not only family and workplace expectations but also our education system push class-advantaged white families to rely on the privilege of whiteness and class-advantaged women's unpaid and often invisible mothering work to navigate school choice. All of this allows individual choices to continue to result in racial segregation and educational inequality.

Placemaking among the White Middle Class

The conversations I had with white mothers map onto school district data, showing that these mothers tend to enroll their children in majority white academic settings, regardless of whether those are public, private, or homeschool options. Yet the same white mothers also emphasize how they seek activities for their children that will ensure they interact with Black and Latine kids. For example, Kimberly, a white homeschooling mother to Anna, Maya, and Cody, tells me:

> I was worried about the role of diversity in home educating. . . . But I'm no longer concerned about that because my kids are getting diverse people . . . through city activities. . . . I think race and class diversity are really valuable, but obviously I don't think it's a priority that everybody can access. There are towns in the state, for example, that are 97 percent white. Clearly, [diversity is] not a priority for everybody, homeschooling or not.

Like Sarah, mentioned earlier in this chapter, Kimberly tries to offset the lack of racial diversity in homeschooling by choosing to live in a racially diverse neighborhood. Though her concern with the educational quality at the public schools, which she describes as lacking "individualized learning," outweighs the value she places on having her children learn in a race- and class-diverse classroom, she seeks out more diverse citywide sport programs for them. It is notable that her phrasing—"getting diverse people"—frames kids of color as an object to acquire and as an enrichment opportunity for her white kids—self-serving rather than framed as caring about racial justice. Kimberly views homeschooling as allowing a more individualized learning program for each child. Her choice is not without ambivalence, though; she recognizes that homeschooling her children contributes to the racial segregation in her racially diverse neighborhood's public schools (where the student body is just about 30 percent white).[21] Still, she seemingly reassures herself that other white families—ones that send their kids to public and private schools—also make many decisions that reproduce racial segregation, especially by living in predominantly white districts. At least she moved to a diverse neighborhood.

In her study involving white class-advantaged families, Margaret Hagerman found that even the most "color-conscious" white families must reckon with what she refers to as the "conundrum of privilege."[22] Among white families who actively provide "color-conscious" racial socialization, teach their children about their own white privilege, and seek to cultivate an anti-racist parenting praxis—choosing to live in race- and class-diverse neighborhoods and enroll their children in integrated neighborhood schools—Hagerman nonetheless found they are reproducing the very inequality they seek to disrupt. For example, they supplement their children's learning through private tutoring, music lessons, summer programs, and international travel—private opportunities that are not available to many other students. The conundrum means understanding their privilege and debating whether and when to leverage it.

I find the conundrum of privilege is reversed among white homeschoolers, who use their privilege to provide education in primarily all-white spaces yet seek out racially diverse supplemental activities. Sarah and Kimberly stand out in that they profess a color-conscious approach to child-rearing and view their schooling decisions as being linked to white privilege, yet they overlook their ability to pick and choose when to consider race as the top priority in their decision-making. They place their white children in all-white academic settings by homeschooling, then seek out Black and Latine children for their child's nonacademic activities (the ones they presumably see as important, but to a lesser degree than scholastic achievement). Here again we see partial white flight: white parents who live in diverse neighborhoods while picking and choosing when their children will interact with children of color.

Mary, a homeschooling mother of five who lives in a primarily white neighborhood, describes how she seeks racial diversity for her children by placing them in extracurricular activities with Latine kids:

> I think it would drive me bonkers if we were only around white people
> all the time. . . . We go to the cathedral in Leeds . . . the English-speaking
> white population is in the minority [there]. . . . Our cathedral is actually
> split between Spanish-speaking masses and English-speaking masses. . . .
> The bottom line and probably the reason we chose to go to that church
> was like, I just don't want my kids to feel like, "Wow, people of color."

Rather than living in a racially diverse neighborhood or sending her
kids to the racially diverse public schools in Leeds where they attend
church, Mary and her husband have chosen to live in a majority white
town and to homeschool. "It's true that we're closest with a handful of
families that are white and homeschooling. All of the homeschoolers are
white," Mary explains. Her appreciation for diversity is subsumed by the
language of personal choice and color blindness.

One mom, Michelle, a white homeschooling mother, told me that
her family lives "in a really white area," and one of the few things she
liked about the private school her daughter had attended was "the mix
of ethnicities." Nonetheless, Michelle ultimately decided to bring her
daughter, Emmy, home for school. Others, like the nonhomeschooling
mother Wendy, explain enrolling their children in extracurricular activities in racially diverse neighboring districts to ensure they have a "non-
white-bread" experience. That so many white homeschooling mothers
express valuing racial integration, while making schooling decisions that
place their children in predominantly white academic settings, helps to
explain the persistence of racial segregation under school choice. These
mothers want their children to have the benefits associated with interacting with students of color, without the associated costs of attending
majority-minority schools, such as fewer resources (larger class sizes,
teaching to the test, fewer "extras" such as art programs), and for some
the perceptions of danger that are linked to attending schools with Black
and Latine students.[23]

White Strategic Schooling

Figure 5.1 breaks down the residencies of the white mothers in my
study: most of those I spoke with live in predominantly white neighborhoods, either homeschooling among other white families or sending

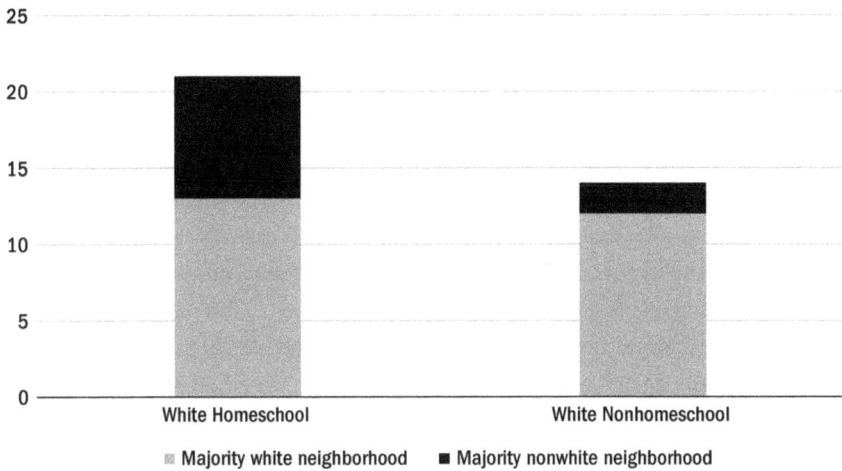

Figure 5.1. White mothers' neighborhoods

their children to the neighborhood's white school. Some of the white homeschoolers live in neighborhoods of color for the diversity but homeschool their children with other white families, engaging in a partial white flight.

By contrast, the previous chapter described Black middle-class families living in predominantly white and middle-class neighborhoods who chose to homeschool to avoid seeing their Black children racially isolated in white schools. What is surprising about white families having more variegated residencies is that I located nonhomeschooling white families for this study by using my connections to middle-class white homeschoolers. Thus, these families are loosely part of the same social network, while making different neighborhood residence and schooling choices. The result is what Margaret Andersen refers to as "diversity without oppression," with white families able to avoid conversations about their role in perpetuating racial inequalities.[24] It's all part of what I call *white strategic schooling*.

Just like Black strategic schooling, white strategic schooling is not practiced just by homeschoolers. White mothers who send their kids to traditional schools tell me they enroll their children in primarily white schools (following ostensibly color-blind logics, including friend recommendations and neighborhood proximity), and they seek out extracurricular activities for their kids that will allow them to interact with kids of color and gain the benefits of diversity. For example, Janet's family moved from one suburban district to another. As she describes:

> [At Greenville public school] there just wasn't a lot of parental involvement . . . they didn't have a lot of peers that could challenge them, and the teachers were really teaching to the test. Even though we were very fortunate to have wonderful teachers, they were teaching to the bottom half of the class, 'cause that's where the need was . . . so we looked into two options: Should we move or should we put the kids in private school? We made the decision to move to a school system that had better schools rather than pay [for private schools].

Janet points to the lack of quality education—teaching to the test, minimal parental involvement, peers who were not academically motivated—in Greenville's public school as her push to explore school choice. While they considered private school, she and her husband decided it was more affordable to move to a different school district—Redding—than pay the high cost of private school tuition. None of this was overtly about race, in Janet's telling, but it is unavoidable that her family's move meant swapping Greenville's 55 percent white public school for Redding's 73 percent white school. Janet's explanation is steeped in color blindness,[25] as though her schooling decisions are not based on common understandings and racial stereotypes about who values education and what kinds of classroom environments are conducive to a child's learning.[26]

Black mothers have to think about race in their schooling strategy because their children experience racial discrimination. White mothers demonstrate the privilege of whiteness in being able to avoid talking about race in making schooling choices, despite the significance of racial inequalities in schooling today.[27] Janet described the Greenville classrooms her family left behind in racially approving terms—"their classrooms kind of looked like the United Nations, which I really liked"—while simultaneously equating educational quality with the whiter, middle-class and upper-middle-class classrooms in Redding. "In Greenville," she said, "we were probably the most educated of [my daughter's] classmates' [families] and . . . some of her friends struggled economically as well." Mothers like Janet are able to be "strategic" around when they prioritize interracial settings; across school type, prioritizing an individualized learning program leads to white academic settings, no matter how much mothers prioritize the value of diversity for children's socialization.

Wendy's family also lives in Redding. She tells me that she and her husband send their sons, Billy and Clayton, to the public schools, saying:

> The public schools are great in terms of academics. . . . It's mostly white with probably 10 percent Asian . . . and then 90 percent white. A very small minority are Black or Hispanic. We joined the Y [YMCA] for a long time because my major was international relations when I was in school and I've always felt compelled to give Billy and Clayton a taste of other cultures. They do get some of the Asian cultures in school, but it's important for me because of the demographics to provide them more of a non-white-bread feel to their lives.

Wendy does not suggest it is the whiteness of the Redding schools that makes the district's academics "great"—to her, that's just an inadvertent consequence of various families' choices around schools and where to live. In other words, like Janet, Wendy demonstrates a color-blind logic in not having to use racial language to explain how racial segregation and the inequalities that ensue are maintained through decisions made by people like them. Then, having made their school decisions, these white moms seek out interracial nonacademic activities for their children—as when Wendy enrolls Billy and Clayton in sports programs at the local YMCA, which draws from Redding as well as a neighboring, predominantly Latine district.

These white mothers do prioritize racial diversity, but they do so in relatively low-stakes settings like sports, church, and music programs. When it comes to high-stakes settings, like academics, they emphasize the need for individualized programs. This suggests that white mothers see racial diversity as one among many available resources to support their intensive mothering.

Existing research identifies the phenomenon of "white debt," which is the assumption that whiteness is lacking, dull, and empty yet superior to "ethnic cultures." White people can address this by cashing in on "color capital" and coding their relationships with nonwhite people as both boons to social status and hedges against claims that they may be racist. This process objectifies people of color, while privileging whites.[28]

I find that white homeschoolers and nonhomeschoolers alike engaged strategies to alleviate their perception that whiteness is both superior and culturally "white bread." In low-stakes settings, their children can gain color capital, while in academic settings they can reap the benefits of white privilege. By picking and choosing, white mothers cultivate experiences for their children aimed at raising "cultural omnivores" who are socially at ease with people of color.[29] Of course, by using the language of consumption and personal enjoyment to describe the extracurriculars they choose,[30] these mothers make racial diversity seem like little more than an add-on to a privileged childhood. Ultimately, their decisions are based on white privilege and the oppression of people of color.

Among my respondents, there were a few white mothers who chose to send their children to more integrated schools, yet their decisions were still made by engaging in white strategic schooling. Take Abby, a mother of three who moved to Riverview because the public schools were known for both racial diversity and academic quality, who tells me:

> Once everybody hit kindergarten age, all three kids, in succession, started at our local public school. We were zoned for one of them . . . and we actually petitioned to go to the one that's slightly physically closer to us. But our neighbor, who was a longtime educator, said, "There are more educated parents at this other one. Go there." Both schools have very, very large percentages of recently immigrated Chinese Asian immigrants. Real low incomes, a lot of free lunch—all of which is great and has been a real plus for our kids. The kind of white-people portion of the school we left was from much rougher neighborhoods, and the white-people portion of the school we went into tended to be more educated, a few more doctors, lawyers.

Abby describes it as a benefit for her children to go to school with low-income Chinese students, drawing on the "model minority myth," which positions Asian Americans as particularly academically driven.[31] Yet her logic also suggests race is deeply linked to class location. Her family switched neighborhood schools because of the class composition of the white students' families. Abby uses racialized and classed understandings to strategically select the school that can best balance racial diversity with class advantage—the one with many low-income Chinese Americans and mostly middle-class whites.

Conclusion: Choice through White Strategic Schooling

Like other race scholars, I find respondents engage with race in ways that appear to render white racial identity as a matter of individual choice. For example, white privilege allows whites to emphasize some portion of their ethnicity on particular holidays ("Kiss me, I'm Irish!" on Saint Patrick's Day, for instance), while accruing zero social or material consequences related to their "ethnic-ness" for the rest of the year.[32] Scholars studying nonhomeschooling white families find that some white parents seek interracial settings to give their child the benefits associated with interacting with students of color, just like the mothers in this study who made sure to enroll their homeschooled white children in diverse but low-stakes after-school settings.[33] Together, these studies highlight that the privilege of whiteness is marked by the ability to seek racial diversity through multiracial neighborhoods, parks, or schools *when you want it*.

The white mothers of Elmford engage in white strategic schooling by being able to pick and choose when to consider race. They opt in when they perceive diversity as a benefit to their child (extracurricular settings), and they opt out when they believe diversity may have negative consequences for their child (academic settings). This is only possible because whites in America are racially "unmarked" or seen as "raceless."[34] By contrast, Black mothers' ability to mobilize full agency under school choice is limited due to the racial discrimination their children face within schools and their work to provide their kids an anti-racist learning environment. They *have* to think about their child's racial identity.

Existing research shows that school segregation is in many ways as prevalent today as it was in the 1950s, before the US civil rights movement, and school choice has only exacerbated this segregation.[35] Specifically, while there have been notable increases in school segregation over the past several decades, since the early 1990s, when school choice took off, there has been greater neighborhood integration yet heightened school segregation, the result of families living in one neighborhood and either sending their children to school in a different neighborhood or else homeschooling.[36] We can begin to understand the persistence of educational segregation, even alongside the diversification of America's school-age children, by bringing in the racial motivations of white families—including homeschoolers—as expressed in the school choices made by white mothers. Research shows, for instance, that white students are the least likely to attend high-poverty schools,[37] with just 8 percent of white public school students attending high-poverty schools in 2014–2015, compared with 45 percent of Black students.[38] White students' public school enrollments have been steadily declining; from 2000 to 2017, the percentage of public school students who were white dropped from 61 percent to 48 percent nationwide, while the percentage of public school students who were Latine increased from 16 percent to 27 percent, and other racial groups remained relatively constant.[39] This change cannot be explained just by increasing racial diversity in the United States—it's also due to fewer whites enrolling their children in public schools.

What alternative options are these white families selecting? Some researchers have pointed to public charter schools;[40] others have focused on private schools,[41] and for the most part homeschools have been sidelined. Yet charters educate only slightly more students than homeschools (6 percent compared with 3.3 percent),[42] and many fewer than private schools (10 percent).[43] This chapter has provided some much-needed qualitative data to round out our understanding of the factors shaping a subset of this growing population, as an increasing number of white families opt out of public schools to homeschool.

My research adds to existing scholarship on partial white flight, which serves to maintain racial segregation and racial inequality even though it valorizes white children's interaction with children of color, whether in majority-minority schools or in multiracial parks.[44] This chapter finds a different form of partial white flight surfacing. Unlike public schooling families who may choose white neighborhoods and schools, some homeschooling families, like Sarah's and Kimberly's, live in racially diverse districts but allow for an all-white education as a by-product of their school choice. Other white homeschooling families, like their nonhomeschool counterparts, live and educate their children in white spaces while seeking racial diversity in other neighborhoods and more low-stakes settings. This is not to suggest that school integration has ever been a "silver bullet" for solving race and class disparities in US education. Indeed, much research shows we need to do much more than simply create integrated schools.[45] However, these mothers' stories add to what we know about how whiteness operates to preserve racial structures.

6

The Contours of Homeschooling

Benefits, Challenges, and Supports

"I like that [my children] are a family unit. I like the fact that they have a lot of flexibility in their schedule," Irma tells me earnestly. Her exuberance captures the satisfaction she expressed in response to my question about homeschool benefits. On an early spring afternoon, I find myself sitting across from Irma in her cozy three-story townhome in a predominantly white neighborhood of Elmford. Irma is a Black homeschooling mother with four children, three of whom are currently homeschooling, while her oldest son, Stephen, finishes his first year at a parochial school just a few blocks from home. This is Stephen's first year in an "institutional school," Irma says, adding that she and her husband had made the decision because Stephen was becoming very "teenagerish." His parents thought the socialization with other teens would be beneficial. Irma continues:

> My daughter doesn't have to be done by four in the afternoon. If there's something she wants to do before that, she obviously has the ability to finish up her school day and do whatever she wants. . . . Because we homeschool they don't have to be in school every second of the day. We have the flexibility. We have that luxury.

Flexibility has been particularly crucial for Irma's family, which has moved all over the world due to her husband's career (he is a professor at an area college and studies religion in different contexts). Homeschooling's flexibility allows them to keep their children's lives relatively consistent and their studies rigorous while also enjoying time together as a family.

Michelle's account was similar. On a wintry evening, this white homeschooling mom shares that, before homeschooling, she was going to her daughter's school "constantly." Freed from that advocacy effort, as well as the half-hour round-trip commute to Emmy's traditional school ("a huge energy and time waster"), Michelle finds homeschooling "a lot less stressful." She concedes that it may be "counterintuitive," but she describes using the extra time to do a load of laundry or start dinner while her daughter is "hunkering down" and working through her homeschooling lessons.

Although the reasons for homeschooling can be very different— for Black families due to racial discrimination, for white families due to individualized learning—across race respondents described similar benefits of homeschooling. Black or white, homeschooling moms repeatedly told me that flexibility and family time were the biggest benefits of their choice—and that it was frustrating that so few people seemed to recognize this when they thought of homeschooling. I, on the other hand, noted that the mothers' accounts routinely overlooked the benefit of their unpaid work for their husbands' careers, which I could only see through piecing together their homeschool journeys.

In this chapter, I will compare the benefits and challenges of homeschooling that mothers described. As is clear from the accounts by Irma and Michelle, homeschooling mothers repeatedly pointed to flexibility in their schedules and the amount of family time afforded as real perks of their school choice, while time commitment and responsibility were commonly reported challenges. Racial differences surface in how mothers described managing the challenges of homeschooling through support: Black mothers described homeschool support through extended kin, whereas white mothers relied on other (white) homeschooling moms for support. These differences offer important indication of how race and racism shape American family life.

The Benefit of Flexibility and Family Time

Viola, a Black married mother of four, describes the rewards of homeschooling as allowing for more family time and catering to individual children's learning needs:

> I like having the kids with me and being able to help them the way they need to be helped. . . . I know it's harder when you're in school and there

are a lot of other kids, but I can pay attention. I mean [my daughter] is one who has needed it most. [In terms of] figuring out what best works for her learning styles. [My son] I'm able to give him the things that he needs and let him play when he is wanting to play.

Women are primarily responsible for carrying out homeschooling. It's an enormous responsibility, yet my respondents insisted it also strengthens their families. While individualized learning was not the primary push out of traditional schools for Black families, Viola does mention it as a benefit of her decision.

Sarah, a white single mother who homeschools her son, describes it as a much more positive experience than public school:

I love the amount of time that I can spend with [my son] and that I see firsthand his progress. I think that is the most rewarding thing for me. . . . When we [public schooled], I was always handing him off to other people to take care. It was kind of depressing, all those things that I was missing. I don't miss them anymore. I am there, day in and day out. It's amazing to see and [to] understand where he is. . . . Our relationship has gotten a lot stronger because of it.

To Sarah, homeschooling fulfills her maternal duty of "being there" for her child. Her comment "I'm there, day in and day out" hints, in other words, at women's gendered understanding of their mothering work and the self-sacrifice they see as required to take care of their families properly.

These accounts exist within a context of contradictions: despite our economy's reliance on working parents, the United States provides few supports for working families. For example, public schools are underfunded and often fail to meet parents' expectations, while after-school day care is too expensive for many families. At the time of this writing, US mothers' labor force participation is at 72.3 percent, yet intensive mothering remains a prominent cultural narrative.[1] The homeschooling mothers I studied had removed themselves from the labor force, though they were still performing their form of stay-at-home mothering within this larger context of cultural tension and lack of support for working families.[2] For Jazmine, a Black married homeschooler with two kids, it's about "keeping the team together," unifying their family bond to resist the external threats to Black child-rearing. Similarly, Grace, a Black married mother of three, tells me:

> Having the time in our day and our routine, having a priority on family so that we have the relationship where we can have those discussions and the time and the priority to work through it, talk about it. . . . Just the fact that we have the freedom to do that, 'cause if school were running our lives, I don't know how well I would even know my children. We would be more disconnected just by virtue of not being together all of the time and not being able to go through all of the ups and downs.

These married Black women's focus on strengthening the family relationship maps onto what Riché Barnes describes as middle-class Black "strategic mothering."[3] In Barnes's research, we see Black women prioritizing marital stability over work stability; here, my Black homeschooling respondents describe a specific focus on nuclear family stability as a reason to opt out of paid labor and public school.

Victoria, a married white mother of one, is among the few in my study who sacralizes her homeschooling choice within the context of her mothering responsibility:

> [Homeschooling] is rewarding. It's fulfilling. I truly believe it's the role that God laid out for me. I clearly want the best for my daughter as a mother, so that would just carry over; I clearly want the best for my daughter by way of her education. I truly feel I'm giving her that. Not to say that if she was to go to a public school she would be getting an inferior education, not at all, but this situation is the best for the three of us.

In Victoria's account, wanting the best for her daughter and honoring her child's individual learning style and personality are joined by what she sees as a divine duty. Still, her core motivations (individualized learning) for homeschooling fit with the drivers of other white homeschooling mothers' decisions. The benefits she identifies now that her family is homeschooling return to the themes of family connection, fulfilling mothering ideals, and enjoying the flexibility to do both.

The Challenges of the Homeschool Responsibility

"I would have plans—'the baby should be napping now'—but then the baby wasn't napping. It was like, 'What do you do?'" Julia humorously recalls being new to what she calls "the juggle." She is a married Black homeschooling mother of seven, and so her busy schedule dictated our interview location: a sandwich shop near her home. Four of her children are now adults (in college or beyond), but that still leaves three to homeschool—and Julia works part-time. On an early spring morning, Julia recalls the struggles of her early days of homeschooling:

> If I had had structure, I think then I might have been able to say to my son, "Go and do this math page." Get over the fact that it's a workbook! Rather than, "Oh, the baby's crying. Well, [son] we can't do the unit study now." The best way to teach in homeschooling is a balanced mixture of both; of structure and the flexible, unit-type studies to spice it up, and each person has to find that balance.

Through years of experience, Julia's homeschooling style evolved and reached that important balance. Still, the enormity of the responsibility—juggling care for her children and designing lesson plans for seven different kids' grade levels, aptitudes, and needs—charges the word *balance* with a certain steady anxiety.

Joy, a widowed white mother of two, describes the size of the homeschool responsibility as a major challenge: "You hate to put your kids as part of your self-worth, but you're responsible for how they look. You're responsible for how they act, and now you're responsible for what they know. You're responsible for every aspect of them." Through homeschooling, Joy has found her mothering responsibilities growing. The education of her children is no longer a duty shared with other adults, like teachers and administrators, but one concentrated on her.

Black and white mothers alike express the challenges of homeschooling in terms of managing the heavy responsibility. This responsibility was intricately woven into cultural narratives of intensive mothering, of raising children as a task placed solely on mothers, rather than the more collective sentiment in many countries with less individualistic cultures.[4] Indeed, Lynette says the hardest part of her alternative schooling decision is managing the self-doubt: "The biggest challenges have always been, 'Am I doing enough?'" Homeschooling allows her to shield her son from the racial hostility he experienced in public school and to individualize his school curriculum—these are clear benefits to Lynette—yet it relies on her ingenuity in developing a curriculum that caters to each child. Constant doubt is a high cost.

Asked about her biggest challenges, Michelle offers that homeschooling means "I'm never 'off.'" She recites her typical schedule by way of explanation:

> I start in the morning, and though [my daughter] is not up yet, I'm doing the housewife stuff. I start the load of laundry, and then I'm figuring out, "OK, these are the things I have prepared that she can choose from," because I prep [lessons] ahead of time and then I'll give her some options. . . . It's not like "Oh, it's four o'clock, we're done." *She* might be done. Now I'm going on to the next thing.

Homeschooling is what we might call unbounded work. Michelle's position as primary educator blends into other reproductive responsibilities (particularly maintaining the home and doing the laundry and other housework) while her husband provides for the family financially. The couple thus has adopted a traditionally gendered division of labor, but the added responsibility of educating their child falls only on Michelle. She sums it up in terms that emphasize both the hard work of homeschooling and her sense that doing it affirms her status as a good mother: when she refers to homeschooling, she emphasizes that it is "a huge time commitment; it's a labor of love, let me tell you!"

The comments mothers in my study made were often double-sided in this way, acknowledging the sacrifices associated with their maternal decisions (regardless of what those decisions are) while also explaining them as "worth it" because they are sacrifices borne for the good of the family. The gendered trope that women, especially mothers, should be selfless is not limited to the home sphere in the United States,[5] where both paid and unpaid reproductive labor—such as providing care for children or the elderly—is typed as "female" and thus extremely devalued.[6] When this labor is paid, as in nursing, teaching, and childcare, it is almost uniformly at lower wages than other, nonreproductive jobs with similar requirements in terms of skills and qualifications.[7] Whether paid or unpaid, much reproductive labor emphasizes the provision of emotional support and face-to-face services that support others' well-being (physical and mental health, and physical, cognitive, and emotional skills).[8] And because women are expected to offer family members this care out of love or a sense of obligation, society deems the relatively paltry market value of such labor as generally appropriate.[9]

As feminist scholars have pointed out, mothers are rewarded for providing care not financially but with reverence—love and money being tidily separate spheres.[10] Michelle, who has a master's degree in communications and left her years-long career to homeschool, refers to her full-time duties as schoolteacher and caregiver to her daughter as a "labor of love." There is no economic compensation as Michelle absorbs this teaching work into her middle-class mothering responsibilities, just as other feminized care labor is characterized as sacrifice for the family or just what a "good" mom, sister, wife, aunt, or daughter does.

Mary, a married white mother of five, is clear that she understands herself as doing a difficult, multifaceted job. Commenting that "in some ways, the most challenging piece is just actually making sure that the things that you want to happen, happen," Mary continues:

> The truth is, being a homeschooling mom is a full-time job. Even though it's a job that happens in the home and I could be doing the dishes while I do it, it still is a big job. . . . I would say the hardest part is being able to manage your time so that everything gets done and that you don't feel like you're shortchanging one aspect of it.

Juggling responsibilities, roles, children, and schedules is, as Mary states, "a full-time job." Others may devalue these efforts, but mothers highlight the seriousness with which they take their maternal duties and the fact that the stakes are high—their children's futures are riding on the moms' ability to innovate, adapt, and succeed.

Hilda, the married Black grandmother who homeschools four grandkids after having homeschooled her three grown children, is experienced in balancing the demands of caring for the younger grandchildren while providing individualized class sessions for older ones. Like Mary, she describes homeschooling as "hard work," adding, "But it's work that

I enter into. I do want to do it because I see the end of the tunnel. I see what's going to happen to them." Despite Hilda's different relationship to her homeschool pupils (as their grandmother), her narrative matches those of the other respondents. Across race, homeschooling is consistently described as both rewarding and taxing. It is what is best for the individual child, and choosing this option is part of fulfilling maternal responsibilities. However, Hilda's and other Black mothers' stories also indicate that they homeschool to protect their children from experiencing racial discrimination in traditional schools.

Many homeschoolers also suggest that the blurring of boundaries between their roles—mother, homemaker, teacher—is quite stressful. Because they are, in fact, home all day, respondents feel responsible not just for educating and caring for children but also for simultaneously accomplishing housework (cooking, cleaning, washing clothes, grocery shopping, and the like). After a full day of caring and teaching, cooking meals, and keeping up with other housework, Michelle and other respondents spend evenings—presumably their leisure time—preparing lesson plans after their children are in bed. Like mothers in Jennifer Lois's study, these mothers admit their work is never "done" and sometimes lean on the fact that homeschooling is temporary to get them through the intense days.[11] Hilda reminds herself that, like her children, her grandchildren will eventually grow up. There will come a day when she is no longer their primary educator and care provider: "I see the end of the tunnel."

Luckily, the resourceful homeschoolers of Elmford seek out support as they navigate the compression of so many responsibilities into a twenty-four-hour day. It's notable, however, that Black and white homeschoolers find that support in different ways.

Black Homeschool Support through Extended Kin

"Black people don't normally homeschool," Jazmine says, and so she feels isolated in her choice. "I don't talk to anyone [about homeschooling] because in my Black group, there's no one to talk to." She might turn to her fellow church congregants, but, she explains, "A lot of the older Black women in my church, they had careers, they send their kids to day care, they send their kids to public schools." When it comes down to it, she sighs, "Homeschooling is very white."

The enormity of the responsibility of homeschooling is amplified for this married Black mother of two by her racial isolation as a home educator—as the choice is for all the Black homeschooling mothers in my study. Jazmine indicates the concerns of white homeschoolers are simply different than those facing Black homeschoolers. She also suggests the cultural narratives around the importance of Black women's workforce participation are distinct from the work-family conflict that dominates narratives of white middle-class women (see chapters 2 and 3). Indeed, in her research with Black professional mothers, Riché Barnes situated her respondents within a web of conflicting stereotypes around work and family. Black women described to Barnes how they face an expected necessity and desire to remain in the paid labor force, regardless of parenting status, as a means for racial and community uplift and protection from exploitation.[12] These opposing tensions are the historical and cultural context with which Black homeschooling mothers contend—and within which they are understood by the predominantly white homeschool community. For Jazmine, keeping her son out of traditional schools and becoming a stay-at-home, homeschooling mother has not been "about ruining [my son's] blackness" but an effort "to keep the team [family] together," yet it has resulted in Jazmine's blackness going unsupported.

Most of the Black homeschoolers in Elmford described this isolation in their interviews. Recall that scholar Dawn Dow described Black middle-class mothers as framing work and family not as oppositional but as integrated mothering responsibilities.[13] As Jazmine articulates, her strategic schooling choices conflict with such integrative cultural narratives, isolating her not only from white homeschoolers but also from Black professional moms. Even so, Jazmine feels strongly that homeschooling is the best choice for her family. In this way, she and the other Black mothers in my study also echo the Black professional women in Barnes's research who "opted out," in that they resisted the strong Black woman myth and expectations to combine work and family, instead focusing on "raising the race."[14] Unlike Barnes, I found that Black homeschooling mothers prioritize family by educating children in the safety of their home rather than in racially risky traditional schools.

Sandy, a Black working-class married woman with three sons, isn't involved in the regional homeschool groups either, although she attributes her isolation to lacking transportation. She tells me that, for support, she and her husband choose to live with her retired mother, who takes the lead on much of the homeschooling for the children, but their situation also feels isolating. As she explains, "That's the challenging part. It's been hard for me to connect to the homeschool community, so my sons don't have playmates except for themselves." With her husband working full-time and using the family's only car during the workday, the local homeschool groups are inaccessible for Sandy.

In contrast to existing research with Black homeschoolers in other parts of the country,[15] Black Elmford mothers describe homeschooling in relative isolation. Almost half of the Black homeschooling mothers I interviewed for this study specifically asked me to put them in touch with each other so they might form a regional Black homeschool support group.

Part of the isolation stems from the relative rarity of Black stay-at-home mothering. Research with nonhomeschooling Black families has found that Black stay-at-home mothers have been uncommon and stigmatized compared with their white counterparts.[16] For some Black families, the support they receive takes the form of what Karen Hansen refers to as *care for*, with extended family members providing practical hands-on care, while others provide *care about*, or emotional support and advice.[17] This supports research showing that many Black middle-class families balance their participation in white spaces by seeking connection through Black communities, which are free from discrimination and affirming of their racial identities.[18] Similarly, I find some participate in the homeschool groups, even though the groups are almost exclusively white. Others seek support primarily through extended kin, who understand the racial implications of their choice in ways that white homeschoolers do not.

Take, for example, Lynette, the Black homeschooling mother of two. She tells me that, for support, "I talk to my parents." Even though initially her parents were "against the whole homeschooling thing," Lynette found they understood her son's experience of racial discrimination and "why I went out." She adds that they "helped me out and told me that I was doing well in protecting him." Even before she started homeschooling, Lynette's parents were involved with her son; she tells me they have "always been supportive of other extracurricular educational activities" and "always . . . a big help." But when it comes to peer support, Lynette has little. She finds that in her local homeschool community, many "parents have been homeschooling their kids because of learning issues of some sort," and they just can't relate to her situation.

Altogether, three Black mothers in my study were able to share some of the education duties of homeschooling with their own parents: Sandy, Hilda's daughter, and Julia (discussed later). Hilda, whose contributions as a caretaker and teacher for her grandchildren allow her daughter and son-in-law to work full-time, nonetheless describes her own isolation, saying, "Homeschool mothers are very lonely." She has attempted networking with other homeschooling families in the region—"downtown Elmford has a homeschool group"—though she quit attending when being the only Black family took its toll. She tells me, "The first year we used to go to some of the activities, [but] white homeschool mothers don't know what to do with Black families. They just don't. Although they were kind, they kept me and the kids at arm's length." Hilda had no illusions that this was about race: she watched other white homeschool mothers "who were brand new" join the group, and the white veterans would "surround them." She states, "I can't afford to get angry or upset, I just go to the next thing. What else is there? What else can I do?" Hilda now tries to seek out other Black families at homeschool conferences. As she explains: "Every time I see a Black family, I run to them. I say, 'Hey, we need each other! Here's my number. Give me your number.'"

Existing research with the Black middle class finds that, similar to their lower-income counterparts, these families rely on support from extended kin, including grandparents, aunts, uncles, nieces, nephews, and cousins, as well as fictive, or non–blood relative kin.[19] For low-income Black families these supports may be particularly crucial for financial survival,[20] while for middle-class families, they may be crucial to providing anti-racist childcare, strengthening family ties, and the like.[21] The responses I heard from Hilda, Lynette, and Sandy suggest that some Black middle-class mothers additionally rely on extended kin to help manage the intensity of homeschooling as a Black family in a primarily white homeschool community.

Julia is another Black mom who turns to her father for homeschooling help, even though he lives in another state. Her dad, a former schoolteacher and chemist, "knows the sciences and math well," and

Julia's children check in with him virtually. Her daughter, Ingrid, as we learned in chapter 2, "scans her work, emails it to granddad, he marks it and sends it back with comments." Not everyone has this kind of experienced parental support, Julia concedes, and she says it is "a huge help . . . because I'm so busy with managing the other things." She may feel unsupported by her white homeschooling counterparts, maybe even misunderstood by her Black nonhomeschooling peers, but her own parent steps in and mitigates some of the stress of the isolation that is a by-product of her schooling strategy.

Extended kin need not be directly involved in teaching kids to provide hugely important support for Black homeschooling moms. Sharon, for instance, is the primary educator to her kids but relies on her parents to provide childcare each week so that she can also attend to her career. Lynette, mentioned earlier, receives emotional support from her parents, around both the discrimination her son faced in school and her decision to teach him at home. Extended kin can provide culturally appropriate support that blends with the more process-oriented help Black mothers might gain from predominantly white regional homeschool groups.

In discussing the challenges of homeschooling, Black mothers point to racial isolation. The problem is that researchers have largely overlooked asking Black mothers about their homeschooling challenges. Limited studies with Black homeschoolers in the Mid-Atlantic and southern United States have found homeschoolers have a well-developed support system of fellow Black homeschoolers,[22] though that only underscores the importance of regional context in homeschooling decisions: in Elmford, there are precious few fellow Black homeschoolers with whom my respondents can build networks. Scholars have reached widespread consensus that homeschoolers rely on homeschool groups and the nuclear family to support their education decisions (especially on mothers' unpaid work),[23] yet my study has identified race as a confounding factor in racially dissonant contexts. Both Black and white mothers report receiving support from other homeschoolers, but this is a primary source of support only for white mothers (mentioned by 13 of 21); Black mothers in my sample were almost as likely to receive help from other homeschoolers (6 of 17) as from extended kin (5 of 17), even though extended family members were often unfamiliar with or skeptical about homeschooling at first (see figure 6.1). Examining Elmford's

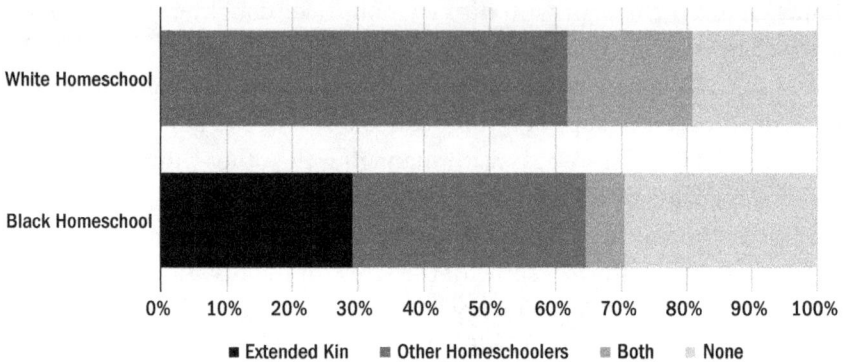

Figure 6.1. Homeschool supports

Black mothers' use of supports in an area without a Black homeschool community offers important new insights on the continued significance of extended kin in these families' lives for providing emotional, teaching, and/or childcare support.

White Homeschool Support through Other Homeschoolers

I met Gail, a white married mother of two kids, on a late fall afternoon at a coffee shop well outside Elmford proper. The place bustled with happy patrons noshing on extravagant baked goods as we settled in at a table near the windows. Gail tells me right up front that her extended family "doesn't support" her in homeschooling (other than an aunt who provides childcare, which allows Gail and her husband to work). Her tight-knit family, she says, is skeptical about homeschooling: "My family's close. I talk to them like at least once a week . . . my aunt watches [my son]. [But] she'll always be like, 'Don't you need a teaching degree [to homeschool]?' And I'm like, 'I have my bachelor's degree in computer science.'" Gail sees her extended family more frequently than many other homeschoolers (weekly as opposed to monthly or annually), but her homeschool community is especially dear to her. She meets up with them "at least once a month."

The frequent contact with Gail's extended family fits with the reliance on extended kin that scholars find is common among the working class (see chapter 3).[24] Indeed, Gail is one of the few working-class homeschoolers I interviewed. She and her husband both work at blue-collar jobs to make ends meet, and though she has a college degree, he does not. While most middle-class white homeschoolers have more distant relationships with kin, as scholars have found in studies of middle-class concerted cultivation,[25] Gail aligns more closely with the relationships that Black homeschoolers report with extended family. At the same time, while most Black homeschoolers described feeling isolated in Elmford's homeschooling community, Gail is able to draw heavily on the support of her white homeschool peers.

Other white mothers also told me their families disapproved of homeschooling. Joan, a white married homeschooler of two kids, thinks very differently about education than the rest of her relatives. She says:

> In my family, if you have boys, you send them to an all-boys prep school where they wear a jacket and tie. They will whip them into shape. They will mold them so that they are successful. . . . That works for [my extended family]. I sort of recoil when I think of that. Homeschooling [is seen as] not very disciplined [in my family]. So, it's like, "Well, your kids need to be disciplined."

Joan does note a lack of discipline and rigor was part of her reasoning for bringing her son home from traditional school, but unlike her extended kin, she did not believe a private school was the right fit. Though she subsequently feels isolated from her family, Joan has become involved in a local homeschool group, and her son has regular play dates with his homeschool friends. The white homeschool community in the region is there for them.

A similar example comes from Kimberly, a white married mother of three, who says, "I definitely have a really good group of homeschooling parents to talk about pedagogy or just challenges, which is great, because people can step up with resources." Meanwhile, Victoria is a sort of homeschool group super-user. She tells me, "I'm in so many different homeschool groups. In particular, I am very active with the Catholic homeschool group. And we're all great friends, and we have lots of activities for the moms and with the kids. I have a great support system." Both white and Black mothers consistently report that these homeschooling groups are usually run by white mothers. White mothers rely on these white homeschoolers to manage the intensity of homeschooling through sharing teaching responsibilities and tips as well as providing emotional support. They seek these supports not out of material necessity for their family but as a result of their choice to opt out of traditional schools to educate their children at home.

Interestingly, white mothers do not talk about receiving extensive help from their extended kin when it comes to homeschooling, but that does not mean extended family are absent from their lives. Six white mothers report providing care to sick or elderly family members on a regular basis while also homeschooling their children. This double care-giving responsibility is a relatively new phenomenon, the result of people living longer and there being scant affordable elder care options. The cohort of mostly women providing this double care has popularly been referred to as the "sandwich generation."[26] For several of these white mothers, their homeschool and elder-care schedules are described as complementary. For example, Karen, a married white homeschooler of three kids, describes her schedule by telling me: "My grandfather's ninety-two, and he lives right next door, so I take care of him, too. And my mom is a widow and needs help, so sometimes I'll run out—and they both need blood checks, so I do that on Mondays." She says that, on other days, "I take a half an hour off for lunch to go sit with my grand-father." It may sound hectic, but Karen finds that her roles as a daughter and granddaughter providing elder care and as a homeschooling mother work out well for her: "I come back [from visiting my grandfather] and [my son] is ready for his math, and then he finishes up what he's got to do and [my daughter] will practice her violin or piano." Clearly, Karen engages in the concerted cultivation child-rearing approach—her kids are enrolled in private music lessons and involved in their church's youth group, and of course their mom oversees their schooling—and she finds time to direct the same attentive care for elderly family members, al-lowing them to live independently rather than in a nursing home or as-sisted living facility. Karen is not a supermom, and I am not attempting to compare research subjects. It does, however, seem obvious to trace some of her capacity to two racially inflected facts: she has a support-ive homeschooling peer group, and she is freed from the racialized se-curity project taken on by every Black mother in my study. In other words, school choice adds labor to the security project of Black mothers because they find themselves having to protect their children from the systemic discrimination their children face in school, while white mothers experience a host of racial privileges that relieve them from some of these insecurities.[27]

Conclusion

This chapter has examined the racial similarities and differences identified by homeschooling mothers in terms of the benefits, challenges, and supports they report. On the whole, the benefits and challenges ascribed to this alternative schooling option look similar across race. Sources of support, which could include emotional support, help with teaching, and/or childcare, diverge in racially patterned ways (figure 6.1). Both Black and white mothers report receiving support from other homeschoolers, but this is a primary source of support only for white mothers, while Black mothers receive support from other homeschoolers just as frequently as from extended family members. As in the cases of Hilda and Julia, Black mothers appear to find extended family crucial for mitigating some of the isolation of homeschooling in a primarily white space, regardless of these family members' inability to give advice on the actual process of homeschooling. Kin provide crucial support for affirming Black identity for these homeschooling women and their children. Meanwhile, though white mothers receive far more help from fellow homeschoolers, they are relatively lacking in support from extended kin. On the contrary, six of these women described providing regular care for sick or elderly family members while also homeschooling.

Having talked to women about why they chose to homeschool, as well as their assessments of its relative benefits and difficulties, I can report that, across race, these American mothers understand themselves as the first, last, and best "social safety net" when academic institutions fail their children. And they are not wrong. In comparison to more robust "welfare states," such as Sweden, Finland, France, and East Germany, where government supports citizen well-being through paid parental leave, publicly supported childcare, and nationalized health care and elder care, the United States has stripped away safety nets and devolved responsibility through welfare retrenchment.[28] Because of this, moms may actually be the best available safety net for their families.

The safety net—in the form of homeschooling—is responding to different problems for different mothers. For white mothers in this study, the primary pull to homeschool is due to a lack of individualized learning in traditional schools, and a major benefit is the ability to provide care to elderly family members while also homeschooling. Black mothers cite racism and discrimination as their primary reason to leave traditional schools, thus providing literal safety for their children, while also noting flexibility and family connection as benefits of homeschooling. Yet providing this care and education for their young and old requires mothers to have access to the financial resources that come with two-parent, class-advantaged households. This presumably leaves single-headed households and those with fewer resources unable to "choose" full-time homeschooling.

A good deal of existing research with class-advantaged families demonstrates that race shapes how people "do" family and seek support. These studies did not involve homeschooling families, but generally found that both Blacks and whites rely on the nuclear family for childcare, whites seek out paid childcare, and Blacks seek childcare from extended kin, partially because of the reasonable concern that they will encounter racial discrimination in paid childcare centers.[29] This chapters extends existing research by considering a different part of childcare—schooling. Consistent with the earlier literature, the mothers in this study reported "doing" family in ways that differ by race; many Black mothers rely on nuclear family and extended kin to "do family" under the challenging circumstances of homeschooling, while most white mothers described relying on the nuclear family in tandem with Elmford's (white) homeschool community. The findings suggest homeschooling may create an added toll on Black families, particularly Black women, who remain on the margins of homeschool networks that might otherwise provide important information, shared experiences, and practical tips about homeschooling. These findings suggest that both Black and white mothers receive crucial homeschool support beyond the bounds of the nuclear family, despite turning to different primary supports.

Scholarship regarding the structure and function of contemporary families has confirmed that, in postindustrial societies like the United States, networks of extended kin, neighbors, and friends have had to adapt to providing support across geographic distances.[30] While extended kin provide enduring, long-term supports, more proximal neighbors and friends often provide more immediate supports.[31] Additionally, multigenerational ties are on the rise for complex reasons, including longer life spans (generations now share more years with each other) and the associated "crisis of care" as longer lives mean more people needing more help in an "age of independence" that conceives of nursing homes and care facilities as last resorts for the class-advantaged elderly.[32] This study, which is the first to examine racial variation in the support networks of homeschooling families, reinvigorates the distinction in support type, finding that support received from kin versus friends or other homeschoolers is shaped by the region's racial hierarchy and makeup.

Conclusion

From Individual to Collective Good

Before Lynette moved to Elmford, she had grown close to a homeschooling family. She recalls her response when she learned about the family's schooling arrangements: "I was like 'What is this? . . . Why don't you just go to school?' Then I realized that school was so far away from everything, and I was like, OK, that's a good reason." She simply hadn't been acquainted with any homeschoolers. Now, several years later and living in a white suburb of Elmford, she is homeschooling her son, Trevor, who faced racial discrimination as a Black boy in the public schools. Without Lynette's familiarity with homeschooling, it may not have seemed like a viable option. Instead, in the middle of the school year, when Trevor needed a change, homeschooling seemed like the least disruptive option in the short term—just to get him through the first grade. Reasoning that she "didn't want him to be afraid of school," she planned for Trevor to return to traditional school for second grade. Now, she's considering keeping him home another year because of the difference between how much her son "loved kindergarten" and his current stance of never wanting to go back to school. Lynette insists, "He's my easygoing kid, too . . . that's why I was like 'OK, they're really messing with my child.'" When I ask what she envisions for Trevor's academic future, she sighs and responds:

> Homeschooling? I'm pretty sure that next year I will keep him home. . . . I just want to make sure that he's OK and not totally traumatized. . . . I'd love to send him to school, but if it's the teachers I'm going to be battling against, I really don't need that. . . . My husband and I were looking into maybe private schools if we stay in this area or elsewhere. We have to figure out . . . a better public school system.

Despite what Lynette had originally intended when pulling Trevor out of school, she is now planning to homeschool him for at least another year. After that, the full range of options are on the table—homeschool, private school, or a different public school. For Lynette and the other Black homeschooling mothers in this study, the decision to homeschool is not necessarily ideal, but it is good enough to be the schooling plan for their foreseeable future.

Friendships with homeschooling families made Maureen, a white mom, amenable to the idea, too. Her daughter, Amelia, was in karate classes with a bunch of homeschooled kids, and Maureen remembers, "I'm like, 'Oh, huh, they don't *look* weird.' . . . '[T]hey don't look like religious crazy people.'" Though she "had never considered homeschooling," Maureen tells me, "I got to know the parents. I really liked them. They were really down-to-earth people. Their kids were delightful." These parents and kids disrupted her assumptions about homeschool families, to the degree that Maureen began asking questions, checking out library books on homeschooling, and talking to her husband about whether it might be good for Amelia. For the record, he initially said she was "nuts." But as Amelia, a fifth grader, continued to struggle with social anxiety and begged to be pulled out to homeschool, her parents finally made the leap. Asked what she foresees for Amelia's schooling future, Maureen is resolute: "We realize now that homeschooling is what we're going to do through high school." She explains, "Education has changed so much. The way we learn has changed so much . . . it just doesn't seem as important to have that same high school experience."

Notably, Maureen, like other white homeschooling mothers, points to a lack of individualized learning in schools' one-size-fits-all model as the primary reason for homeschooling her child. This aligns with Kate Averett's finding in her study of Texan homeschoolers. She discovers that across political and religious affiliation parents hold a common understanding of childhood that embraces the need for individualized learning.[1] Yet my research exposes something new: unlike these white homeschoolers, the Black homeschooling moms living around Elmford, like Lynette, emphasized racial discrimination as the primary driver behind their decision.

In decades past, women like Lynette and Maureen might have homeschooled only if they held strict religious or countercultural beliefs. Today, the pushes and pulls of homeschooling are different, and school choice policies encourage all families to find the right "fit" for their children. In other words, homeschooling has gone mainstream. Every homeschooling family I met for this study already knew someone else in their social network who homeschooled before they made the switch. The familiarity was an undeniable part of what made homeschooling seem like a viable option for these families. I cannot know whether the class-advantaged mothers in my study will keep their kids at home for school in the long term, but in the short term, at least, home education is their response to what they see as the failures of traditional school.

Another big change in homeschooling is that, unlike families in the 1980s and 1990s who started their kids off with homeschooling, the families I interviewed were more frequently homeschooling as a response to previous experiences in mainstream schools. Their kids start at a public school, charter school, or private school, and these mothers respond to the conditions in those schools by switching to home education. Black mothers engage in Black strategic schooling (building on Riché Barnes's "strategic mothering," which captures the way that Black professional women prioritize marital stability over work stability),[2] in which racial hostility in traditional schools convinced them that homeschooling is the only way to provide an anti-racist learning environment. Black strategic schooling finds Black mothers privileging their child's schooling stability over other responsibilities. Notably, many live in primarily white neighborhoods and send their children to white schools. Those nonhomeschool Black mothers reflect similar experiences with mainstream schools, but their interventions are different—they have fewer class resources to offset their income if they were to homeschool. Also, unlike the homeschoolers, these mothers are more likely to live in majority-minority neighborhoods, meaning racial isolation is not a challenge as it is for the Black homeschoolers. Under school choice, Black class-advantaged mothers can bring their children home, though this means the discrimination their children faced in school is generally pushed under the rug. Schools don't really have to address systemic racism when these Black mothers protect their children from racial hostility by refusing to expose them to more of it and choosing to homeschool instead.

White strategic schooling, on the other hand, came into focus differently as I interviewed white homeschooling moms. They too described bringing their children home as a response to traditional school, though not in response to racism, but to what they saw as a cookie-cutter curriculum that was insufficiently tailored to their children. Instead of a *push* out of the schools, white mothers felt *pulled* to customizing their unique child's education. White strategic schooling hinges on several aspects of white privilege, not least that white mothers are free from having to consider their child's race in the decision-making process. Regardless of their intent, many make decisions that place their children in white academic settings, whether homeschool or nonhomeschool. Some of the white homeschooling families in my study practice a form of partial white flight, responding to the whiteness of homeschooling by choosing to live in majority-minority neighborhoods, while white nonhomeschoolers tend to live in white neighborhoods and send their children to white schools. Some mothers, who express concern about the lack of racial diversity in their children's lives, enroll their children in racially diverse low-stakes settings, like sports programs, while avoiding diverse high-stakes settings, like academics. These sentiments reflect that way that whiteness is made invisible, not seen as a race, by white respondents. White mothers don't have to think of their children as raced, which allows them to avoid taking responsibility for racial injustice or working to mitigate racial segregation and inequalities as they make decisions they see as not directly "about race." By contrast, Black mothers don't have the ability to pick and choose when to consider the impact of race in their parenting choices, and they must confront the systemic racism embedded within school praxis.

The School Choice Landscape

School choice is presented as a race-neutral or "color-blind" policy allowing parents to act as consumers in the education marketplace. But in a society and education system suffused with racial injustices and inequalities, the policy of, process of, and options available through school choice are inexorably raced. The US civil rights era was key in setting up school choice as a sort of escape route for white families to avoid integrated schools, and the Supreme Court's *Yoder* decision in

1972, which stated that parents' religious practices warrant protection from state interference, added a nonracial reason to pull their children from traditional schools. Other white families sought out homeschooling as a public school alternative when their children's schools were affected by integrationist busing programs.[3]

The dramatic increase in the number of white families turning to homeschools since the 1970s fits with Maureen's initial impression—not necessarily weirdos and "religious crazy people," they were nonetheless mostly white and countercultural hippies or Christian families.[4] Situated at opposite ends of the political spectrum, these groups responded to their displeasure with mainstream society and government-led public schools by coming to the same decision. As homeschool legislation and leaders emerged in the 1970s and 1980s, so did homeschool organizations and support groups.[5] Regardless of their intent, the rise in homeschooling families further entrenched white flight and countered public schools' integration efforts. Throughout the 1990s, homeschooling was so nearly exclusive to white families that it is a recognized contributor to the persistence of racial segregation in American public schools.[6]

Beginning in the 1980s, under the Reagan administration, we have seen a rollback of the welfare state in all realms of family life, with specific shifts in educational debates from integration to academic achievement as captured by rigid metrics.[7] Political leaders devolving educational responsibility from the state to the family have favored neoliberal market logics in which education is publicly financed but privately provided in business-model schools. School reform, consequently, has focused on instituting "accountability" in the form of national-level testing and scoring for schools and passing that information along to parents operating as individual consumers selecting from competing education providers. As the cultural anthropologist and education scholar Ujju Aggarwal argues, school choice has moved from a way to redistribute resources across schools and toward redistributing "universal rights as individual choices."[8] Making the right school choice for a child is the task of parents, the state has alleged, and given the gendering of reproductive labor, it is more precisely the task of mothers. And because mothers' social location mobilizes and forecloses school choice options, school choice is "guaranteeing the continued production of a tiered citizenship"—it is reproducing and amplifying race, gender, and class inequalities.[9] At the same time, the homeschool population is slowly becoming more heterogeneous,[10] with a notable rise in Black and other families of color educating their kids at home.[11] The emphasis on parental choice, advances in technology (including the growth of online homeschool curricula and classes, sure to proliferate in the wake of the COVID-19 pandemic), and this racial diversification have made home-schooling mainstream.[12]

Still, direct comparisons return us to the image of mothers navigating school choice under unequal conditions. The Black mothers in my study, like Lynette, were undertaking school choice to avoid having their children experience further racial hostility. This is not the kind of school choice government officials describe but an urgent decision made under duress. White mothers like Maureen, however, can choose homeschool-ing to better tailor education to their children. When anxiety overwhelms Maureen's daughter, they make home the new school. In the meantime, as with other school choice options, low-income students and students of color are far less able to choose homeschooling and may be left behind to deal with inflexible curricula and racial discrimination.[13]

In comparing homeschool and nonhomeschool families within the same broad social network, I have demonstrated that material resources are central to Black mothers' strategies as the managers of their children's education. Usually, the time and energy to homeschool and navigate school transfers is available only to two-parent households with enough wealth for one parent to leave the paid workforce. Single-headed house-holds have fewer resources, though the parents in these households surely share the same concerns about their children's education as their more class-advantaged counterparts. So, too, do Black families (whose house-hold wealth is, on average, 10 percent that of the average white American family),[14] and Black women in particular (in part because they remain at the low-water mark in the US wage gap by both race and gender). In addition, when white families decide to homeschool, they frequently pursue a sort of partial white flight, moving their children to classrooms that are less race and class diverse—whether they are in a different school or nested within a homeschool community. Though white parents may try to counter a school's homogeneity by enrolling their children in race-diverse extracurricular activities, the fact remains that traditional schools become further segregated and inequalities continue to accrue.

School-Family-Work Conflict

Like other forms of education, homeschooling is deeply shaped by families' local context. Though across race, class, and school type, mothers lead school choice decisions, homeschoolers rely most heavily on mothers' unpaid labor (and fathers' uninterrupted career paths). Existing studies of gender inequality in parenting,[15] including of those who homeschool,[16] have problematized the rhetoric of choice, explaining how it obscures structural inequalities embedded in the organization of work and family. When policy makers and pundits talk of work-family conflict, it is generally as an individual concern confronted by mothers alone, not as a conflict embedded in the very organization of our workplaces and construction of class-inflected notions of "good" mothering. The ubiquity of the intensive mothering and choice narratives offers a cultural justification for some women who choose to opt out of careers to care for children and the home.[17]

Of course, "mothering" is neither universal nor unchanging. As intersectional theorists explain, studying mothering by considering how gender, race, and class operate in tandem is crucial for understanding women's stories, circumstances, and lives.[18] Research on the experiences of Black middle-class mothers decenters white mothering within the literature and offers crucial interventions to family scholarship by mapping the historical context that gives rise to contemporary strategies. For example, rather than intensive mothering, Dawn Dow describes Black middle-class mothering as integrated with employment responsibilities.[19] This is because Black middle-class mothers have qualitatively different social contexts than white middle-class mothers or Black working-class and poor mothers. Like other Black mothers, their children will experience racism and discrimination through schooling, employment, and law enforcement. Unlike low-income Black mothers, their class resources provide options, yet their class status cannot carry the same material resources and security as those of white middle-class mothers because every aspect of their lives will still be touched by racism.[20]

Bringing schools, another dominant institution shaping American family life, into the work-family conflict extends this earlier research on choice rhetoric. My study starts with the experiences of class-advantaged homeschooling mothers, comparing their schooling logics with those of class-advantaged nonhomeschooling mothers and examining how education decisions are connected to understandings of mothering. Schools also draw on women's time, and so a work-family-school conflict better captures the tensions faced by both Black and white mothers and identifies the competing pressures under which they "choose" to prioritize children's education over their own career paths and identities. Left unexamined is the lesson this prioritization instills in their own children (particularly daughters but also sons)—to see their mother in servitude to their child's education and in sacrifice to her career, while their fathers lean into professional lives. Thus, a second notable finding of this study is that school choice policy is written not only as if it were race-neutral but also as if gender is uninvolved. It goes without saying that the intersectionality of the issue—the way the choice is navigated in racially gendered ways—is entirely overlooked. The fact that I have found both Black and white class-advantaged women absorb the extensive work of navigating school choice into their mothering work obviates the ostensible gender neutrality on its own. Further, as women's career decisions are shaped by inflexible workplaces and school choice policies that make them responsible for the quality of their children's education (in racialized ways), the pressures are compounded by the way that insecurity manifests among class-advantaged families.

The Color of Insecurity

What I call the *racialized security shift* exposes how Black and white mothers explain rectifying their concern over their children's future stability through the reproductive labor mothers do to navigate school choice. Importantly, these concerns are *racialized*, since being Black in America adds specific uncertainties for children's futures whereas whiteness alleviates uncertainties for white children. This term builds on Marianne Cooper's work, in which she finds mothers often do the labor of worrying about their families' instability by building resilience in their children to prepare them to navigate our economically and politically insecure times (see chapter 3).[21] My study not only confirms that worrying about children's futures is labor done by mothers but also illuminates how this worry work—this racialized security shift—is exacerbated by school choice, since mothers are tasked with securing children's future stability in class- and race-inflected ways.

I spoke to these mothers at a time when violence inflicted on Black individuals and communities was becoming more broadly salient in the United States. Regularly broadcast through mainstream news, accounts of race and racial oppression have moved to the fore of our national consciousness. What would become Black Lives Matter was founded by Alicia Garza, Patrisse Cullors, and Opal Tometi in response to the acquittal of George Zimmerman in the shooting death of teenager Trayvon Martin in 2013. Today, Black Lives Matter is a global movement against police brutality and the callousness of white America toward the oppression and murder of Black people. This context is crucial for understanding the schooling strategies mothers described to me, particularly the uniformity of Black mothers' responses, that those who chose to homeschool did so to protect their child from discrimination in their traditional schools and classrooms. This is also the context within which white mothers make school choices that capitalize on their racial privilege in not seeing whiteness as a race and leaving the implications unaddressed. Even when class resources are available, other status markers—race and gender—are implicated in these families' schooling decisions, leaving enormous social inequalities intact.

Where Do We Go from Here?

When I give presentations on this research, I am often asked what I suggest we do to create equality across families and schools. This is an almost inconceivably large question, but a wealth of social science research has considered it. We are not lacking in good ideas for creating change. Rather, we seem to lack a sustained commitment to work together across communities to implement these changes. As Prudence Carter and Kevin Welner suggest, shifting national focus away from education's Black-white "achievement gap" would free us up to consider its deeper source—the "opportunity gap."[22] I have followed their excellent lead by focusing not on student academic achievement outcomes but on the gap between the opportunities available to seemingly comparable Black and white families. Class resources certainly matter, yet even when we hold class resources relatively constant, mothers' decisions are shaped by white students' privilege and Black students' marginalization and criminalization. Indeed, it's the symbolic capital that comes with whiteness that makes whiteness a credential under school choice and strips Black mothers of their full suite of options.

Producing real change and addressing inequalities at many different wellsprings means more than educating policy makers, teachers, administrators, students, and parents about race and racism. It will require the abandonment of the deficit thinking that views students of color as failing due to essentialist arguments about biological or cultural deficiency rather than racial oppression and stereotyping. It will mean refusing assimilationist rhetoric that suggests if students of color just learned to behave like white students in the classroom, they would succeed, too. An antideficit perspective will mean recognizing the value that Black and Brown students and families brings to schools based on their varied experiences in the world.[23] It will mean recognizing that students' different social locations within the racial hierarchy will shape their challenges in school and beyond. And it will require that we deconstruct the whitewashed curricula that allow for a collective overlook (or outright denial) when it comes to our racial past, present, and future.[24] The opposite of a deficit is a credit, an abundance. Holding Black History Month once a year implies that there is only enough Black history to require a month of recognition; an abundance-based curriculum would fundamentally shift education to not just "tolerate" but engage and celebrate diversity, including epistemological diversity across cultures. One education visionary, Paulo Freire, even calls for literacy to be measured in terms of political awareness. Such innovative curricula can enable disadvantaged groups by offering tools for empowerment, but they can also enable advantaged groups by increasing their cultural awareness (particularly about how their privilege operates through others' disenfranchisement) and opening up the intellectual benefit of a more panoramic worldview.[25]

When scholars speak of institutions as racist, and when I speak of schools as racist, it is not about a few lone teachers or parents or administrators with outdated racial ideas. No, schools are embedded within raced, gendered, and classed schemata that have become durable structures linked to resources.[26] I see this, for instance, in the disparate power afforded to families when exercising school choice. Existing research finds that low-income families of color face constraints in their ability to exercise empowerment, agency, and control under school choice.[27] I extend this work to find that, despite their socioeconomic resources, Black middle-class families are similarly hamstrung in school choice. Further, because mothers, not fathers, do this work, the process exacerbates gendered divisions of labor. Thus, we have a group of primarily women navigating school choice in ways that are circumscribed by their racial groups, such that whiteness is a credential giving whites access to a full range of schooling choices and blackness affords only the ability to seek the least discriminatory option. Understanding organizations as shaped by the interaction of race, class, and gender allows us to turn to the structure of these schools. Seemingly race-, class-, and gender-neutral policies and ways of organizing education smuggle in white and class privilege, along with gender inequality. The significance of these patterns cannot be overlooked.

Creating change will also require many frank conversations about race and racism, especially when it is expressed in "nonracial" terms, and about classed and gendered labor. To disrupt these patterns of inequality, in which segregation and tracking provide unequal access to high-quality schools, we can foster policies that promote integrated communities and schools. These might include affordable housing programs, or school policies that prioritize diversity and even support "de-tracking," so that all students have the opportunity to take college preparation classes.[28] To equalize opportunity, after all, policies cannot start at the end point: we cannot create educational equality by simply changing school choice processes, just as we cannot force it by measuring educational outcomes. We must address the root causes of those outcomes.

Janelle Scott and her colleagues have proposed several concrete suggestions for education reform that build from the lessons learned by past presidential administrations.[29] For example, the Obama administration used competitive grants to encourage schools' voluntary race and class integration efforts, and these were shut down by the Trump administration. Looking at the data to compare those policy periods is likely to provide useful direction to legislators. The Obama administration had also put into place antidiscrimination policies that required the investigation and assessment of complaints to place those incidents within the context of larger patterns of discrimination. During the time of my data collection (2014–2016), these policies were on the books but clearly were not doing enough to prevent Black students from becoming targets of racial discrimination. What does it tell us that Black class-advantaged mothers were, in those same years, telling me about removing their children from the racist environments of their local schools?

All the cracks and vulnerabilities in a system become more apparent in a crisis. As I write, we see the disparate impacts of COVID-19 throughout this country. Not only are the consequences of infection unevenly distributed across the population such that people of color are both more likely to be exposed to the virus and more likely to die from it,[30] but the consequences of public health efforts have been unevenly distributed. As schools moved to online instruction, those with fewer resources, disproportionately educating lower-income and students of color, were unprepared for the increased expenditures of safety precautions and poorly positioned to provide their students with the technology they may need to participate in education from home.[31] The lack of resources along with the added labor that has come with the pandemic, helps to explain why teachers are burned out and leaving their jobs.[32] Clearly, structural change cannot come quickly enough, and policy reforms will be piecemeal and inadequate. Yet they are a necessary first step.

Moving away from high-stakes testing is another way to lessen the opportunity gap among students. Standardized testing is popular, in large part, because it's convenient. No matter how often social scientists object, most people agree that "numbers don't lie." They want to score schools to make easier comparisons between school districts, to make simpler choices about resource allocations and school closures. But this reduces children to vessels, empty and waiting to be filled up with a specific set of facts. Currently, it is primarily white and wealthy schools that can focus on developing critical thinking skills; while low-income, majority-minority schools cannot risk losing funding and thus pressure their teachers to "teach to the test." This not only is harmful for students but also pushes quality teachers out of their careers—the pressure is just so taxing.[33] The testing, in fact, is one reason cited by the white class-advantaged mothers in my study—they believe their children need individualized learning, which is all but impossible when schools are hewing to the Common Core (the set of national math and English curriculum standards).[34] On the other hand, the simple provision of the necessary material resources for each student—current textbooks, up-to-date buildings, smaller class sizes, technology, and tutoring services—would improve student learning and draw teachers into the profession rather than push them out.

Amanda Lewis and John Diamond have urged would-be change makers to focus on disparate impacts rather than intentional discrimination.[35] As they and many others have pointed out, the racial discrimination embedded in our institutions is rarely experienced as blatant and intentional but rather as subtle, unintentional, and even apparently "nonracial" practices.[36] In other words, stamping out intentional discrimination is unlikely to address the problem of racial inequalities in schools. Had I not interviewed both Black and white mothers and triangulated their accounts with neighborhood and school district data, I would not have seen just how enormously school choice decisions are shaped by race. These mothers are confronting the same schooling options yet making their decisions in response to racially structured schools. A focus on disparate impacts, bolstered by a "power-aware" perspective, would better acknowledge and address how schooling policies and practices and schooling decisions work to reproduce inequalities.[37]

As I mentioned at the beginning of this book, as a sociologist it is not for me to argue *for* or *against* homeschooling. Rather, I focus on homeschooling to examine this underresearched phenomenon at the nexus of school and family, two of our most prominent social institutions. As sociologist Kate Averett posits: "Rather than asking . . . whether homeschooling is a problem . . . the more fruitful question is whether school choice is a problem," since homeschooling is the epitome of the current educational policies that support school choice.[38] Beyond examining the schooling strategies of Black and white homeschoolers and their nonhomeschooling counterparts, this study has sought to understand how these mothers' strategies are shaped by social, legal, cultural, and economic forces—by their networks, careers, race, and neighborhoods, as well as cultural scripts about mothering, racial uplift, and academic achievement. My findings suggest that real educational reform must recognize the full range of options available under school choice rather than continue to treat homeschooling as a niche practice with little to tell us about the promise and perils of the other available choices.

Challenging Individualism

In her research with white families and their engagement with diversity, Margaret Hagerman identifies a mismatch between what white parents *say* and what they *do*.[39] A mismatch surfaces in my data as well. White mothers claim to "value diversity," while making residential and schooling decisions that support segregation. Whites wield their power under seemingly nonracial policies in ways that mobilize their racial power, not recognizing how their whiteness gives them schooling options that Black families have been denied. This upholds the invisibility of whiteness as unmarked by race while positioning people of color as racial tokens.[40] For white homeschoolers and nonhomeschoolers alike, their contribution to segregation is a sort of partial white flight, since some live in racially diverse neighborhoods and attend white (home)schools, while others choose white neighborhoods and schools yet enroll their children in neighboring districts for more diverse extracurricular activities. This partial white flight allows white mothers to pick and choose to interact with children of color when it benefits their white child while avoiding the moral conundrum of being a "good" white who values diversity yet has no contact with people of color.[41] Unless white families recognize and begin to give up some of their privilege, racial inequalities will continue to stymie equal access to schooling opportunities.

Both race and gender are socially constructed, not biologically determinate, categories and concepts. Indeed, the power that comes with whiteness and manhood and the disenfranchisement that goes along with blackness and womanhood have been constructed through historical, legal, and social means. Still, social constructs have real, and hugely consequential, outcomes in every domain of one's life—economic, political, social, and educational.[42] Intersectional theorists argue that studying how *multiple* categories of difference operate in tandem allows us to see how power works in uneven, overlapping ways;[43] the privilege of one group is not "free-floating" but directly linked to the disadvantage of another group.[44] In other words, inequalities are relational. In my study, white class-advantaged families' privilege is directly linked to Black class-advantaged families' constraints. The opportunities that white middle-class children experience through their mothers' navigation of school choice are what leave Black middle-class children disadvantaged within the traditional school system, despite their mothers' protective efforts. Again, disrupting inequality will require those with privilege to cede some of it. As Hagerman suggests, white parents "rejecting the idea that their own child is more innocent and special and deserving than other people's children" is one crucial way that whites can challenge the racial inequality of the United States, but it will still mean little if they refuse to give up some of their racial power.[45] White parents must be willing to resist centering themselves and their status in their engagement with families of color and instead listen and work collaboratively to confront racial injustice. This might involve sending their children to majority-minority schools and involving themselves to benefit children collectively rather than individually. Individualist thinking cannot get us to the collective, interdependent thinking that asks what all children need to secure safety, care, and quality education. And thinking alone cannot get us to a redistribution of opportunity.

"Having it all," Dawn Dow suggests, may not mean being a mother who can work, provide the best possible anti-racist education for her child, and keep her marriage alive and well, but, rather, being a mother who shares the responsibilities of work, family, and education with spouses, extended family, education professionals, and community members.[46] The familiar sentiment "it takes a village to raise a child" might actually work to mitigate the overwhelming burden of child-rearing that is so normalized as a *woman's* burden. It could help relieve essentialist notions of who can best perform this reproductive labor. And it might even help us reconfigure mothers' work-family-school conflict, but it also requires explicit support from workplaces, schools and the state. For example, family-friendly policies could support the collective good by providing paid parental leave for both mothers and fathers (thus decoupling caregiving and breadwinning from gender) and by ensuring that high-quality childcare and educational facilities are accessible to all children.

Cultural narratives about good mothering encourage women to prioritize their child—their unique, individual child—over everything else, including their own needs, ambitions, and aptitudes. But if we are truly concerned about the collective, good mothering must actually be good for mothers (and fathers!). We need parents who are happy and feel supported in the important job of raising children to be productive citizens, as well as in any other important job they may hold, from software developer to intergenerational caretaker or educator.

ACKNOWLEDGMENTS

Writing this book would not have been possible without the support and guidance of many individuals. First and most important, I would like to express my deepest gratitude to my adviser and mentor, Joya Misra. It was truly an honor to work with such a brilliant scholar and the most kind and compassionate mentor I could ask for. I am forever indebted to her for the guidance, patience, and support she showed me throughout this long process. I am especially grateful that she always reminded me of the intersectional approach that I wanted to take in the project, while her gift at explaining the complexities of social life in clear and concrete ways helped me cultivate this eye in my research. Without her as an inspiration, I would not be where I am today, nor would I have written this book.

I am grateful to Naomi Gerstel, Jennifer Lundquist, and Miliann Kang, who also served as invaluable mentors on this project. Their scholarship and feedback over the past twelve years have been hugely influential in my development as a scholar and in the shaping of this book. Miliann Kang's tutelage through the mothering research group, along with reading countless drafts, helped to make me the scholar I am today. She understood my vision for the project long before I was able to clearly articulate it. Naomi Gerstel's grooming of me as a family scholar but also her interest in the project despite the ups and downs I faced in graduate school kept me going. Her detailed feedback on countless drafts and her eye toward family scholarship hugely shaped the project. Jennifer Lundquist coached me especially through the school choice chapters, offering invaluable feedback that helped me conceptualize why homeschoolers can actually assist us in understanding larger patterns of school segregation. Without these incredible scholars, I would not have completed this project.

I would also like to thank the faculty of the Sociology Department and Women, Gender, and Sexuality Studies at the University of

Massachusetts, Amherst, as well as the faculty in the Sociology Department at Hamilton College from whom I received invaluable feedback. I extend special thanks to Maureen Perry-Jenkins, Aline Sayer, Gisele Litalian, and all of those at UMass's Center for Research on Families for their support and feedback on this project. I also must thank Kysa Nygreen, who provided expert guidance very early on, as well as Michelle Budig, Dan Chambliss, Steve Ellingson, Matt Grace, Janice Irvine, Yagmur Karakaya, Jaime Kucinskas, Alex Manning, Noriko Milman, Millie Thayer, Melissa Wooten, Jon Wynn, and Robert Zussman, all of whom provided crucial feedback on the project at various stages.

I would be remiss to not also thank several UMass colleagues and friends. I am forever grateful for the incredible strength of the intellectual community I have been a part of through the Sociology Department. I am indebted to the Simones, a group of feminist sociologists who welcomed me into their community and have provided intellectual and emotional sustenance: Sharla Alegria, Irene Boeckmann, Laura Heston, Melissa Hodges, Elisa Martinez, Sarah Miller, Mary Scherer, Chris Smith, and Abby Templer-Rodriguez. In addition, I send a special thanks to Celeste Curington, Misun Lim, Juyeon Park, Cassaundra Rodriguez, and Ryan Turner for their intellectual support and friendship over the years. Each in their own way has inspired me to stay true to the sociologist I want to become.

A portion of this book appears in the journal *Sociology of Race and Ethnicity* and thus has benefited from the constructive feedback of the editors and anonymous reviewers. I would like to extend special thanks to David Brunsma for his editorial expertise. Beth Berry provided her editing eye on earlier drafts of this work. Later, Letta Page offered her incredible writing and editing skills to develop the prose and clarity of my arguments. Hannah Peterson, my research assistant at Hamilton College, helped me clarify the language to reach an undergraduate audience. Kaja Bielecka also generously shared their careful and critical eye, helping to polish the manuscript in later stages of revision.

I am incredibly grateful to Ilene Kalish, my editor at New York University Press, and her team for their guidance and advice throughout this process. I also thank the anonymous reviewers who read my manuscript and provided extensive feedback that has greatly sharpened the clarity and analytic contributions of my work.

I am also forever grateful to my parents, siblings, grandmother, god-mother, and five nibblings for the unwavering love they have provided throughout this long journey. I thank Mama, who first gave me the ability to see the strength in women's voices and has always encouraged me in finding the courage to use my own. She also showed me how to juggle work and family, despite the structural barriers we face. I thank Papa for providing tech support no matter what time of the day or night I might be asking, and for being one of my biggest cheerleaders. I thank Grandmom for her unyielding belief in me and in my autonomy as a woman. I thank Suna for being the dear sibling and role model that they are, listening to my anxieties, but always encouraging me onward. They also showed me the importance of finding and following my path, whatever that might be. I thank my brother Gene for reminding me of the importance of compassion. I thank Jesse for being such a loving big brother, leading the way, while reminding me of our roots. I thank Lisa for being such a positive force and providing endless big-sister support.

Completing this book while becoming a mother was at times challenging but was made possible by my parents and by Suna, Coral, Izzy, and Cori, who graciously provided childcare so that I could write, write, write. My son, Sasha, has offered new meaning and inspiration to my research by giving me the privilege of being his mother. He has taught me the importance of efficiency while bringing me love and joy every single day. Finally, I thank my partner, Tim, who has been and remains an incredible source of love and inspiration. From late night social theory conversations to discussions about the nitty gritty of research methods, to reading countless chapter drafts, Tim has provided the unwavering support of a spouse, friend, and colleague, and for that I am forever grateful. He has always valued my work equally as his own, despite structural forces working against us in this regard. Tim is also a wonderful father to our Sasha. He made having a child seem possible. I am so glad we found each other and look forward to our adventures together.

Last, but certainly not least, I thank the women who volunteered to participate in this study, without whom this manuscript would not have been possible. To them, I am eternally grateful.

APPENDIX A

Tables

TABLE A.1. Interviewee Demographic and Employment Information

	Black Homeschool (*n* = 17)	White Homeschool (*n* = 21)	Black Conventional (*n* = 15)	White Conventional (*n* = 14)
Marital Status				
Partnered	94% (16)	90% (19)	60% (9)	100% (14)
Single/divorced	6% (1)	10% (2)	40% (6)	0 (0)
Religion				
Religious	88% (15)	67% (14)	86% (13)	29% (4)
Secular	12% (2)	33% (7)	14% (2)	71% (10)
Education				
High school/+	0% (0)	0% (0)	73% (11)	29% (4)
College/+	100% (17)	100% (21)	27% (4)	71% (10)
Employment				
No paid	47% (8)	38% (9)	27% (4)	29% (4)
Part-time paid	47% (8)	48% (10)	20% (3)	42% (6)
Full-time paid	6% (1)	14% (2)	53% (8)	29% (4)
Partner Education				
High school/+	56% (9)	21% (4)	67% (6)	14% (2)
College/+	43% (7)	79% (15)	33% (3)	86% (12)
Partner Employment				
No paid/retired	0% (0)	11% (2)	0% (0)	0% (0)
Part-time paid	0% (0)	0% (0)	0% (0)	0% (0)
Full-time paid	100% (16)	89% (17)	100% (9)	100% (14)
Household Income				
A. Under $30,000	6% (1)	10% (2)	13% (2)	0% (0)
B. $30,000–$74,999	41% (7)	33% (7)	47% (7)	13% (2)
C. $75,000–$200,000	47% (8)	43% (9)	40% (6)	87% (13)
D. Above $200,000	6% (1)	14% (3)	0% (0)	0% (0)
Social Class				
Working class	18% (3)	19% (4)	60% (9)	27% (4)
Middle class	76% (13)	71% (15)	40% (6)	73% (11)
Upper middle class	6% (1)	10% (2)	0% (0)	0% (0)

TABLE A.2. Interviewee and Household Employment and Education Details

	Black Interrupted Career (*n* = 23)	Black Steady Career (*n* = 9)	White Interrupted Career (*n* = 28)	White Steady Career (*n* = 7)
Marital Status				
Partnered	87% (20)	55% (5)	93% (26)	86% (6)
Single	13% (3)	45% (4)	7% (2)	14% (1)
Education				
High school/+	22% (5)	75% (6)	14% (4)	0% (0)
College/+	78% (18)	25% (2)	86% (24)	100% (7)
Employment				
Interrupted	48% (11)	0% (0)	50% (14)	0% (0)
Pulled back	52% (12)	0% (0)	50% (14)	0% (0)
Steady	0% (0)	100% (9)	0% (0)	100% (7)
Partner Education				
High school/+	20% (4)	80% (4)	20% (5)	29% (2)
College/+	80% (16)	20% (1)	80% (21)	71% (5)
Partner Employment				
No paid/retired	0% (0)	0% (0)	8% (2)	0% (0)
Part-time paid	0% (0)	0% (0)	0% (0)	0% (0)
Full-time paid	100% (20)	100% (5)	92% (24)	100% (6)
School Type				
Homeschool	70% (16)	11% (1)	68% (19)	29% (2)
Conventional	30% (7)	89% (8)	32% (9)	71% (5)
Social Class				
Working class	26% (6)	67% (6)	21% (6)	29% (2)
Middle class	70% (16)	33% (3)	71% (20)	71% (5)
Upper middle class	4% (1)	0% (0)	8% (2)	0% (0)

APPENDIX B

The Study

For this research I conducted in-depth interviews with 96 Black and white families, mostly mothers who lived in and around the city of Elmford, a pseudonym for a midsize city located in the northeastern United States. I wanted to include an equal number of homeschool and nonhomeschool families from the same region to make this comparison robust. As such, the focal interviews include 67 respondents—17 Black homeschoolers, 21 white homeschoolers, 15 Black nonhomeschoolers, and 14 white nonhomeschoolers—living in Elmford. In the process of seeking the Black homeschool interviewees, I conducted 29 interviews with interracial homeschoolers and Black homeschoolers living outside of the study region. All interviewees had at least one school-age child (between five and eighteen years old) at the time of the interview. Among the 46 respondents who identified as religious (29 of 38 homeschool and 17 of 29 nonhomeschool), levels of piousness varied. Most interviewees described attending weekly worship, but a few homeschool families also employed religious curricula and engaged in daily prayer.

While I was not explicitly seeking middle-class respondents, the majority of the 67 focal interviews were with middle-class (45 total; 19 Black and 26 white) or upper-middle-class (3 total; 1 Black and 2 white) families. Fifty-seven of the 67 respondents identified their household as heterosexual and married, one respondent as lesbian and married, and 9 respondents identified as single-parent households (widowed, divorced, or single). All homeschool respondents (38 of 38) held at least a college degree, as did nearly half of the nonhomeschool respondents (14 of 29).

Like other schooling studies, I measure social class by considering household income, as well as the education and occupation of each respondent and their partner.[1] Respondents are identified as middle-class when they hold a bachelor's degree or more, and they and/or their partner works in jobs that demand at least a college degree, such as schoolteacher, lawyer, or professor. Upper-middle-class families are those who meet the middle-class criteria and also earn a household income of above $200,000 per year. When asked to place their household within an annual income range, most respondents fell within this country's two middle income brackets of over $30,000 but below $200,000. Three Black respondents and two white respondents earned below this range, while one Black respondent and three white respondents earned above this range (see table A.1, appendix A).

Among the 67 focal interviews, the class advantage and regional focus control for differences, making the homeschool and nonhomeschool comparison meaningful. Together, these data situate each group in relation to the others, which has allowed me to examine how regional school choice politics are understood and navigated by class-advantaged families.

Research Design

I purposefully designed the study to center the stories of mothers, which allows me to unpack the meaning they hold around schooling decisions. I do not provide systematic observations or interviews with children or other family members (such as spouses or extended family). However, as youth scholars document, rather than passive subjects who quietly follow their parents, children can be assumed to be actively involved in school choice, shaping their parents' decisions and their own futures.[2] In short, children's voices matter in families' decisions about schooling. Indeed, several homeschooling mothers described how their children asked to be homeschooled before parents had made the decision to do so. For example, Lynette told me, "My son begged me to pull him out," and Maureen recalled how her daughter "petitioned" to stay home by writing a persuasive essay on the topic. This suggests the active role children play in their schooling futures.

In the process of meeting with mothers in coffee shops, at their homes, or on video calls, I was often introduced to their children. Some were kept busy completing homework or coloring while I talked to their moms; others were interested in the conversation and would listen, or in some cases chime in with questions or opinions. Mothers didn't always bring their children to an interview, but many did. While it is not examined in this book, children's role in shaping their lives (including their education) is a topic other scholars' have explored.[3] It is certainly worthy of further exploration, particularly as it relates to homeschooled children.

The voices of fathers are also absent from this study. I mostly did not interview men, nor did I observe them. This was not because I asked to speak exclusively with mothers but rather the result of who volunteered to participate in my study. The propensity of mothers, but not fathers, to volunteer to be interviewed about child-rearing is consistent with prior parenting research.[4] Despite the absence of fathers, I developed a sense of their presence within the family through how mothers talked about their husbands, and some interviews that were conducted in the home allowed me to meet the husband. In two instances, husbands joined their wives for the interview. Collectively, these accounts demonstrate that while mothers highlight the extensive labor involved in navigating school choice for their children, husbands influenced these decisions, even if through their lack of involvement.

Studying across racial groups and school types meant that I needed to design an interview guide that would be relevant to the varied experiences of all four groups: Black, white, homeschool, and traditional school. To develop questions, I followed the lead of other interview studies that have used similar cross-group comparisons.[5] In particular, I was attentive to asking the same questions for each group but wording them in a way that would accommodate the variety of responses I anticipated. For example, the question about mothers' approaches to child-rearing asks, "What do you think is the image of a good mother and good father in American society?" When necessary, I would then follow up with "What images do family, friends, neighbors, and school administrators seem to hold"? Next I would ask, "Can you describe your own image of a good mother and a good father?" While this set of questions is broad, I designed it with anticipated variation across Black and white families' responses since existing research suggests that both groups may recognize the cultural pressures of intensive mothering, where work and family are at odds with good mothering. Yet Black mothers may find that the members of their community hold an integrative understanding of mothering whereas white mothers may express the consistency of intensive mothering throughout their community (see the Interview Guide in appendix C).[6]

Another example of a question designed to be relevant across race and school type is, "When you face a particular challenge or joy of parenting or schooling, with whom do you talk about it?" With this question I hoped to get a sense of the support respondents drew on to manage child-rearing. I anticipated that responses could vary by race and school type, since existing research finds middle-class Black families are more likely to draw on extended kin and community members for support, while middle-class white families rely on nuclear family members.[7] As such, I designed this question with the intention of capturing such variation. I avoided asking something about the involvement of certain people (extended family, spouse, friends), which could be leading, or asking more broadly where one turns for support, which could result in vague responses. Instead, I asked respondents to describe the specific examples of challenges they face, what support they drew from to navigate these challenges, and from whom the support came.

Recruitment

In the spring of 2014, I located respondents through contacting the eighteen homeschool organizations listed on the state's homeschool website and identified as located in the Elmford region. I used respondent-driven sampling to interview other homeschoolers and conventional schoolers through these initial contacts. In addition to interviews, for one weekend in spring 2014 and again in spring 2016, I attended an annual state-run homeschool conference, observing the various sessions, exploring the homeschool textbook exhibit hall, and introducing myself to homeschoolers. This allowed me to collect additional interviews and better understand the homeschool context of the region. These tactics were fruitful for locating white homeschoolers to interview.

Because I was interested in drawing comparisons between Black and white homeschoolers and found that those who initially responded to my interview request were white, I began also asking white homeschoolers what they knew about the changing demographics of homeschooling, particularly the growth of Black homeschool families (see question 27 in the Interview Guide, appendix C).[8] Many of the white homeschoolers responded to this question by stating that they had noticed this growth, yet none of them said they knew Black homeschoolers well enough to put me in touch. This is unsurprising and maps onto existing research that finds social networks tend to be racially homogeneous. Specifically, even when whites claim to know people of color, they do not know them well.[9]

Based on my assessment of the eighteen local homeschool groups' online descriptions, none identified as explicitly for homeschooling families of color, and this was confirmed through my interview with Leslie, a Black homeschooling mother. She explained that when her family first moved to Elmford, they were "part of a co-op with [twelve to thirteen] Black kids." They were involved with this group "for two years," but "[the group] folded when the host took a full-time job and sent her kids off to public school." Although the former group members remain friends, Leslie explains that the group itself dissolved. My exchange with Leslie left me wondering if Elmford-based Black homeschoolers were just not involved in homeschool groups and therefore if I would have better luck locating this population through some other route. This led me to contact—by emailing, calling, and posting flyers—Elmford's Black churches and cultural organizations about the study. In addition, I reached out to a national Black homeschool organization, National Black Home Educators, asking if they would share my information with its membership. These channels led to some responses and interviews. From there, I snowball sampled for additional interviews, asking each person if they would invite two or three of their friends to participate in the study.

Once I began piecing together that the Black homeschool network was not regionally bound as it seemed to be for white families, I decided to interview Black homeschoolers regardless of their regional location, hoping that some would have connections to Black homeschoolers in the Elmford area. Many of the Black homeschoolers from Elmford said they didn't know any other Black homeschoolers in their region. However, they were willing to put me in touch with a Black homeschooler they knew from a different part of the country. Notably, most of these women asked if I would put them in touch with other Black homeschoolers in Elmford, which I eventually did. This speaks to the isolation these mothers experienced, as has been described in the Black homeschoolers' narratives in chapter 6.

Through this recruitment strategy, I eventually spoke with 17 Black homeschooling mothers from Elmford and an additional 29 homeschooling families of color located around the country (I do not include these additional interviews in this book's analysis because of the race and regional variation). The 17 focal interviews center on homeschooling mothers who identify as Black, Black American, or African American and live in the greater Elmford region. Ten other families of color were interviewed who identified as interracial homeschool families. This included four Asian-white homeschool families, three Black-white homeschool families, and three homeschool families in which the parents were white and had adopted Black children. In addition to these 10 interviews, I spoke with 19 Black homeschoolers from different places around the country. In total, 5 were homeschooling in Maryland; 3 in Georgia; 2 in Florida; 2 in New Jersey; and 1 each in Tennessee, North Carolina, Delaware, Michigan, Alabama, Texas, and Pennsylvania.

Data Analysis

I audio-recorded, transcribed, and coded all interviews using NVivo, a qualitative data analysis software. I also wrote detailed descriptive and analytic memos throughout the research process, from which I drew for analysis. I used an iterative approach when coding the data, paying attention to theoretical expectations while remaining open to meanings that emerged from the interviews themselves.[10] This led to initial topics, then through multiple rounds of coding developed into salient themes.[11] These themes included respondents' articulation of their approach to parenting, as well as how they navigated schooling, childcare, and employment.

After situating the study historically—as is common for sociological books—chapters 2 and 3 focus on themes surrounding parenting strategies and the relationship to mothers' employment. The second half of the book explores how families navigate schooling their children. In terms of parenting, central themes that I found emerging from the transcripts include ideas around protective parenting, opting out of employment, and notable variations based on race and school type. I found that the theme of schooling strategies surfaced in transcripts with key differences based on race: Black mothers sought to protect their children from racism in schools, and white mothers sought to individualize their children's education without considering race.

Rather than observing families' daily lives, I talked with mothers, which offered depth for understanding the belief and meaning they hold behind their navigation of school choice.[12] I refer to respondents' interviews as in-depth in that they are relatively lengthy and involve taking the time to build rapport. Indeed, interviews lasted between thirty minutes to two hours or more, although most averaged sixty minutes, which resulted in an average of roughly twenty-seven single-spaced pages of transcript per interview. Through the interviews I asked a set of initial questions, with follow-up questions available to allow the respondents to reflect on their answers and add further thoughts. For example, I opened with a broad question ("Can you walk me chronologically through each of your children's schooling experiences from prekindergarten through their current situation?") and then followed up with more questions based on the mother's response. Replies to this initial question often led me to jump to later questions in the interview guide when a mother touched on other questions through this initial one. This open-ended conversational approach allowed me to gain more depth through responses from mothers and is distinct from more structured interview approaches that seek shorter responses and follow a set order.[13]

As is the nature with in-depth interviewing, the study sample is much smaller than those in quantitative studies in which thousands of survey responses are often collected. The shortcoming of interviews as compared with surveys are that the findings are not generalizable to a larger population. Yet, the strength of interviews, and of qualitative research more generally, is the depth with which we can study the social world. Kristin Luker describes this as our ability to "examine a grain of sand very, very closely to show how the world is reflected in it."[14] Rather than generalizing to a larger population, through these interviews I tested and generated theory, or ideas that can be applied logically, not statistically, to a larger population. To do this I continued data collection until theoretical saturation was reached—when interviews confirmed previous findings, leading to consistent explanations.[15]

Talking about Race

The way interviewees responded to questions about race maps onto existing research in notable ways. Very often I found whites engaging in the four frames of color-blind racism: abstract liberalism (regarding people as making individual choices and using this as justification for racial inequalities), naturalization (explaining away racial phenomena as natural occurrences), cultural racism (relying on culturally based arguments to explain racial inequalities), and minimization of racism (claiming that racial discrimination is no longer a factor in explaining today's racial inequalities).[16] For example, when asked to explain how it came to be that her daughter's friend group is primarily white and middle-class, Maureen, a white middle-class homeschooling mother, drew on abstract liberalism to explain: "Well, we live in suburban [Elmford] so most of the kids are white suburban kids . . . [because we homeschool] she's not forced to socialize with people just because she's in the same classroom with them. She's really able to choose her friends based on friend qualities." Here Maureen suggests that her daughter's friend group is based on the individual neighborhood choices of her family and the personal "quality" of friends. This explanation ignores the relationship between the whiteness of her daughter's friend group and the structural segregation practices that result in benefits for white children, at the expense of people of color.[17]

Dominant ideologies, like color-blind racism, impact members of all groups (dominant and subordinate) but not necessarily in the same way.[18] Indeed, while I found color-blind racism more prominent among whites, Black respondents also used color-blind frames although to a lesser extent and sometimes in contradictory ways. For example, in one part of her interview, Hilda, a Black middle-class homeschooling grandmother, explains that white people are homeschooling because they're "wanting the best for their children . . . the best social environment and the best educational environment and they just don't know that Black kids are the best for them. . . . I honestly don't think it's racism . . . they're not prejudiced." Here Hilda uses a bit of abstract liberalism (individual choices that are framed as not being part of larger patterns) and naturalization (this is a natural logic of parents) to explain away white homeschoolers' contributions to racial segregation and the negative impacts on Black (and white) children. Yet later in the interview, Hilda describes the discrimination she faced from white homeschoolers: "They kept me and the kids at arm's length. . . . I'm seeing other [white] homeschool mothers who are brand-new come in and they're surrounding them." She lets out a sigh and says, "I can't afford to get angry or upset, I just go to the next thing. What else can I do?" Unlike her first example, here Hilda's statement exposes race and racism as shaping white homeschoolers' interactions with her and her grandchildren, indicating the impact of race in their lives and disrupting color-blind logics.

Many white respondents appeared uncomfortable talking about race, and some admitted they never had to think about it in this way. For example, in her interview, Maureen says she "doesn't know" how race has shaped her daughter's experience with friends because she had never thought about it. Whites also demonstrated discomfort when asked to talk about race through their hesitation, using many "ums" and "ahs" in their responses. For instance, when asked about how the whiteness of his daughter's friend group shaped their experience, Steve (the only white homeschooling father I interviewed) said: "Ah, um. I, I, I don't, I don't really think of, I don't really think of that actually. I just try to be active, I, I think you make most of your friends through, through mutual interests and not, and not necessarily through age or ethnicity . . . we just try to do a lot of different activities that they want to do anyway and um sort of, and let friendships go from there." Steve is not alone in expressing the sentiment that race does not shape his children's friend group. This sentiment was expressed by many white and some Black mothers. What is different between the two groups, however, is that most white respondents appeared unfamiliar with "seeing" their race and were often uncomfortable when asked to talk about it—a pattern that is consistent with existing research on whiteness.[19]

In contrast to white respondents, most Black mothers demonstrated little hesitation when asked to talk about how race shapes their experience even if they sometimes used color-blind logics in explaining their children's friend groups. This difference is a "perception gap" where whites consider racism having ended with the 1960s civil rights era, whereas people of color see the continuation of racial discrimination. This signals both the discomfort that whites may feel when talking about race and the privilege of not having really thought directly about their race.[20] In what was said and not said, these differences and the sometimes subtle and indirect ways of talking about race by white respondents demonstrate respondents' racial understandings of the world.

As the interviewer, I found white respondents' discomfort when talking about race to be challenging to navigate. My goal when asking these questions was to make white mothers feel comfortable enough that they would genuinely address the question without inducing such discomfort that they would end the interview early. As such, I asked this question about race partway through the interview (question 14 in the Interview Guide), not at the beginning because I wanted time to build rapport. I also did not place this question at the end of the interview because I hoped that most of the potential discomfort elicited by the question would be overcome by the end, so that respondents would help me recruit additional participants. I suspect my strategy worked since none of the respondents—white or Black—ended the interview early due to a question that I asked. A few respondents did go into the interview stating they only had so much time in their schedule to speak with me, and so we ended early for that reason.

Positionality

In this study, I was guided by feminist approaches to research, which center the narratives of those who have been historically marginalized.[21] Most participants were privileged by class status, yet their experiences of marginalization due to race and gender were common in the narratives they shared. As qualitative researchers have well documented, the race, class, and gender of the researcher and the study participant shape every aspect of the research process.[22] Drawing from Patricia Hill Collins, throughout the research I reflected on how my insider/outsider status as a white class-advantaged woman shaped the study, from design to rapport building.[23] My outsider status was most obvious with regard to race and parental status. Black respondents generously shared their stories of navigating school choice and helped me locate additional Black homeschoolers. Most of these respondents appeared comfortable in their conversations with me, although I imagine some hesitation could have existed for respondents given my position within the dominant racial group. One case in which I wondered if part of the respondent's hesitation was due to my being white was that of Juanita, a Black widowed homeschooling mother of two. I had approached Juanita at the homeschool conference to see if she would be willing to be interviewed. Although initially she agreed, scheduling the interview ended up involving several false starts. I contacted her a few times by phone and text message after the conference, and it wasn't until a third try, several months later, that she responded to schedule the interview. Once we met for the interview, she seemed to relax into the conversation, disclosing information at the end that she requested be kept off the record, which I attribute to the importance she placed on sharing her story but also the rapport we had built.

Other Black mothers seemed to use the interview as an opportunity to educate me on experiences of Black Americans in a white-dominant and anti-Black society. For example, Julia, a Black homeschooling mother of seven kids, explained how being Black and homeschooling has meant being divided between two worlds, extended family and the white homeschool community:

> We came from an area . . . with just about all people of African descent . . . and that was our world. So, when we came here and we had our children, there ended up being this clash of worlds, because our children grew up in a white middle-class church, neighborhood, homeschooling. . . . And so our children grew up between two worlds. . . . [They] appreciate their roots and of course they love their grandparents and their cousins, through us. But, I believe their world has definitely been shaped more by . . . the [way the] homeschooling community thinks, and pretty much the way white middle-class America thinks. It's affected them.

I can't know how the interview would have been different if I were Black instead of white. The level of detail that Julia provided may have been glossed over if I were of the same race as her. For instance, she might have assumed that I understood this division between two worlds and therefore would not have explained what she meant in such detail, or she might not have felt the need to share this comment at all. At the same time, Black respondents also may have left out certain experiences, anticipating that I would not fully understand or relate to them.

Being childless when I conducted the interviews likely also shaped my interactions with respondents. Although I did not disclose my parental status unprompted, some women asked if I was a mother myself. I suspect that I received more detailed responses from some respondents since they knew I had no experience in raising a child of my own. It has now been several years since I collected the interviews, and I have just welcomed my first child into the world. Joining my respondents in identifying as a mother has certainly brought new meaning to the mothering narratives respondents shared with me.

My insider status was most prominent regarding my own education, given that I had been homeschooled and also attended public school as a child. My experience being homeschooled led to many rapport-building opportunities with homeschool respondents. For example, when I disclosed at the beginning of the interview that I had been homeschooled until ninth grade, at which point I attended the local public high school, many of the homeschool respondents would follow up to ask how I liked that alternative school experience. Usually, this seemed to lead homeschoolers to feel more comfortable in sharing their stories with me.

Still, in some cases, respondents appeared to become more comfortable after the interview got underway. For example, Elizabeth, a white married homeschooling mother of four children, was one of the most hesitant respondents with whom I spoke. Her responses started out relatively short, but I could see her relaxing into the conversation as things progressed. It wasn't until the very end of the interview that I learned her hesitation was linked to concerns she had about the information from the interview getting into government hands. This became clear when I asked if she would be willing to share my request for interviews with other homeschoolers. She replied:

> Because of the nature of homeschooling. Because sometimes there's legal issues going on, there may be more reluctance if someone's currently homeschooling, saying too much for fear that something could get out. . . . But it's good that I went through this first because then I can tell people, you know she's a nice gal . . . [she's] not gonna ask you certain questions about things that you might not want to answer.

Elizabeth proceeded to describe how other homeschoolers she knew were so concerned about "legal issues" that they wouldn't put their names on any of the homeschool listservs for fear of being questioned. While she differentiated herself from these families, the amount of time she spent talking about what she saw as the state's overreach into the lives of homeschoolers made it clear that she held similar concerns. Elizabeth's fear of government intervention into the homeschooling of her kids helps to explain her hesitation.

It was because of interviews with homeschoolers like Elizabeth that I decided to not disclose the state within which I conducted interviews, let alone the city. Because I wanted to talk to a diverse range of home-schoolers, I needed the respondents to trust that I was not going to expose their identity. Given the relatively high homeschool regulation in the study region, I suspect some homeschoolers might have been more concerned about my disclosing their identity than if I was studying homeschoolers in states with very low homeschool regulation, such as Texas or Illinois.[24] Overall, my insider/outsider status proved important for developing skillful interactions with respondents—whether to probe past assumed understanding based on commonalities or to focus on building rapport due to salient differences or hesitation.

APPENDIX C

Interview Guide

Introduction: I am conducting a study that looks at parents' experiences with child-rearing and decisions around schooling their children. In this interview I plan to ask you questions about your children's schooling, more general questions about child-rearing, your and your spouse's (if married) employment and education experiences, and closing with some basic demographic questions.

SCHOOLING EXPERIENCES
1. Can you walk me chronologically through each of your children's schooling experiences from prekindergarten through their current situation?
   a. Specifically what kind of schooling programs was he/she enrolled in, for how long, and why?
   b. What were you happy/unhappy about regarding their experience in each schooling program? Why?
   c. What kinds of schooling programs do you foresee your child(ren) attending in the coming years (high school/college)?
2. Besides the programs your child(ren) have attended, what other schooling options have you/do you consider for you child(ren)?
   Why? Why did you not end up choosing these options?
3. What is it about your child(ren)'s current school program that made you choose this schooling option for them?
4. Can you describe the [school type] curriculum your child follows? PROBES
   a. Math, science, art, music, social studies programs, etc.
5. Can you give me a sense of how your day and your child's day are structured or organized?

   a. How are you involved in your child's day around schooling and
      extracurriculars?
6. How are decisions about your child's daily schedule/activities
   made (after-school activities, childcare)?
   Who is involved? Why?
7. Can you describe the process you go through to receive approval to
   homeschool your child?
   What do you think of this process? Is it effective? Not effective?
8. What do you most and least enjoy about your child's current
   schooling situation? Why?

Parenting Experiences

9. As a parent, what do you see your role being in your child's
   education?
10. What do you think is the image of a good mother and good father
    in American society?
    a. Popular culture.
    b. Family members, friends, neighbors, school administrators.
11. Can you describe your own image of a good mother and a good
    father?
    a. How is it different than the image in American society?
12. When you face a particular challenge or joy of parenting or school-
    ing, with whom do you talk about it?
    a. What is their relationship to you?
    b. Can you give me a specific example of something you brought
       to these people and what you discussed?
13. Who are the people most involved in your and your child's daily
    life and schooling?
    a. What is their relationship to you?
    b. In what ways are these people involved in your lives?
14. Can you describe the demographics of your children's friend/peer
    groups in terms of race, class, ethnicity, or other factors?
15. How do you think these demographics shape your child's
    experiences?
16. How do you think your race, class, and ethnicity influence your
    relations with other families? With educators, administrators,
    teachers, parents?

Employment and Education Experiences

17. Have you ever been employed outside of the home? (If yes, move to question 18; if no, skip to question 20.)
18. Can you walk me through your employment timeline, describing your employment before and after you became a parent?
    (IF HOMESCHOOLING)
    a. Can you describe how you and your partner came to the decision for you to be the full-time homeschooling parent?
    b. What factors were weighed? Why?
19. Can you describe the parental leave you took from your place of employment when having your child(ren)?
20. Can you tell me about your education?
21. Can you tell me about your current and past relationship status?
    If partnered:
    a. Can you describe your partner's employment experience before and after having kids?
    b. Did he/she take any time off from work upon the arrival of your child(ren)?
    c. Can you tell me about your partner's education?

Demographic Information

22. How would you describe your socioeconomic status?
23. What is the town name of your current place of residence?
24. Of the following four income brackets, which one does your household fall into?
    a. Under $29,999 per year.
    b. Between $30,000 and $74,999 per year.
    c. Between $75,000 and $199,999.
    d. Above $200,000.
25. What year were you born?
26. If I have any further questions for you, is it OK if I contact you for clarification?

For Homeschoolers:

27. Recent news and research on homeschooling suggest that there is an increasing number of African American homeschoolers. What are your thoughts on this? What do you know about this?

28. Do you know of any homeschool or nonhomeschool parents who you think would be interested in participating in this study? If yes, would you be willing to either pass my information on to them or provide me their name and contact information?

    1. Name_____

       Contact Information_____

    2. Name_____

       Contact Information_____

    3. Name_____

       Contact Information_____

29. Do you have any questions for me?

Thank you for your time!

NOTES

INTRODUCTION

1 Hays 1996.
2 Public charter schools are defined as publicly funded schools that are governed by a group or organization under the legislation of the state or district (NCES 2020a).
3 V. Ray 2019; Wooten and Couloute 2017.
4 Dwyer and Peters 2019; B. D. Ray 2010.
5 Dwyer and Peters 2019; Gaither (2008) 2017; Stevens 2001.
6 Dwyer and Peters 2019; Gaither (2008) 2017; Stevens 2001.
7 Mineo 2020.
8 NCES 2017b.
9 NCES 2017b.
10 NCES 2017b.
11 Averett 2021; Duhaney 2022; Sopelsa, Bellamy-Walker, and Reuters 2022.
12 To protect the confidentiality of study respondents and their families, all the names of places and people are pseudonyms.
13 P. H. Collins 1994, 56; C. W. Cooper 2007.
14 Barnes 2016.
15 Underhill 2018.
16 C. W. Cooper 2007.
17 Barnes 2016; Christopher 2012; Damaske 2011; Dow 2016c, 2019; Florian 2018; Glauber 2007; Hays 1996; Stone 2007.
18 M. Cooper 2014; Pugh 2015.
19 M. Cooper 2014; Pugh 2015.
20 Averett 2021; Lois 2013; Stevens 2001.
21 Giles 2014; Glenn, Chang, and Forcey 1994.
22 Budig, Misra, and Boeckmann 2012; C. Collins 2020; Utrata 2015.
23 Coontz 2005.
24 Zelizer 1994.
25 Coontz 2005; Glenn, Chang, and Forcey 1994; Zelizer 2011.
26 Glenn, Chang, and Forcey 1994; Roberts 1997; Weinbaum 2019.
27 Branch 2011.
28 Utrata 2015.
29 Glenn, Chang, and Forcey 1994.
30 L. S. Davis 2021; Hays 1996; Lindemann 2022; Sandberg 2013.

31 Stone 2007.

32 Damaske 2011; Stone 2007.

33 Damaske 2011.

34 Averett 2021; Blair-Loy 2003; Hays 1996; Lois 2013; Macdonald 2010; Stone 2007; J. Williams 2000.

35 Glenn, Chang, and Forcey 1994. See also Blum and Deussen 1996; P. H. Collins 2000; Dill 1994; Edin, Kefalas, and Furstenberg 2011; Hondagneu-Sotelo and Avila 1997; Huang 2019; Moon 2003; Parreñas 2010; Peng and Wong 2013; Roschelle 1997.

36 Barnes 2016; Dow 2019; Lacy 2004, 2007.

37 Dow 2016c.

38 Annamma et al. 2019; Ferguson 2000; Goff et al. 2014; Lewis and Diamond 2015; Morris 2012; Morris and Perry 2016, 2017; Rios 2011; Skiba et al. 2002; Skiba et al. 2011; Sykes et al. 2015.

39 NCES 2019.

40 Dow 2019.

41 Barnes 2016; Carter 2005; C. W. Cooper 2007, 2009; Dow 2019; Lacy 2004; Manning 2019; Pattillo-McCoy 1999.

42 Lareau 2011.

43 Calarco 2018.

44 Adler and Adler 1994; Delpit 1995; Dumais 2019; Dumais and Ward 2010; Hoff, Laursen, and Tardif 2002; Vincent and Ball 2007; Weininger, Lareau, and Conley 2015; Wildhagen 2009.

45 Emerson, Chai, and Yancey 2001; Goyette 2017; Hagerman 2018; Holme 2002; Lareau and Goyette 2014.

46 Cucchiara 2013; Kimelberg 2014.

47 Averett 2021; Blume Oeur 2018; Lipman 2003.

48 Averett 2021; Berends 2015.

49 Whitty 2002; Whitty, Power, and Halpin 1998.

50 Bankston and Caldas 2000; Billingham and Hunt 2016; Sikkink and Emerson 2008.

51 P. H. Collins 2000.

52 Choo and Ferree 2010; P. H. Collins 2000; Misra, Curington, and Green 2020.

53 Misra, Curington, and Green 2020.

54 Anderson, Caughy, and Owen 2021; Hagerman 2018.

55 Barnes 2016; Christopher 2012; Damaske 2011; Dow 2019; Hays 1996; Lois 2013; Reich 2016; Stone 2007; Villalobos 2014.

56 For Epstein (1995), the integration of schools, families, and communities can lead to positive outcomes for students' learning.

57 Dow 2019, 126–127.

58 Lareau and Weininger 2008; Lois 2013.

59 I also did not conduct interviews with the children in respondents' families, despite children certainly being actively involved in their schooling trajectories. See appendix B for more details on this study design decision.

60 Similar to other studies on schooling, I measure social class by considering household income, and the education and occupation of each respondent and their partner (Lareau 2011). Respondents are identified as middle-class when they hold at least a bachelor's degree, and they and/or their partners work in jobs that demand at least a college degree, such as schoolteacher, lawyer, and professor. The upper-middle-class women in my study are those meeting the middle-class criteria and also earning an annual household income above $200,000 per year.

61 Choo and Ferree 2010, P. H. Collins 2000; Misra, Curington, and Green 2020.

CHAPTER 1. ELMFORD HOMESCHOOLING

1 Stevens 2001.

2 Lois 2013.

3 Fields-Smith and Kisura 2013; Mazama and Lundy 2012.

4 Averett 2021.

5 Murphy 2014.

6 B. D. Ray 2010.

7 Jenkins 1998; Prue 1997; Sorey and Duggan 2008.

8 de Oliveira, Watson, and Sutton 1994; Galloway and Sutton 1995; Gray 1993; B. D. Ray 2009.

9 In his national study, Collom found that homeschooling minimizes the race- and class-based academic achievement gap found in public schools. He writes that "the two great divides that public school children face—race and class—are inconsequential for student achievement among home-educated children" (2005, 329). Yet the fact that on average homeschooling parents have more human and economic capital than the national average suggests homeschooling is primarily accessible to class-advantaged families (NCES 2017b). Like Carter and Welner along with other scholars studying nonhomeschooling, I argue that examining homeschooling within the context of the opportunity gap is more useful than within the context of the achievement gap (Carter and Welner 2013; Ochoa 2013). In other words, rather than focus on homeschool students' academic outcomes, to understand educational disparities, it's more effective to consider for whom homeschooling is seen as a viable option.

10 Chatham-Carpenter 1994; McCulloch et al. 2006; B. D. Ray 2009.

11 Medlin 2000; B. D. Ray 2009; Saunders 2009; Smedley 1992.

12 Dwyer and Peters 2019; Gaither (2008) 2017.

13 H. A. Williams 2005.

14 Dwyer and Peters 2019; Gaither (2008) 2017.

15 Gaither (2008) 2017, 57.

16 Coontz 1988; Zelizer 1994.

17 D. R. Berry and Gross 2020; Branch 2011; Dill 1994; Roberts 1997.

18 Ingersoll 2019.

19 Coontz 2005; Griswold 1993; Gutman 1976.

20 Du Bois (1903) 1989.
21 Billingsley 1994; Branch 2011; Wilkerson 2010.
22 Banks 2006; D. R. Berry and Gross 2020; Giddings 1984.
23 D. R. Berry and Gross 2020.
24 Dwyer and Peters 2019; Stambach and David 2005.
25 Grant 1998; Salem 1990; Stambach and David 2005.
26 Dwyer and Peters 2019.
27 Gaither (2008) 2017.
28 Mills 1959, 1.
29 Dwyer and Peters 2019.
30 Stulberg 2008.
31 Van DeBurg 1992.
32 Hatton 1977; Jackson 1978; O'Shea 1977; Stulberg 2008.
33 Stulberg 2008.
34 Stulberg 2008.
35 Farley, Richards, and Wurdock 1980. Part of the decrease in white students is attributed to a decline in white fertility.
36 Clotfelter 1976, 2004; Levy 2009; Reardon and Owens 2014.
37 Dwyer and Peters 2019.
38 Coleman, Kelly, and Moore 1975; Orfield 2001; Reardon and Owens 2014; Welch and Light 1987.
39 There is variation by city, with larger districts with more students of color showing more entrenched segregation than smaller districts (Reardon and Owens 2014).
40 Logan and Oakley 2004; Orfield 1983.
41 The *Yoder* case was a major legal win for homeschoolers. Yet it should be noted that three states—Oklahoma, Nevada, and Utah—passed homeschool laws before the 1972 case.
42 Aurini and Davies 2005; Collom and Mitchell 2005; Dwyer and Peters 2019; Gaither (2008) 2017; Renzulli, Werum, and Kronberg 2020; Stevens 2001.
43 Mayberry 1988; Stevens 2001.
44 Rachel Carson's *Silent Spring*, published in 1962, documented the adverse effects of pesticide use.
45 Gaither (2008) 2017.
46 Heidenry 2011.
47 Renzulli, Werum, and Kronberg 2020.
48 Levy 2009.
49 Ravitch 2010; Renzulli, Werum, and Kronberg 2020; Vinovskis 2009.
50 Hinnant-Crawford 2019.
51 Kantor and Lowe 2006; Lipman 2003.
52 Braun, Chapman, and Vezzu 2010.
53 Successful reforms were measured through specific areas: improving assessment and standards, bolstering school performance data collection, supporting teacher

training, retention and evaluation, turning around low-performing schools (McGuinn 2012).

54 Dwyer and Peters 2019; NCES 2017b.

55 Fields-Smith and Kisura 2013; Mazama and Lundy 2012; NCES 2017b.

56 National Black Home Educators 2022.

57 Kamenetz 2020.

58 S. Berry 2017; Rizzo 2019.

59 Kamenetz 2020.

60 Due to the relatively small number of homeschoolers within the region compared with their nonhomeschooling counterparts, all identifying information about the region has been removed to maintain respondents' confidentiality.

61 I have developed the historical context of Black schooling in Elmford based on 2016 data from the US Census Bureau, the Department of Education, and three studies that focused on the city and were published in *Equity and Excellence in Education* and the *Journal of Urban History*.

62 Fong and Faude 2018.

63 Cohen et al. 2022.

64 Lois 2013; Murphy 2014; Stevens 2001.

65 Fields-Smith and Kisura 2013; Mazama and Lundy 2012.

CHAPTER 2. THE SHAPE OF WOMEN'S WORK

1 Dow 2016a.

2 Folbre 2001.

3 Hartman 2007; Roberts 1997; Weinbaum 2019.

4 Barnes 2016; Blair-Loy 2003; Damaske 2011; Dow 2019; Hays 1996; Stone 2007.

5 Doan and Quadlin 2019; England 2010, 2011; Folbre and Nelson 2000; Hartmann 1981; Hochschild 1989.

6 Budig, Misra, and Boeckmann 2012; C. Collins 2020; Utrata 2015.

7 There were two exceptions: two respondents had husbands who had retired from state employment, although choosing to retire was not influenced by their fathering status.

8 Stone 2007.

9 Budig and England 2001.

10 Lareau 2011.

11 Duffy 2005; Glenn 1992.

12 Folbre 2001.

13 Bianchi et al. 2000; Bianchi and Milkie 2010; Bianchi, Robinson, and Milkie 2006; Blair-Loy et al. 2015; Hochschild 1989; Perry-Jenkins and Gerstel 2020; Sayer 2005; Sayer, Bianchi, and Robinson 2004.

14 Blair-Loy et al. 2015; Cahusac and Kanji 2014; England 2010; Perry-Jenkins and Gerstel 2020.

15 Ehrenreich and Hochschild 2003; Macdonald 2010; Parreñas 2015; Romero 2011; Zimmerman, Litt, and Bose 2006.

16 Jacobs and Gerson 2004; Neumark 2000; Pugh 2015.
17 Aumann, Galinksy, and Matos 2011; Cahusac and Kanji 2014; Cha 2010; Cha and Weeden 2014; Clawson and Gerstel 2014; Kossek et al. 2014; Lambert 2008.
18 Hegewisch et al. 2014; Rose and Hartmann 2004.
19 Blair-Loy 2003; for a more recent study on the topic see Cahusac and Kanji 2014.
20 Benard and Correll 2010; Berdahl and Moon 2013; Stone and Hernandez 2013.
21 Aggarwal 2014; Berends 2015.
22 Braun, Chapman, and Vezzu 2010; Hursh 2007.
23 For an exception, see Stambach and David 2005; Griffith and Smith 2005.
24 Fong and Faude 2018; Rich and Jennings 2015.
25 Friedman 2013; Hofferth, Kinney, and Dunn 2009; Hofferth and Sandberg 2001; Kaufman and Gabler 2004; Lareau 2011; White and Gager 2007.
26 Friedman 2013; Hofferth, Kinney, and Dunn 2009; Hofferth and Sandberg 2001; Kaufman and Gabler 2004; Lareau 2011; White and Gager 2007.
27 Friedman 2013; Hofferth, Kinney, and Dunn 2009; Hofferth and Sandberg 2001; Kaufman and Gabler 2004; Lareau 2011; White and Gager 2007..
28 Macdonald 2010.
29 Hattery 2001.
30 C. W. Cooper 2007.
31 Such arrangements also may rely on the caregiving work of less privileged women, such as nannies, domestic workers, daycare workers and the like (Ehrenreich and Hochschild 2003; Glenn 1992; Macdonald 2010; Parreñas 2000; Peng and Wong 2013; Romero 2011).
32 Friedman 2013; Hofferth, Kinney, and Dunn 2009; Hofferth and Sandberg 2001; Kaufman and Gabler 2004; Lareau 2011; White and Gager 2007.
33 C. W. Cooper 2007.
34 C. W. Cooper 2007.

CHAPTER 3. PROTECTIVE MOTHERING

1 Barnes 2016; Dow 2019.
2 Orbuch 1997.
3 M. Cooper 2014; Nelson 2010; Pugh 2015.
4 Pugh 2015.
5 Horsman 1986.
6 As sociologist Sabrina Strings (2019) traces, the kernels of this notion emerged in the seventeenth century through writings of French physician and traveler François Bernier, based on perceived biological differences. While many European men before Bernier had written about their contact with people from outside of Europe, Bernier was the first to create a system of human classification based on skin color. This initiated the use of skin color, hair texture, and facial features as evidence of cultural deficiency, particularly of Africans.
7 P. H. Collins 2000; Morgan 2004; Strings 2019.
8 Strings 2019.

9 Brown 2015; Hartman 2007; J. Jones 2010; Roberts 1997; Sharpe 2016; Tillet 2012; Weinbaum 2019.
10 Morgan 2004.
11 Hartman 2007; Roberts 1997; Weinbaum 2019.
12 Bell 2014; Cade 1970; A. Davis 1990; McCann 1994; Roberts 1997.
13 Lois 2013.
14 P. H. Collins 2000; Dean, Marsh, and Landry 2013; Dow 2019; S. A. Hill 2001; Stack 1974.
15 Hofferth and Sandberg 2001; Kaufman and Gabler 2004; Lareau 2011; White and Gager 2007.
16 Shapiro 2017.
17 Afflerback et al. 2013; Beck 1992; Curran 2013; Mythen 2005.
18 M. Cooper 2008.
19 Damaske 2011.
20 M. Cooper 2014; Hays 1996; Lareau 2011; Nelson 2010; Pugh 2015.
21 Dow 2016c.
22 Dow 2016b.
23 P. H. Collins 2000; Moynihan (1965) 2003; Randles 2020.
24 Alexander 2010; Edin, Kefalas, and Furstenberg 2011; Pager 2003; Randles 2020; Stack 1974.
25 Edin, Kefalas, and Furstenberg 2011; Silva 2013.
26 Hays 1996.
27 Lois 2013.
28 M. Cooper 2014; Nelson 2010; Villalobos 2014.
29 M. Cooper 2014.
30 Villalobos 2014.
31 Blair-Loy 2003; Hays 1996; Stone 2007.
32 Gerson 2009; Pedulla and Thébaud 2015.
33 Gerson 2009; Pedulla and Thébaud 2015.
34 Dean, Marsh, and Landry 2013; Griswold 1993; S. A. Hill 2001; Hossain and Roopnarine 1993; Kamo and Cohen 1998; Landry 2002; Wilkie 1993.
35 Hartman 2007; Weinbaum 2019.
36 Beck 1992; M. Cooper 2008; Giddens 1991; Pugh 2015; Villalobos 2014.
37 Damaske 2011.

CHAPTER 4. "THEY MADE ME FEEL LIKE HE WAS A TERRORIST"
1 These details are based on 2016 data from the Department of Education.
2 Dow 2016b; Downey and Pribesh 2004; Feagin and Sikes 1994; Ferguson 2000; Morris and Perry 2016; Pattillo 2015; Staples and Johnson 1993; Tatum 2003.
3 P. H. Collins 1994; C. W. Cooper 2007.
4 Alexander 2010; A. Davis 2003; Muñiz 2021.
5 Alexander 2010.
6 Alexander 2010; Garland 2001.

7 Rocque 2012.

8 Bridges 2022; Katsiyannis, Whitford, and Ennis 2018; Rocque 2012.

9 Everytown for Gun Safety 2021; Solnit 2022.

10 Triplett, Allen, and Lewis 2014: 354.

11 DeSilver 2014. Since then, multiple-victim school-based violent deaths have increased (see Frederique 2020).

12 Triplett, Allen, and Lewis 2014.

13 Importantly, many scholars have critiqued the pipeline metaphor as failing to capture the array of forces—which may function more as a web, nexus, or mixing of factors than as a pipeline—that lead to a disproportionate number of Black and Latine youth to be mixed up in the carceral state. Alternative language to the pipeline includes the youth control complex (Rios 2011), enclosures (Sojoyner 2013), or the carceral continuum (Shedd 2015). To read more about these critiques, see Annamma 2018; Meiners 2007; Pitcher and Shahjahan 2017; Sojoyner 2013; Waterman, Lowe, and Shotton 2018.

14 Sykes et al. 2015, 1. Throughout the book, I use *Latine*, a gender-neutral term for Latino/Latina that refers to people from Spanish-speaking countries. I use this language as opposed to "Latinx" since the letter x is not found in Spanish while the letter e is found in Spanish, making "Latine" more suitable language for reflecting the people it represents (for more information, see Carbajal 2020).

15 NCES 2020c.

16 Reynolds et al. 2008.

17 King and Schindler 2021, 30.

18 Sawchuk 2021.

19 King and Schindler 2021.

20 King and Schindler 2021, 29.

21 L. Hill 2017; Mendez 2003; Noguera 2008; Rocque 2010; Skiba et al. 2002; Skiba et al. 2011; Wallace et al. 2008.

22 NCES 2019, 2020c.

23 Annamma et al. 2019; Ferguson 2000; Goff et al. 2014; Skiba et al. 2002; Skiba et al. 2011.

24 NCES 2019, 2020c.

25 P. H. Collins 2000.

26 P. H. Collins 2000; Dow 2016b; Rios 2011.

27 Bernstein 2011; Ferguson 2000; Lewis and Diamond 2015; Morris and Perry 2016; Noguera 2008. Morris and Perry (2017) also find racial bias in the disproportionate disciplining of African American girls.

28 Ferguson 2000.

29 Annamma et al. 2019; Ispa-Landa 2013; N. Jones 2009.

30 NCES 2019.

31 Annamma et al. 2019, 229.

32 Hemez, Brent, and Mowen 2019; Moody 2016; Schiff 2018; Wadhwa 2016.

33 See Pyne 2019. The good news is that it doesn't have to be this way. Educators and advocates alike have provided a wealth of suggestions for changing the climate of schools by shifting away from a law enforcement approach and toward a holistic approach that provides alternatives to suspensions and expulsions. Such alternatives include putting more focus on building community and a sense of belonging within the school, between parents, students, teachers, and health professionals, while also providing more support for teachers, school counselors, nurses, and social workers to be culturally relevant to the particular students who attend the school (Anyon et al. 2014; L. Hill 2017; Reynolds et al. 2008).

34 This lack of gender variation could well be due to the nature of my data, which rely on mothers' accounts of their interactions in schools. Thus, rather than suggesting this study shows gender is less important in these interactions, it is more likely that the lack of gender variation is due to the absence of observational data.

35 V. Ray 2019; Wooten 2006; Wooten and Couloute 2017.

36 Stewart 2020.

37 Blume Oeur 2018; Ferguson 2000; Lewis and Diamond 2015; Morris 2012; Morris and Perry 2016; Noguera 2008.

38 Noguera 2008, xxiii.

39 Skiba et al. 2002; Wallace et al. 2008.

40 Acker 1990, 2006; V. Ray 2019; Stewart 2020; Wooten 2006; Wooten and Couloute 2017.

41 Farkas and Morgan 2018; Hibel, Farkas, and Morgan 2010; Katusic et al. 2001; Mendez 2003; Moody 2016; Oswald et al. 2003; Ramey 2015.

42 Annamma 2014; L. Hill 2017.

43 Esposito 1999; Togut 2011.

44 Berends 2015; Golann 2015.

45 Gill et al. 2001; Golann 2015.

46 C. W. Cooper 2007; Fields-Smith and Kisura 2013; Pattillo 2015; Suizzo, Robinson, and Pahlke 2008; A. D. Williams et al. 2017.

47 A. D. Williams et al. 2017.

48 C. W. Cooper 2007.

49 M. Cooper 2014; Hays 1996; Lareau 2011; Nelson 2010; Pugh 2015.

50 Wooten and Couloute 2017, 8.

51 C. W. Cooper 2007, 2009.

52 Pugh 2015.

53 Hunter and Robinson 2018, 179.

54 Hunter and Robinson 2018.

55 The details presented throughout this section on the demographics of respondents' school and neighborhood are based on 2016 data from the US Census Bureau or the Department of Education. Here white is categorized as "non-Hispanic white" and distinct from Hispanic or Latine white-identifying individuals.

56 Frazier 1957; Lacy 2004, 2007; Landry 1978; Landry and Marsh 2011; Martin 2010; K. S. Moore 2005; Pattillo 2005; Pattillo-McCoy 1999.

57 Massey and Denton 1993.

58 C. W. Cooper 2007; A. D. Williams et al. 2017.

59 Dow 2019.

60 Dow 2019; Lacy 2004; Martin 2010; K. S. Moore 2005; Pattillo-McCoy 1999; Tatum 1987.

61 Shapiro 2017.

62 Blume Oeur 2018; Ferguson 2000; Ispa-Landa 2013; Lewis and Diamond 2015; Morris 2012; Morris and Perry 2016, 2017; Noguera 2008.

63 Ginwright 2002; Martin 2010; K. S. Moore 2005.

64 Lacy 2004.

65 C. W. Cooper 2005, 175.

66 Averett 2021.

67 These two types of homeschool decisions—starting from the beginning or bring-ing children home after experience in nonhomeschools—resemble a distinction made by Jennifer Lois (2013) in her study of white homeschooling mothers in the Pacific Northwest. Lois found 19 of 24 mothers from her sample were "first-choicers" who saw homeschooling as a logical extension of their mothering work and did so from the beginning, while the remaining 5 mothers were "second-choicers" who struggled with the pros and cons of homeschooling and found themselves homeschooling more due to circumstance after trying nonhome-schools. Notably, I found a slightly larger number of "second-choicers" (9 of 17) than "first-choicers" (8 of 17) in Elmford than Lois found in her research. I speculate these differences could be attributed to region (Northeast versus Northwest homeschooling), race (Lois focused on white homeschoolers, whereas I compared similar numbers of Black and white homeschoolers), or changes over time (my data were collected from 2014 to 2016; her data were collected primarily in the early 2000s).

68 Fields-Smith and Kisura 2013; Mazama and Lundy 2012.

69 Annamma et al. 2019; Blume Oeur 2018; Dow 2016b; Ferguson 2000; Ispa-Landa 2013; N. Jones 2009; Lewis and Diamond 2015; Morris and Perry 2016; Noguera 2008.

70 Dow 2016a.

71 Massey and Denton 1993.

72 Hunter and Robinson 2018, 171.

73 Du Bois (1903) 1989, 10.

CHAPTER 5. "I WISH IT WAS A BIT MORE DIVERSE"

1 Even within schools that are integrated, tracking resegregates students along racial lines (Cucchiara 2013; E. Frankenberg and Orfield 2012; Hagerman 2018; Lewis and Diamond 2015; Ochoa 2013).

2 Bankston and Caldas 2000; Billingham and Hunt 2016; Dougherty et al. 2009; Emerson, Chai, and Yancey 2001; Hagerman 2014; Jiménez and Horowitz 2013; Kimelberg 2014; Lareau and Goyette 2014; Roda and Wells 2013.

3 Bonilla-Silva 2015, 78.

4 Billingham and Hunt 2016.

5 Hagerman 2014; McClelland and Linnander 2006.

6 Hagerman 2014; Billingham and Hunt 2016; Bunyasi 2015.

7 Hagerman 2014.

8 Ferguson 2000; Rios 2011.

9 Do mothers consider how their decisions may disadvantage their children (particularly their daughters) by role modeling that education is prioritized through a mother's servitude and career sacrifice? While I did not ask this question, and it was not addressed through conversation, it is certainly worth wondering whether women ever felt conflicted by the unspoken "lessons" their children may be learning from such decisions. Future research might explore this question.

10 V. Ray 2019; Wooten 2006; Wooten and Couloute 2017.

11 Stewart 2020.

12 Downey and Pribesh 2004; Ferguson 2000; Lewis and Diamond 2015; Morris and Perry 2017.

13 Hemez, Brent, and Mowen 2019; Schiff 2018; Wadhwa 2016; Wolf and Kupchik 2017.

14 Budig, Misra, and Boeckmann 2012; C. Collins 2020; Utrata 2015.

15 Damaske 2011; Hays 1996; Stone 2007.

16 Damaske 2011.

17 Lois 2013; also see Hays 1996, Blair-Loy 2003, Stone 2007, and Damaske 2011 for the link between women's mothering expectations and employment pathways.

18 Cucchiara 2013; Davies and Quirke 2007; Goldring and Phillips 2008; Holme 2002; Kantor and Lowe 2006; Lareau and Goyette 2014; Roda and Wells 2013.

19 Camera 2020.

20 Kahlenberg 2012; Orfield and Lee 2006; Rothstein 2015.

21 Like the school district data presented in chapter 4, the demographic information here is based on respondents' school and neighborhood information as captured in the 2016 US Census Bureau and the Department of Education.

22 Hagerman 2018, 130–131.

23 Bankston and Caldas 2000; Billingham and Hunt 2016.

24 Andersen 1999; Burke 2011.

25 Bonilla-Silva 2022; Hagerman 2018.

26 Cucchiara 2013; Davies and Quirke 2007; Goldring and Phillips 2008; Hagerman 2018; Holme 2002; Kantor and Lowe 2006; Lareau and Goyette 2014; Roda and Wells 2013.

27 Logan, Zhang, and Oakley 2017; Orfield and Lee 2006.

28 Hughey 2012.

29 Khan 2011; Underhill 2018.

30 Burke 2011.

31 Chou and Feagin 2008.

32 Bonilla-Silva 2022; Gallagher 2003; Waters 1990.

33 Underhill 2018; Woody 2020.
34 R. Frankenberg 2001.
35 Orfield et al. 2016.
36 Coughlan 2018.
37 High-poverty public schools are those with 75 percent or more of their students eligible for free or reduced-price lunch, a government measure that includes children from families with annual incomes that are 130 percent to 185 percent below the poverty line (NCES 2017a).
38 The likelihood of attending high-poverty public schools for other racial groups is also relatively high: 33 percent of multiracial students, 25 percent of American Indian/Alaska Native students, and 18 percent of Asian/Pacific Islander students (NCES 2017a).
39 NCES 2020c.
40 Bankston et al. 2013; Jennings 2010; Johnston 2014; Kleitz et al. 2000; Renzulli and Evans 2005; Renzulli, Parrott, and Beattie 2011.
41 Bankston and Caldas 2000; Cowen et al. 2013; Davies and Quirke 2007; Goldring and Phillips 2008.
42 Dwyer and Peters 2019; NCES 2020a; NCES 2017b.
43 NCES 2020b.
44 Cucchiara 2013; Posey-Maddox 2014; Underhill 2018; Woody 2020.
45 Carter and Welner 2013.

CHAPTER 6. THE CONTOURS OF HOMESCHOOLING

1 US Bureau of Labor Statistics 2020.
2 Christopher 2012; Dow 2016c, 2019; Hays 1996.
3 Barnes 2016.
4 Budig, Misra, and Boeckmann 2012; C. Collins 2020; Utrata 2015.
5 Damaske 2011.
6 Duffy 2005; Glenn 1992.
7 England, Budig, and Folbre 2002.
8 Duffy 2005; England, Budig, and Folbre 2002; Fisher and Tronto 1990; Folbre 2001; Hochschild 1998.
9 Folbre 2001; Folbre and Nelson 2000.
10 England, Budig, and Folbre 2002; Folbre 2001; Folbre and Nelson 2000.
11 Lois 2013.
12 Barnes 2016.
13 Dow 2016c.
14 Barnes 2016.
15 Fields-Smith and Kisura 2013; Mazama and Lundy 2012.
16 Barnes 2016.
17 Hansen 2005.
18 Dow 2019; Lacy 2007.

19 P. H. Collins 1994; Dow 2016a, 2016c; Gerstel 2011; Sarkisian and Gerstel 2004; Taylor et al. 2017; Uttal 1999.
20 P. H. Collins 1994; Stack 1974.
21 Dow 2016a, 2016c; Uttal 1999.
22 Fields-Smith and Kisura 2013; Mazama and Lundy 2012.
23 Lois 2013; Stevens 2001.
24 Gerstel 2011; Hansen 2005; Lareau 2011.
25 Lareau 2011.
26 Calhoun 2020.
27 M. Cooper 2014; Pugh 2015.
28 Boeckmann, Misra, and Budig 2015; Brewer 2001; C. Collins 2020; Lyon and Glucksmann 2008; Thébaud 2010.
29 C. W. Cooper 2009; Damaske 2011; Dow 2016a, 2016c; Gerstel 2011; Uttal 1999.
30 Litwak and Szelenyi 1969.
31 Hansen 2005.
32 Hansen 2005.

CONCLUSION

1 Averett 2021.
2 Barnes 2016.
3 Levy 2009.
4 Mayberry 1988; Stevens 2001.
5 Gaither (2008) 2017.
6 Levy 2009; Renzulli, Werum, and Kronberg 2020.
7 Hinnant-Crawford 2019.
8 Aggarwal 2014, 102.
9 Aggarwal 2014, 102.
10 Dwyer and Peters 2019; NCES 2017b.
11 Fields-Smith and Kisura 2013; Mazama and Lundy 2012; NCES 2017b.
12 Averett 2021.
13 Aggarwal 2014.
14 Shapiro 2017.
15 Christopher 2012; Stone 2007; J. Williams 2000.
16 Lois 2013; Stevens 2001.
17 Hays 1996; Stone 2007.
18 Glenn, Chang, and Forcey 1994.
19 Dow 2016c.
20 Barnes 2016; Dow 2016c.
21 M. Cooper 2014.
22 Carter and Welner 2013.
23 C. W. Cooper 2009; Lipman 2003; Ochoa 2013.
24 Carter and Welner 2013.

25 P. H. Collins 2009; Freire 1970.

26 Acker 1990, 2006; V. Ray 2019; Wooten 2006; Wooten and Couloute 2017.

27 Aggarwal 2014; C. W. Cooper 2007; Pattillo 2015.

28 Carter and Welner 2013; Tyson 2013.

29 Scott et al. 2020.

30 Centers for Disease Control and Prevention 2022.

31 Mervosh 2021; Simon 2021.

32 Cray 2022.

33 Carter and Welner 2013.

34 Cohen et al. 2022.

35 Lewis and Diamond 2015.

36 Bonilla-Silva 2022; DiTomaso 2013; Lewis and Diamond 2015.

37 For more on this power-aware perspective, see Ochoa 2013.

38 Averett 2021, 181.

39 Hagerman 2018.

40 R. Frankenberg 2001.

41 Underhill 2018.

42 Omi and Winant 1994; West and Zimmerman 1987.

43 Choo and Ferree 2010; P. H. Collins 2000; Misra, Curington, and Green 2020.

44 Misra, Curington, and Green 2020.

45 Hagerman 2018, 209.

46 Dow 2019.

APPENDIX B

1 Calarco 2018; Lareau 2011.

2 Corsaro 2011; Hagerman 2016; Lewis 2003; V. Moore 2001.

3 Barker and Weller 2003; Best 2007; Hagerman 2018.

4 Lareau and Weininger 2008; Lois 2013.

5 Christopher 2012; Damaske 2011; Lareau 2011.

6 Christopher 2012; P. H. Collins 2000; Dill 1994; Hays 1996.

7 Christopher 2012; Lois 2013; Uttal 1999.

8 Fields-Smith and Kisura 2013; Huseman 2015; Mazama 2016; NCES 2017b; B. D. Ray 2009.

9 Bonilla-Silva, Goar, and Embrick 2006; Chesler, Peet, and Sevig 2003; Tatum 2003.

10 Charmaz 2014.

11 Saldaña 2009.

12 Weiss 1994.

13 Gerson and Damaske 2021.

14 Luker 2008, 125.

15 Glaser and Strauss 1967.

16 Bonilla-Silva 2022, 148–151.

17 Bonilla-Silva 2022; DiTomaso, Parks-Yancy, and Post 2011.

18 Bonilla-Silva 2022, 302–303.
19 Bonilla-Silva 2022; Bonilla-Silva and Zuberi 2008.
20 Bonilla-Silva and Zuberi 2008; Chesler, Peet, and Sevig 2003.
21 P. H. Collins 1986; Hesse-Biber 2007; Riessman 1987; Smith 1990; Sprague 2005.
22 Bonilla-Silva and Zuberi 2008; P. H. Collins 1986; Hesse-Biber 2007.
23 P. H. Collins 1986, 2000; Mann and Kelley 1997.
24 Averett 2021; Homeschool Legal Defense Association 2022; Stevens 2001.

REFERENCES

Acker, Joan. 1990. "Hierarchies, Jobs, Bodies: A Theory of Gendered Organizations." *Gender & Society* 4(2):139–158.

———. 2006. "Inequality Regimes: Gender, Class, and Race in Organizations." *Gender & Society* 20(4):441–464.

Adler, Patricia A., and Peter Adler. 1994. "Social Reproduction and the Corporate Other: The Institutionalization of Afterschool Activities." *Sociological Quarterly* 35(2):309–328.

Afflerback, Sara, Shannon K. Carter, Amanda Koontz Anthony, and Liz Grauerholz. 2013. "Infant-Feeding Consumerism in the Age of Intensive Mothering and Risk Society." *Journal of Consumer Culture* 13(3):387–405.

Aggarwal, Ujju. 2014. "The Politics of Choice and the Structuring of Citizenship Post-*Brown v. Board of Education*." *Transforming Anthropology* 22(2):92–104.

Alexander, Michelle. 2010. *The New Jim Crow: Mass Incarceration in the Age of Colorblindness*. New York: New Press.

Andersen, Margaret L. 1999. "The Fiction of 'Diversity without Oppression': Race, Ethnicity, Identity, and Power." In *Critical Ethnicity: Countering the Waves of Identity Politics*, edited by Mary L. Kenyatta and Robert H. Tai, 5–20. Totowa, NJ: Rowman and Littlefield.

Anderson, Leslie A., Margaret O'Brien Caughy, and Margaret T. Owen. 2021. "'The Talk' and Parenting While Black in America: Centering Race, Resistance, and Refuge." *Journal of Black Psychology* 48(3–4): 475–506.

Annamma, Subini Ancy. 2014. "Disabling Juvenile Justice: Engaging the Stories of Incarcerated Young Women of Color with Disabilities." *Remedial and Special Education* 35(5):313–324.

———. 2018. *The Pedagogy of Pathologization: Dis/abled Girls of Color in the School-Prison Nexus*. New York: Routledge.

Annamma, Subini Ancy, Yolanda Anyon, Nicole M. Joseph, Jordan Farrar, Eldridge Greer, Barbara Downing, and John Simmons. 2019. "Black Girls and School Discipline: The Complexities of Being Overrepresented and Understudied." *Urban Education* 54(2):211–242.

Anyon, Yolanda, Jeffrey M. Jenson, Inna Altschul, Jordan Farrar, Jeanette McQueen, Eldridge Greer, Barbara Downing, and John Simmons. 2014. "The Persistent Effect of Race and the Promise of Alternatives to Suspension in School Discipline Outcomes." *Children and Youth Services Review* 44:379–386.

Aumann, Kerstin, Ellen Galinsky, and Kenneth Matos. 2011. *The New Male Mystique: National Study of the Changing Workforce*. New York: Families and Work Institute.

Aurini, Janice, and Scott Davies. 2005. "Choice without Markets: Homeschooling in the Context of Private Education." *British Journal of Sociology of Education* 26(4):461–474.

Averett, Kate Henley. 2021. *The Homeschool Choice: Parents and the Privatization of Education*. New York: New York University Press.

Banks, Nina. 2006. "Uplifting the Race through Domesticity: Capitalism, African-American Migration, and the Household Economy in the Great Migration Era of 1916–1930." *Feminist Economics* 12(4):599–624.

Bankston, Carl L., III, and Stephen J. Caldas. 2000. "White Enrollment in Nonpublic Schools, Public School Racial Composition, and Student Performance." *Sociological Quarterly* 41(4):539–550.

Bankston, Carl L., III, Diane Ravitch, Michael J. Petrilli, Linda A. Renzulli, Christopher Bonastia, and Maria Paino. 2013. "Charter Schools." *Contexts* 12(3):16–25.

Barker, John, and Susie Weller. 2003. "Is It Fun? Developing Children Centred Research Methods." *International Journal of Sociology and Social Policy* 23(1–2):33–58.

Barnes, Riché J. Daniel. 2016. *Raising the Race: Black Career Women Redefine Marriage, Motherhood, and Community*. New Brunswick, NJ: Rutgers University Press.

Beck, Ulrich. 1992. *Risk Society: Towards a New Modernity*. London: Sage.

Bell, Ann V. 2014. *Misconception: Social Class and Infertility in America*. New Brunswick, NJ: Rutgers University Press.

Benard, Stephen, and Shelley J. Correll. 2010. "Normative Discrimination and the Motherhood Penalty." *Gender & Society* 24(5):616–646.

Berdahl, Jennifer L., and Sue H. Moon. 2013. "Workplace Mistreatment of Middle Class Workers Based on Sex, Parenthood, and Caregiving." *Journal of Social Issues* 69(2):341–366.

Berends, Mark. 2015. "Sociology and School Choice: What We Know after Two Decades of Charter Schools." *Annual Review of Sociology* 41:159–180.

Bernstein, Robin. 2011. *Racial Innocence: Performing American Childhood from Slavery to Civil Rights*. New York: New York University Press.

Berry, Daina Ramey, and Kali Nicole Gross. 2020. "Black Women's History in the US: Past and Present." *Not Even Past: Resources for Teaching Women's History*, University of Texas at Austin. http://repositories.lib.utexas.edu.

Berry, Susan. 2017. "Homeschool Advocates to Betsy DeVos: We Want to Be Left Alone by Federal Government." *BreitBart*, May 17. www.breitbart.com.

Best, Amy L., ed. 2007. *Representing Youth: Methodological Issues in Critical Youth Studies*. New York: New York University Press.

Bianchi, Suzanne M., and Melissa A. Milkie. 2010. "Work and Family Research in the First Decade of the 21st Century." *Journal of Marriage and Family* 72(3):705–725.

Bianchi, Suzanne M., Melissa A. Milkie, Liana C. Sayer, and John P. Robinson. 2000. "Is Anyone Doing the Housework? Trends in the Gender Division of Household Labor." *Social Forces* 79(1):191–228.

Bianchi, Suzanne M., John P. Robinson, and Melissa A. Milkie. 2006. *Changing Rhythms of American Family Life*. New York: Russell Sage Foundation.

Billingham, Chase M., and Matthew O. Hunt. 2016. "School Racial Composition and Parental Choice: New Evidence on the Preferences of White Parents in the United States." *Sociology of Education* 89(2):99–117.

Billingsley, Andrew. 1994. *Climbing Jacob's Ladder: The Enduring Legacy of African-American Families*. New York: Simon and Schuster.

Blair-Loy, Mary. 2003. *Competing Devotions: Career and Family among Women Executives*. Cambridge, MA: Harvard University Press.

Blair-Loy, Mary, Arlie Hochschild, Allison J. Pugh, Joan C. Williams, and Heidi Hartmann. 2015. "Stability and Transformation in Gender, Work, and Family: Insights from the Second Shift for the Next Quarter Century." *Community, Work and Family* 18(4):435–454.

Blum, Linda M., and Theresa Deussen. 1996. "Negotiating Independent Motherhood: Working-Class African American Women Talk about Marriage and Motherhood." *Gender & Society* 10(2):199–211.

Blume Oeur, Freeden. 2018. *Black Boys Apart: Racial Uplift and Respectability in All-Male Public Schools*. Minneapolis: University of Minnesota Press.

Boeckmann, Irene, Joya Misra, and Michelle Budig. 2015. "Cultural and Institutional Factors Shaping Mothers' Employment and Working Hours in Postindustrial Countries." *Social Forces* 93(4):1301–1333.

Bonilla-Silva, Eduardo. 2015. "More Than Prejudice: Restatement, Reflections, and New Directions in Critical Race Theory." *Sociology of Race and Ethnicity* 1(1):73–87.

———. 2022. *Racism without Racists: Color-Blind Racism and the Persistence of Racial Inequality in America*. 6th ed. Lanhma, MD: Rowman and Littlefield.

Bonilla-Silva, Eduardo, Carla Goar, and David Embrick. 2006. "When Whites Flock Together: The Social Psychology of White Habitus." *Critical Sociology* 32(2–3):229–254.

Bonilla-Silva, Eduardo, and Tukufu Zuberi. 2008. *White Logic, White Methods: Racism and Methodology*. Plymouth, UK: Rowman and Littlefield.

Branch, Enobong Hannah. 2011. *Opportunity Denied: Limiting Black Women to Devalued Work*. New Brunswick, NJ: Rutgers University Press.

Braun, Henry, Lauren Chapman, and Sailesh Vezzu. 2010. "The Black-White Achievement Gap Revisited." *Education Policy Analysis Archives* 18(21):1–99.

Brewer, Loretta. 2001. "Gender Socialization and the Cultural Construction of Elder Caregivers." *Journal of Aging Studies* 15(3):217–235.

Bridges, Tristan. 2022. "Counting Mass Shootings is a National Emergency." *Inequality by (Interior) Design*, May 31. https://inequalitybyinteriordesign.wordpress.com.

Brown, Kimberly Juanita. 2015. *The Repeating Body: Slavery's Visual Resonance in the Contemporary*. Durham, NC: Duke University Press.

Budig, Michelle J., and Paula England. 2001. "The Wage Penalty for Motherhood." *American Sociological Review* 66(2):204–255.

Budig, Michelle J., Joya Misra, and Irene Boeckmann. 2012. "The Motherhood Penalty in Cross-National Perspective: The Importance of Work-Family Policies and Cultural Attitudes." *Social Politics* 19(2):163–193.

Bunyasi, Tehama Lopez. 2015. "Color-Cognizance and Color-Blindness in White America: Perceptions of Whiteness and Their Potential to Predict Racial Policy Attitudes at the Dawn of the Twenty-First Century." *Sociology of Race and Ethnicity* 1(2):209–224.

Burke, Meghan A. 2011. "Discursive Fault Lines: Reproducing White Habitus in a Racially Diverse Community." *Critical Sociology* 38(5):645–668.

Cade, Toni. 1970. "The Pill: Genocide or Liberation" In *The Black Woman: An Anthology*, edited by Toni Cade, 162–169. New York: New American Library.

Cahusac, Emma, and Shireen Kanji. 2014. "Giving Up: How Gendered Organizational Cultures Push Mothers Out." *Gender, Work and Organization* 21(1):57–70.

Calarco, Jessica McCrory. 2018. *Negotiating Opportunities: How the Middle Class Secures Advantages in School*. New York: Oxford University Press.

Calhoun, Ada. 2020. "Gen-X Women Are Caught in a Generational Tug-of-War." *The Atlantic*, January 7. www.theatlantic.com.

Camera, Lauren. 2020. "DeVos Says School Choice Is Coming, Like It or Not." *U.S. News & World Report*, October 20. www.usnews.com.

Carbajal, Paloma Celis. 2020. "From Hispanic to Latine: Hispanic Heritage Month and the Terms That Bind Us." *New York Public Library Blog*, September 29. www.nypl.org.

Carter, Prudence L. 2005. *Keepin' It Real: School Success beyond Black and White*. New York: Oxford University Press.

Carter, Prudence L., and Kevin G. Welner, eds. 2013. *Closing the Opportunity Gap: What America Must Do to Give Every Child an Even Chance*. New York: Oxford University Press.

Centers for Disease Control and Prevention. 2022. "Risk for COVID-19 Infection, Hospitalization, and Death by Race/Ethnicity." Accessed February 28, 2022. www.cdc.gov.

Cha, Youngjoo. 2010. "Reinforcing Separate Spheres: The Effect of Spousal Overwork on Men's and Women's Employment in Dual-Earner Households." *American Sociological Review* 75(2):303–329.

Cha, Youngjoo, and Kim A. Weeden. 2014. "Overwork and the Slow Convergence in the Gender Gap in Wages." *American Sociological Review* 79(3):457–484.

Chatham-Carpenter, April. 1994. "Home vs. Public Schoolers: Differing Social Opportunities." *Home School Researcher* 10(1):15–24.

Charmaz, Kathy. 2014. *Constructing Grounded Theory*. 2nd ed. Thousand Oaks, CA: Sage.

Chesler, Mark A., Melissa Peet, and Todd Sevig. 2003. "Blinded by Whiteness: The Development of White College Students' Racial Awareness." In *White Out: The Continuing Significance of Racism*, edited by Ashely W. Doane and Eduardo Bonilla-Silva, 215–230. New York: Routledge.

Choo, Hae Yeon, and Myra Marx Ferree. 2010. "Practicing Intersectionality in Sociological Research: A Critical Analysis of Inclusions, Interactions, and Institutions in the Study of Inequalities." *Sociological Theory* 28(2):129–149.

Chou, Rosalind S., and Joe R. Feagin. 2008. *The Myth of the Model Minority: Asian Americans Facing Racism*. Oxfordshire: Routledge.

Christopher, Karen. 2012. "Extensive Mothering: Employed Mothers' Constructions of the Good Mother." *Gender & Society* 26(1):73–96.

Clawson, Dan, and Naomi Gerstel. 2014. *Unequal Time: Gender, Class, and Family in Employment Schedules*. New York: Russell Sage Foundation.

Clotfelter, Charles T. 1976. "School Desegregation, 'Tipping,' and Private School Enrollment." *Journal of Human Resources* 11(1):28–50.

———. 2004. "Private Schools, Segregation, and the Southern States." *Peabody Journal of Education* 79(2):74–97.

Cohen, Julie, Ethan Hutt, Rebekah Berlin, and Emily Wiseman. 2022. "The Change We Cannot See: Instructional Quality and Classroom Observation in the Era of Common Core." *Educational Policy*:36(6):1261–1287.

Coleman, James S., Sara D. Kelly, and John A. Moore. 1975. *Trends in School Segregation, 1968–73*. Washington, DC: Urban Institute.

Collins, Caitlyn. 2020. *Making Motherhood Work: How Women Manage Careers and Caregiving*. Princeton, NJ: Princeton University Press.

Collins, Patricia Hill. 1986. "Learning from the Outsider Within: The Sociological Significance of Black Feminist Thought." *Social Problems* 33(6):S14–S32.

———. 1994. "Shifting the Center; Race, Class, and Feminist Theorizing about Motherhood." In *Mothering: Ideology, Experience, and Agency*, edited by Evelyn Nakano Glenn, Grace Chang, and Linda Rennie Forcey, 45–65. New York: Routledge.

———. 2000. *Black Feminist Thought: Knowledge, Consciousness, and the Politics of Empowerment*. New York: Routledge.

———. 2009. *Another Kind of Public Education: Race, Schools, the Media, and Democratic Possibilities*. Boston: Beacon Press.

Collom, Ed. 2005. "The Ins and Outs of Homeschooling: The Determinants of Parental Motivations and Student Achievement." *Education and Urban Society* 37(3):307–335.

Collom, Ed, and Douglas E. Mitchell. 2005. "Home Schooling as a Social Movement: Identifying the Determinants of Homeschoolers' Perceptions." *Sociological Spectrum* 25(3):273–305.

Coontz, Stephanie. 1988. *The Social Origins of Private Life: A History of American Families, 1600–1900*. New York: Verso.

———. 2005. *Marriage, a History: How Love Conquered Marriage*. London: Penguin.

Cooper, Camille Wilson. 2005. "School Choice and the Standpoint of African American Mothers: Considering the Power of Positionality." *Journal of Negro Education* 74(2):174–189.

———. 2007. "School Choice as 'Motherwork': Valuing African American Women's Educational Advocacy and Resistance." *International Journal of Qualitative Studies in Education* 20(5):491–512.

———. 2009. "Parent Involvement, African American Mothers, and the Politics of Educational Care." *Equity and Excellence in Education* 42(4):379–394.

Cooper, Marianne. 2008. "The Inequality of Security: Winners and Losers in the Risk Society." *Human Relations* 61(9):1229–1258.

———. 2014. *Cut Adrift: Families in Insecure Times*. Berkeley: University of California Press.

Corsaro, William A. 2011. *The Sociology of Childhood*. 3rd ed. Thousand Oaks, CA: Pine Forge Press.

Coughlan, Ryan W. 2018. "Divergent Trends in Neighborhood and School Segregation in the Age of School Choice." *Peabody Journal of Education* 93(4):349–366.

Cowen, Joshua M., David J. Fleming, John F. Witte, Patrick J. Wolf, and Brian Kisida. 2013. "School Vouchers and Student Attainment: Evidence from a State-Mandated Study of Milwaukee's Parental Choice Program." *Policy Studies Journal* 41(1):147–168.

Cray, Kate. 2022. "America Is Desperate for Substitute Teachers." *The Atlantic*, January 27. www.theatlantic.com.

Cucchiara, Maia. 2013. "'Are We Doing Damage?': Choosing an Urban Public School in an Era of Parental Anxiety." *Anthropology and Education Quarterly* 44(1):75–93.

Curran, Dean. 2013. "Risk Society and the Distribution of Bads: Theorizing Class in the Risk Society." *British Journal of Sociology* 64(1):44–62.

Damaske, Sarah. 2011. *For the Family? How Class and Gender Shape Women's Work*. New York: Oxford University Press.

Davies, Scott, and Linda Quirke. 2007. "The Impact of Sector on School Organizations: Institutional and Market Logics." *Sociology of Education* 80(1):66–89.

Davis, Angela. 1990. "Racism, Birth Control, and Reproductive Rights." In *From Abortion to Reproductive Freedom: Transforming a Movement*, edited by Marlene Gerber Fried, 15–26. Boston: South End Press.

———. 2003. *Are Prisons Obsolete?* New York: Seven Stories Press.

Davis, Lisa Selin. 2021. "It's 2021. Why Is 'Supermom' Still Around?" *New York Times*, June 4. www.nytimes.com.

Dean, Paul, Kris Marsh, and Bart Landry. 2013. "Cultural Contradiction or Integration? Work-Family Schemas of Black Middle Class Mothers." *Advances in Gender Research* 17:137–158.

Delpit, Lisa. 1995. *Other People's Children: Cultural Conflict in the Classroom*. New York: New Press.

de Oliveira, Paulo C. M., Timothy G. Watson, and Joe P. Sutton. 1994. "Differences in Critical Thinking Skills among Students Educated in Public Schools, Christian Schools, and Home Schools." *Home School Researcher* 10(4):1–8.

DeSilver, Drew. 2014. "Why Timely, Reliable Data on Mass Killings Is Hard to Find." Washington, DC: Pew Research Center.

Dill, Bonnie Thornton. 1994. "Fictive Kin, Paper Sons, and Compadrazgo: Women of Color and the Struggle for Family Survival." In *Women of Color in U.S. Society*, edited by Maxine Baca Zinn and Bonnie Thornton Dill, 149–169. Philadelphia: Temple University Press.

DiTomaso, Nancy. 2013. *The American Non-dilemma: Racial Inequality without Racism*. New York: Russell Sage Foundation.

DiTomaso, Nancy, Rochelle Parks-Yancy, and Corinne Post. 2011. "White Attitudes toward Equal Opportunity and Affirmative Action." *Critical Sociology* 37(5):615–629.

Doan, Long, and Natasha Quadlin. 2019. "Partner Characteristics and Perceptions of Responsibility for Housework and Child Care." *Journal of Marriage and Family* 81(1):145–163.

Dougherty, Jack, Jeffrey Harrelson, Laura Maloney, Drew Murphy, Russell Smith, Michael Snow, and Diane Zannoni. 2009. "School Choice in Suburbia: Test Scores, Race, and Housing Markets." *American Journal of Education* 115(4):523–548.

Dow, Dawn Marie. 2016a. "Caring for Them Like Family: How Structure and Culture Simultaneously Influence Contemporary African American Middle- and Upper-Middle-Class Mothers' Kin and Community Child Care Choices." *Sociology of Race and Ethnicity* 2(1):72–86.

———. 2016b. "The Deadly Challenges of Raising African American Boys: Navigating the Controlling Image of the 'Thug.'" *Gender & Society* 30(2):161–188.

———. 2016c. "Integrated Motherhood: Beyond Hegemonic Ideologies of Motherhood." *Journal of Marriage and Family* 78(1):180–196.

———. 2019. *Mothering While Black: Boundaries and Burdens of Middle-Class Parenthood*. Oakland: University of California Press.

Downey, Douglas B., and Shana Pribesh. 2004. "When Race Matters: Teachers' Evaluations of Students' Classroom Behavior." *Sociology of Education* 77(4):267–282.

Du Bois, W. E. B. (1903) 1989. *The Souls of Black Folk: Essays and Sketches*. New York: Bantam Books.

Duffy, Mignon. 2005. "Reproducing Labor Inequalities: Challenges for Feminists Conceptualizing Care at the Intersections of Gender, Race, and Class." *Gender & Society* 19(1):66–82.

Duhaney, Patrina. 2022. "Why Does Critical Race Theory Make People So Uncomfortable?" *The Conversation*, March 8. https://theconversation.com.

Dumais, Susan A. 2019. "The Cultural Practices of First-Generation College Graduates: The Role of Childhood Cultural Exposure." *Poetics* 77(December):1–14.

Dumais, Susan A., and Aaryn Ward. 2010. "Cultural Capital and First-Generation College Success." *Poetics* 38(3):245–265.

Dwyer, James G., and Shawn F. Peters. 2019. *Homeschooling: The History and Philosophy of a Controversial Practice*. Chicago: University of Chicago Press.

Edin, Kathryn, Maria Kefalas, and Frank Furstenberg. 2011. *Promises I Can Keep: Why Poor Women Put Motherhood before Marriage, with a New Preface*. Berkeley: University of California Press.

Ehrenreich, Barbara, and Arlie Russell Hochschild. 2003. *Global Woman: Nannies, Maids, and Sex Workers in the New Economy*. New York: Metropolitan Books.

Emerson, Michael O., Karen J. Chai, and George Yancey. 2001. "Does Race Matter in Residential Segregation? Exploring the Preferences of White Americans." *American Sociological Review* 66(6):922–935.

England, Paula. 2010. "The Gender Revolution: Uneven and Stalled." *Gender & Society* 24 (2):149–166.

———. 2011. "Missing the Big Picture and Making Much Ado about Almost Nothing: Recent Scholarship on Gender and Household Work." *Journal of Family Theory and Review* 3(1):23–26.

England, Paula, Michelle Budig, and Nancy Folbre. 2002. "Wages of Virtue: The Relative Pay of Care Work." *Social Problems* 49(4):455–473.

Epstein, Joyce L. 1995. "School/Family/Community Partnerships: Caring for the Children We Share." *Phi Delta Kappan* 76(9):701–712.

Esposito, Cynthia. 1999. "Learning in Urban Blight: School Climate and Its Effect on the School Performance of Urban, Minority, Low-Income Children." *School Psychology Review* 28(3):365–377.

Everytown for Gun Safety. 2021. "Twelve Years of Mass Shootings in the United States." *Everytown Research & Policy*, June 4. https://everytownresearch.org/.

Farkas, George, and Paul L. Morgan. 2018. "Risk and Race in Measuring Special Education Need." *Contexts* 17(4):72–74.

Farley, Reynolds, Toni Richards, and Clarence Wurdock. 1980. "School Desegregation and White Flight: An Investigation of Competing Models and Their Discrepant Findings." *Sociology of Education* 53(3):123–139.

Feagin, Joseph R., and Melvin P. Sikes. 1994. *Living with Racism: The Black Middle-Class Experience*. Boston: Beacon Press.

Ferguson, Ann Arnett. 2000. *Bad Boys: Public Schools in the Making of Black Masculinity*. Ann Arbor: University of Michigan Press.

Fields-Smith, Cheryl, and Monica Wells Kisura. 2013. "Resisting the Status Quo: The Narratives of Black Homeschoolers in Metro-Atlanta and Metro-DC." *Peabody Journal of Education* 88(3):265–283.

Fisher, Berenice, and Joan Tronto. 1990. "Toward a Feminist Theory of Caring." In *Circles of Care: Work and Identity in Women's Lives*, edited by Emily K. Abel and Margaret K. Nelson, 35–62. Albany: State University of New York Press.

Florian, Sandra M. 2018. "Motherhood and Employment among Whites, Hispanics, and Blacks: A Life Course Approach." *Journal of Marriage and Family* 80(1):134–149.

Folbre, Nancy. 2001. *The Invisible Heart: Economics and Family Values*. New York: New Press.

Folbre, Nancy, and Julie A. Nelson. 2000. "For Love or Money—Or Both?" *Journal of Economic Perspectives* 14(4):123–140.

Fong, Kelley, and Sarah Faude. 2018. "Timing Is Everything: Late Registration and Stratified Access to School Choice." *Sociology of Education* 91(3):242–262.

Frankenberg, Erica, and Gary Orfield, eds. 2012. *The Resegregation of Suburban Schools: A Hidden Crisis in American Education*. Cambridge, MA: Harvard Education Press.

Frankenberg, Ruth. 2001. "The Mirage of an Unmarked Whiteness." In *The Making and Unmaking of Whiteness*, edited by Birgit Brander Rasmussen, Eric Klinenberg, Irene J. Nexica, and Matt Wray, 72–96. Durham, NC: Duke University Press.

Frazier, E. Franklin. 1957. *Black Bourgeoisie*. New York: Simon and Schuster.

Frederique, Nadine. 2020. "What Do the Data Reveal about Violence in Schools." November 13. National Institute of Justice. https://nij.ojp.gov/.

Freire, Paulo. 1970. *Pedagogy of the Oppressed*. New York: Bloomsbury Publishing.

Friedman, Hilary Levey. 2013. *Playing to Win: Raising Children in a Competitive Culture*. Berkeley: University of California Press.

Gaither, Milton. (2008) 2017. *Homeschool: An American History*. New York: Palgrave Macmillan.

Gallagher, Charles A. 2003. "Color-Blind Privilege: The Social and Political Functions of Erasing the Color Line in Post Race America." *Race, Gender and Class* 10(4):22–37.

Galloway, Rhonda A. Scott, and Joe P. Sutton. 1995. "Home Schooled and Conventionally Schooled High School Graduates: A Comparison of Aptitude for and Achievement in College English." *Home School Researcher* 11(1):1–9.

Garland, David. 2001. *The Culture of Control: Crime and Social Order in Contemporary Society*. Chicago: University of Chicago Press.

Gerson, Kathleen. 2009. *The Unfinished Revolution: How a New Generation Is Reshaping Family, Work, and Gender in America*. New York: Oxford University Press.

Gerson, Kathleen, and Sarah Damaske. 2021. *The Science and Art of Interviewing*. New York: Oxford University Press.

Gerstel, Naomi. 2011. "Rethinking Families and Community: The Color, Class, and Centrality of Extended Kin Ties." *Sociological Forum* 26(1):1–20.

Giddens, Anthony. 1991. *Modernity and Self-Identity: Self and Society in the Late Modern Age*. Stanford, CA: Stanford University Press.

Giddings, Paula. 1984. *When and Where I Enter: The Impact of Black Women on Race and Sex in America*. New York: William Morrow.

Giles, Melinda Vandenbeld, ed. 2014. *Mothering in the Age of Neoliberalism*. Bradford, ON: Demeter Press.

Gill, Brian P., P. Michael Timpane, Karen E. Ross, and Dominic J. Brewer. 2001. *Rhetoric versus Reality: What We Know and What We Need to Know about Vouchers and Charter Schools*. Santa Monica, CA: Rand Education.

Ginwright, Shawn A. 2002. "Classed Out: The Challenges of Social Class in Black Community Change." *Social Problems* 49(4):544–562.

Glaser, Barney, and Anslem Strauss. 1967. *The Discovery of Grounded Theory Strategies for Qualitative Research*. Chicago: Aldine.

Glauber, Rebecca. 2007. "Marriage and the Motherhood Wage Penalty among African Americans, Hispanics, and Whites." *Journal of Marriage and Family* 69(4):951–961.

Glenn, Evelyn Nakano. 1992. "From Servitude to Service Work: Historical Continuities in the Racial Division of Paid Reproductive Labor." *Signs* 18(1):1–43.

Glenn, Evelyn Nakano, Grace Chang, and Linda Rennie Forcey. 1994. *Mothering: Ideology, Experience, and Agency*. New York: Routledge.

Goff, Phillip Atiba, Matthew Christian Jackson, Brooke Allison Lewis Di Leone, Carmen Marie Culotta, and Natalie Ann DiTomasso. 2014. "The Essence of Innocence: Consequences of Dehumanizing Black Children." *Journal of Personality and Social Psychology* 106(4):526–545.

Golann, Joanne W. 2015. "The Paradox of Success at a No-Excuses School." *Sociology of Education* 88(2):103–119.

Goldring, Ellen B., and Kristie J. R. Phillips. 2008. "Parent Preferences and Parent Choices: The Public-Private Decision about School Choice." *Journal of Education Policy* 23(3):209–230.

Goyette, Kimberly A. 2017. *Education in America*. Oakland: University of California Press.

Grant, Julia. 1998. *Raising Baby by the Book: The Education of American Mothers*. New Haven, CT: Yale University Press.

Gray, Steven. 1993. "Why Some Parents Choose to Home School." *Home School Researcher* 9(4):1–12.

Griffith, Alison I., and Dorothy E. Smith. 2005. *Mothering for Schooling*. New York: Routledge.

Griswold, Robert L. 1993. *Fatherhood in America: A History*. New York: Basic Books.

Gutman, Herbert G. 1976. *The Black Family in Slavery and Freedom: 1750–1925*. New York: Random House.

Hagerman, Margaret Ann. 2014. "White Families and Race: Colour-Blind and Colour-Conscious Approaches to White Racial Socialization." *Ethnic and Racial Studies* 37(14):2598–2614.

———. 2016. "Reproducing and Reworking Colorblind Racial Ideology: Acknowledging Children's Agency in the White Habitus." *Sociology of Race and Ethnicity* 2(1):58–71.

———. 2018. *White Kids: Growing Up with Privilege in a Racially Divided America*. New York: New York University Press.

Hansen, Karen V. 2005. *Not-So-Nuclear Families: Class, Gender, and Networks of Care*. Piscataway, NJ: Rutgers University Press.

Hartman, Saidiya. 2007. *Lose Your Mother: A Journey along the Atlantic Slave Route*. New York: Farrar, Straus and Giroux.

Hartmann, Heidi I. 1981. "The Family as the Locus of Gender, Class, and Political Struggle: The Example of Housework." *Signs* 6(3):366–394.

Hattery, Angela J. 2001. "Tag-Team Parenting: Costs and Benefits of Utilizing Non-overlapping Shift Work in Families with Young Children." *Families in Society: The Journal of Contemporary Human Services* 82(4):419–427.

Hatton, Barbara R. 1977. "Schools and Black Community Development: A Reassessment of Community Control." *Education and Urban Society* 9(2):215–233.

Hays, Sharon. 1996. *The Cultural Contradictions of Motherhood*. New Haven, CT: Yale University Press.

Hegewisch, Ariane, Claudia Williams, Heidi Hartmann, and Stephanie Keller Hu-diburg. 2014. *The Gender Wage Gap 2013: Differences by Race and Ethnicity, No Growth in Real Wages for Women*. Washington, DC: Institute for Women's Policy Research.

Heidenry, Margaret. 2011. "My Parents Were Home-Schooling Anarchists." *New York Times*, November 13. www.nytimes.com.

Hemez, Paul, John J. Brent, and Thomas J. Mowen. 2019. "Exploring the School-to-Prison Pipeline: How School Suspensions Influence Incarceration during Young Adulthood." *Youth Violence and Juvenile Justice* 18(3):235–255.

Hesse-Biber, Sharlene Nagy. 2007. *Handbook of Feminist Research: Theory and Praxis*. Thousand Oaks, CA: Sage.

Hibel, Jacob, George Farkas, and Paul L. Morgan. 2010. "Who Is Placed into Special Education?" *Sociology of Education* 83(4):312–332.

Hill, Leah. 2017. "Disrupting the Trajectory: Representing Disabled African American Boys in a System Designed to Send Them to Prison." *Fordham Urban Law Journal* 45(1):201–239.

Hill, Shirley A. 2001. "Class, Race, and Gender Dimensions of Child Rearing in African American Families." *Journal of Black Studies* 31(4):494–508.

Hinnant-Crawford, Brandi N. 2019. "Legislating Instruction in Urban Schools: Unin-tended Consequences of Accountability Policy on Teacher-Reported Classroom Goal Structures." *Urban Education*, April 2. doi.org/10.1177/0042085919838004.

Hochschild, Arlie. 1989. *The Second Shift: Working Families and the Revolution at Home*. New York: Penguin Group.

———. 1998. *The Managed Heart: Commercialization of Human Feeling*. Berkeley: University of California Press.

Hoff, Erika, Brett Laursen, and Twila Tardif. 2002. "Socioeconomic Status and Parent-ing." In *Handbook of Parenting*. Vol. 2, *Biology and Ecology of Parenting*, edited by Marc H. Bornstein, 231–253. Mahwah, NJ: Lawrence Erlbaum.

Hofferth, Sandra, David Kinney, and Janet Dunn. 2009. "The Hurried Child: Myth vs. Reality." In *Life Balance: Multidisciplinary Theories and Research*, edited by Kathleen Matuska and Charles Christiansen, 183–206. Bethesda, MD: AOTA Press.

Hofferth, Sandra L., and John F. Sandberg. 2001. "How American Children Spend Their Time." *Journal of Marriage and Family* 63(2):295–308.

Holme, Jennifer Jellison. 2002. "Buying Homes, Buying Schools: School Choice and the Social Construction of School Quality." *Harvard Educational Review* 72(2):177–205.

Homeschool Legal Defense Association. 2022. "Homeschool Laws by State." Accessed May 2, 2022. https://hslda.org.

Hondagneu-Sotelo, Pierrette, and Ernestine Avila. 1997. "I'm Here but I'm There: The Meanings of Latina Transnational Motherhood." *Gender & Society* 11(5):548–571.

Horsman, Reginald. 1986. *Race and Manifest Destiny: The Origins of American Racial Anglo-Saxonism*. Cambridge, MA: Harvard University Press.

Hossain, Ziarat, and Jaipaul L. Roopnarine. 1993. "Division of Household Labor and Child Care in Dual-Earner African-American Families with Infants." *Sex Roles* 29:571–583.

Huang, Shu-Yi. 2019. *Being a Mother in a Strange Land: Motherhood Experiences of Chinese Migrant Women in the Netherlands*. Newcastle upon Tyne: Cambridge Scholars Publishing.

Hughey, Matthew W. 2012. "Color Capital, White Debt, and the Paradox of Strong White Racial Identities." *Du Bois Review* 9(1):169–200.

Hunter, Marcus Anthony, and Zandria F. Robinson. 2018. *Chocolate Cities: The Black Map of American Life*. Oakland: University of California Press.

Hursh, David. 2007. "Assessing No Child Left Behind and the Rise of Neoliberal Education Policies." *American Educational Research Journal* 44(3):493–518.

Huseman, Jessica. 2015. "The Rise of Homeschooling among Black Families." *The Atlantic*, February 17. www.theatlantic.com.

Ingersoll, Hannah. 2019. "Legally a Lady." *Contexts* 18(3):20–25.

Ispa-Landa, Simone. 2013. "Gender, Race, and Justifications for Group Exclusion: Urban Black Students Bussed to Affluent Suburban Schools." *Sociology of Education* 86(3):218–233.

Jackson, Pamela Irving. 1978. "Community Control, Community Mobilization, and Community Political Structure in 57 U.S. Cities." *Sociological Quarterly* 19(4):577–589.

Jacobs, Jerry A., and Kathleen Gerson. 2004. *The Time Divide: Work, Family and Gender Inequality*. Cambridge, MA: Harvard University Press.

Jenkins, Toni P. 1998. "The Performance of Home-Schooled Students in Community Colleges." PhD diss., Texas A&M University.

Jennings, Jennifer L. 2010. "School Choice or Schools' Choice? Managing in an Era of Accountability." *Sociology of Education* 83(3):227–247.

Jiménez, Tomás R., and Adam L. Horowitz. 2013. "When White Is Just Alright: How Immigrants Redefine Achievement and Reconfigure the Ethnoracial Hierarchy." *American Sociological Review* 78(5):849–871.

Johnston, Joseph B. 2014. "Resisting Charters: A Comparative Policy Development Analysis of Washington and Kentucky, 2002–2012." *Sociology of Education* 87(4):223–240.

Jones, Jacqueline. 2010. *Labor of Love, Labor of Sorrow: Black Women, Work, and the Family, from Slavery to the Present*. New York: Basic Books.

Jones, Nikki. 2009. *Between Good and Ghetto: African American Girls and Inner-City Violence*. Piscataway, NJ: Rutgers University Press.

Kahlenberg, Richard D. 2012. "From All Walks of Life: New Hope for School Integration." *American Educator* 36(4):2–14.

Kamenetz, Anya. 2020. "DeVos to Use Coronavirus Relief Funds for Home Schooling 'Microgrants.'" National Public Radio, April 29. www.npr.org.

Kamo, Yoshinori, and Ellen L. Cohen. 1998. "Division of Household Work between Partners: A Comparison of Black and White Couples." *Journal of Comparative Family Studies* 29(1):131–145.

Kantor, Harvey, and Robert Lowe. 2006. "From New Deal to No Deal: No Child Left Behind and the Devolution of Responsibility for Equal Opportunity." *Harvard Educational Review* 76(4):474–502.

Katsiyannis, Antonis, Denise K. Whitford, and Robin Parks Ennis. 2018. "Historical Examination of United States Intentional Mass School Shootings in the 20th and 21st Centuries: Implications for Students, Schools, and Society." *Journal of Child and Family Studies* 27(8):2562–2573.

Katusic, Slavica K., Robert C. Colligan, William J. Barbaresi, Daniel J. Schaid, and Steven J. Jacobsen. 2001. "Incidence of Reading Disability in a Population-Based Birth Cohort, 1976–1982, Rochester, Minn." *Mayo Clinical Proceedings* 76(11):1081–1092.

Kaufman, Jason, and Jay Gabler. 2004. "Cultural Capital and the Extracurricular Activities of Girls and Boys in the College Attainment Process." *Poetics* 32(2):145–168.

Khan, Shamus Rahman. 2011. *Privilege: The Making of an Adolescent Elite at St. Paul's School*. Princeton, NJ: Princeton University Press.

Kimelberg, Shelley McDonough. 2014. "Middle-Class Parents, Risk, and Urban Public Schools." In *Choosing Homes, Choosing Schools*, edited by Annette Lareau and Kimberly A. Goyette, 207–235. New York: Russell Sage Foundation.

King, Ryan, and Marc Schindler. 2021. "Reconsidering Police in Schools." *Contexts* 20(4):28–33.

Kleitz, Bretten, Gregory R. Weiher, Kent Tedin, and Richard Matland. 2000. "Choice, Charter Schools, and Household Preferences." *Social Science Quarterly* 81(3):846–854.

Kossek, Ellen Ernst, Leslie B. Hammer, Erin L. Kelly, and Phyllis Moen. 2014. "Designing Work, Family and Health Organizational Change Initiatives." *Organizational Dynamics* 43(1):53–63.

Lacy, Karyn R. 2004. "Black Spaces, Black Places: Strategic Assimilation and Identity Construction in Middle-Class Suburbia." *Ethnic and Racial Studies* 27(6):908–930.

———. 2007. *Blue-Chip Black: Race, Class, and Status in the New Black Middle Class*. Berkeley: University of California Press.

Lambert, Susan. 2008. "Passing the Buck: Labor Flexibility Practices That Transfer Risk onto Hourly Workers." *Human Relations* 61(9):1203–1227.

Landry, Bart. 1978. "A Reinterpretation of the Writings of Frazier on the Black Middle Class." *Social Problems* 26(2):211–222.

———. 2002. *Black Working Wives: Pioneers of the American Family Revolution*. Berkeley: University of California Press.

Landry, Bart, and Kris Marsh. 2011. "The Evolution of the New Black Middle Class." *Annual Review of Sociology* 37:373–394.

Lareau, Annette. 2011. *Unequal Childhoods: Class, Race, and Family Life*. Berkeley: University of California Press.

Lareau, Annette, and Kimberly A. Goyette. 2014. *Choosing Homes, Choosing Schools*. New York: Russell Sage Foundation.

Lareau, Annette, and Elliott B. Weininger. 2008. "Time, Work, and Family Life: Re-conceptualizing Gendered Time Patterns through the Case of Children's Organized Activities." *Sociological Forum* 23(3):419–454.

Levy, Tal. 2009. "Homeschooling and Racism." *Journal of Black Studies* 39(6):905–923.

Lewis, Amanda E. 2003. *Race in the Schoolyard: Negotiating the Color Line in Classrooms and Communities*. New Brunswick, NJ: Rutgers University Press.

Lewis, Amanda E., and John B. Diamond. 2015. *Despite the Best Intentions: How Racial Inequality Thrives in Good Schools*. New York: Oxford University Press.

Lindemann, Danielle. 2022. "What Reality TV Reveals about Motherhood." *The Atlantic*, February 13. www.theatlantic.com.

Lipman, Pauline. 2003. "Chicago School Policy: Regulating Black and Latino Youth in the Global City." *Race, Ethnicity and Education* 6(4):331–355.

Litwak, Eugene, and Ivan Szelenyi. 1969. "Primary Group Structures and Their Functions: Kin, Neighbors, and Friends." *American Sociological Review* 34(4):465–481.

Logan, John R., and Deirdre Oakley. 2004. *The Continuing Legacy of the Brown Decision: Court Action and School Segregation, 1960–2000*. Albany, NY: Lewis Mumford Center for Comparative Urban and Regional Research, University at Albany.

Logan, John R., Weiwei Zhang, and Deirdre Oakley. 2017. "Court Orders, White Flight, and School District Segregation, 1970–2010." *Social Forces* 95(3):1049–1075.

Lois, Jennifer. 2013. *Home Is Where the School Is: The Logic of Homeschooling and the Emotional Labor of Mothering*. New York: New York University Press.

Luker, Kristin. 2008. *Salsa Dancing into the Social Sciences: Research in an Age of Info-Glut*. Cambridge, MA: Harvard University Press.

Lyon, Dawn, and Miriam Glucksmann. 2008. "Comparative Configurations of Care Work across Europe." *Sociology* 42(1):101–118.

Macdonald, Cameron Lynne. 2010. *Shadow Mothers: Nannies, Au Pairs, and the Micropolitics of Mothering*. Berkeley: University of California Press.

Mann, Susan A., and Lori R. Kelley. 1997. "Standing at the Crossroads of Modernist Thought: Collins, Smith, and the New Feminist Epistemologies." *Gender & Society* 11(4):391–408.

Manning, Alex. 2019. "The Age of Concerted Cultivation: A Racial Analysis of Parental Repertoires and Childhood Activities." *Du Bois Review* 16(1):5–35.

Martin, Lori Latrice. 2010. "Strategic Assimilation or Creation of Symbolic Blackness: Middle-Class Blacks in Suburban Contexts." *Journal of African American Studies* 14(2):234–246.

Massey, Douglas S., and Nancy A. Denton. 1993. *American Apartheid: Segregation and the Making of the Underclass*. Cambridge, MA: Harvard University Press.

Mayberry, Maralee. 1988. "Characteristics and Attitudes of Families Who Homeschool." *Education and Urban Society* 21(1):32–41.

Mazama, Ama. 2016. "African American Homeschooling Practices: Empirical Evidence." *Theory and Research in Education* 14(1):26–44.

Mazama, Ama, and Garvey Lundy. 2012. "African American Homeschooling as Racial Protectionism." *Journal of Black Studies* 43(7):723–748.

McCann, Carole R. 1994. *Birth Control Politics in the United States, 1916–1945*. Ithaca, NY: Cornell University Press.

McClelland, Katherine, and Erika Linnander. 2006. "The Role of Contact and Information in Racial Attitude Change among White College Students." *Sociological Inquiry* 76(1):81–115.

McCulloch, Donald S., Sarah Slocum, Cadia Kolegue, and Sarah Montaudo. 2006. "Cynicism, Trust, and Internal-External Locus of Control among Home Educated Students." *Academic Leadership* 4(4):1–4.

McGuinn, Patrick. 2012. "Stimulating Reform: Race to the Top, Competitive Grants and the Obama Education Agenda." *Educational Policy* 26(1):136–159.

Medlin, Richard G. 2000. "Home Schooling and the Question of Socialization." *Peabody Journal of Education* 75(1–2):107–123.

Meiners, Erica R. 2007. *Right to Be Hostile: Schools, Prisons, and the Making of Public Enemies*. New York: Routledge.

Mendez, Linda. 2003. "Predictors of Suspension and Negative School Outcomes: A Longitudinal Investigation." *New Directions for Youth Development* 99:17–33.

Mervosh, Sarah. 2021. "The Pandemic Hurt These Students the Most." *New York Times*, July 28. www.nytimes.com.

Mills, C. Wright. 1959. *The Sociological Imagination*. New York: Oxford University Press.

Mineo, Liz. 2020. "A Warning on Homeschooling." *Harvard Gazette*, May 15. www.news.harvard.edu.

Misra, Joya, Celeste Vaughan Curington, and Venus Mary Green. 2020. "Methods of Intersectional Research." *Sociological Spectrum* 41(1):9–28.

Moody, Myles. 2016. "From Under-diagnoses to Over-representation: Black Children, ADHD, and the School-to-Prison Pipeline." *Journal of African American Studies* 20(2):152–163.

Moon, Seungsook. 2003. "Immigration and Mothering: Case Studies from Two Generations of Korean Immigrant Women." *Gender & Society* 17(6):840–860.

Moore, Kesha S. 2005. "What's Class Got to Do with It? Community Development and Racial Identity." *Journal of Urban Affairs* 27(4):437–451.

Moore, Valerie. 2001. "'Doing' Racialized and Gendered Age to Organize Peer Relations: Observing Kids in Summer Camp." *Gender & Society* 15(6):835–58.

Morgan, Jennifer L. 2004. *Laboring Women: Reproduction and Gender in New World Slavery*. Philadelphia: University of Pennsylvania Press.

Morris, Edward W. 2012. *Learning the Hard Way: Masculinity, Place, and the Gender Gap in Education*. New Brunswick, NJ: Rutgers University Press.

Morris, Edward W., and Brea L. Perry. 2016. "The Punishment Gap: School Suspension and Racial Disparities in Achievement." *Social Problems* 63(1):68–86.

———. 2017. "Girls Behaving Badly? Race, Gender, and Subjective Evaluation in the Discipline of African American Girls." *Sociology of Education* 90(2):127–148.

Moynihan, Daniel Patrick. (1965) 2003. "The Negro Family: The Case for National Action." In *Welfare: A Documentary History of U.S. Policy and Politics*, edited by Gwendolyn Mink and Rickie Solinger, 226–238. New York: New York University Press.

Muñiz, Julissa O. 2021. "Exclusionary Discipline Policies, School-Police Partnerships, Surveillance Technologies and Disproportionality: A Review of the School to Prison Pipeline Literature." *Urban Review* 53(5):735–760.

Murphy, Joseph. 2014. "The Social and Educational Outcomes of Homeschooling." *Sociological Spectrum* 34(3):244–272.

Mythen, Gabe. 2005. "Employment, Individualization and Insecurity: Rethinking the Risk Society Perspective." *Sociological Review* 53(1):129–149.

National Black Home Educators. 2022. "Our Vision." Accessed March 22, 2022. www .nbhe.net.

National Center for Education Statistics (NECS). ———. 2017a. "Concentration of Public School Students Eligible for Free or Reduced-Price Lunch." Washington, DC: Institute of Education Sciences.

———. 2017b. "Parent and Family Involvement in Education: Results from the National Household Education Surveys Program of 2016." Washington, DC: Institute of Education Sciences.

———. 2019. "Status and Trends in the Education of Racial and Ethnic Groups." Washington, DC: Institute of Education Sciences.

———. 2020a. "Fast Facts: Charter Schools." Washington, DC: Institute of Education Sciences.

———. 2020b. "Private School Enrollment." Washington, DC: Institute of Education Sciences.

———. 2020c. "Racial/Ethnic Enrollment in Public Schools." Washington, DC: Institute of Education Sciences.

Nelson, Margaret K. 2010. *Parenting Out of Control: Anxious Parents in Uncertain Times*. New York: New York University Press.

Neumark, David, ed. 2000. *On the Job: Is Long-Term Employment a Thing of the Past?* New York: Russell Sage Foundation.

Noguera, Pedro A. 2008. *The Trouble with Black Boys: And Other Reflections on Race, Equity, and the Future of Public Education*. San Francisco: Jossey-Bass.

Ochoa, Gilda L. 2013. *Academic Profiling: Latinos, Asian Americans, and the Achievement Gap*. Minneapolis: University of Minnesota Press.

Omi, Michael, and Howard Winant. 1994. *Racial Formation in the United States*. 2nd ed. New York: Routledge.

Orbuch, Terri L. 1997. "People's Accounts Count: The Sociology of Accounts." *Annual Review of Sociology* 23:455–478.

Orfield, Gary. 1983. *Public School Desegregation in the United States, 1968–1980*. Washington, DC: Joint Center for Political Studies.

———. 2001. *Schools More Separate: Consequences of a Decade of Resegregation*. Cambridge, MA: The Civil Rights Project at Harvard University.

Orfield, Gary, Jongyeon Ee, Erica Frankenberg, and Genevieve Siegel-Hawley. 2016. *Brown at 62: School Segregation by Race, Poverty and State*. Los Angeles: The Civil Rights Project at UCLA.

Orfield, Gary, and Chungmei Lee. 2006. *Racial Transformation and the Changing Nature of Segregation*. Cambridge, MA: The Civil Rights Project at Harvard University.

O'Shea, David W. 1977. "Community Control of Urban Schools: Lessons from the Suburban Experience." *Journal of Sociology and Social Welfare* 4(8):1284–1299.

Oswald, Donald P., Al M. Best, Martha J. Coutinho, and Heather A. L. Nagle. 2003. "Trends in the Special Education Identification Rates of Boys and Girls: A Call for Research and Change." *Exceptionality* 11(4):223–237.

Pager, Devah. 2003. "The Mark of a Criminal Record." *American Journal of Sociology* 108(5):937–975.

Parreñas, Rhacel Salazar. 2000. "Migrant Filipina Domestic Workers and the International Division of Reproductive Labor." *Gender & Society* 14(4):560–581.

2010. "Transnational Mothering: A Source of Gender Conflict in the Family." *North Carolina Law Review* 88(5):1825–1856.

———. 2015. *Servants of Globalization: Migration and Domestic Work*. 2nd ed. Stanford, CA: Stanford University Press.

Pattillo, Mary. 2005. "Black Middle-Class Neighborhoods." *Annual Review of Sociology* 31:305–329.

———. 2015. "Everyday Politics of School Choice in the Black Community." *Du Bois Review* 12(1):41–71.

Pattillo-McCoy, Mary. 1999. *Black Picket Fences: Privilege and Peril among the Black Middle Class*. Chicago: University of Chicago Press.

Pedulla, David S., and Sarah Thébaud. 2015. "Can We Finish the Revolution? Gender, Work-Family Ideals, and Institutional Constraint." *American Sociological Review* 80(1):116–139.

Peng, Yinni, and Odalia M. H. Wong. 2013. "Diversified Transnational Mothering via Telecommunication: Intensive, Collaborative, and Passive." *Gender & Society* 27(4):491–513.

Perry-Jenkins, Maureen, and Naomi Gerstel. 2020. "Work and Family in the Second Decade of the 21st Century." *Journal of Marriage and Family* 82(1):420–453.

Pitcher, Erich N., and Riyad A. Shahjahan. 2017. "From Pipelines to Tasting Lemonade: Reconceptualizing College Access." *Educational Studies* 53(3):216–232.

Posey-Maddox, Linn. 2014. *When Middle-Class Parents Choose Urban Schools: Class, Race, and the Challenge of Equity in Public Education*. Chicago: University of Chicago Press.

Prue, Irene M. 1997. "A Nation-Wide Survey of Admissions Personnel's Knowledge, Attitudes, and Experiences with Home Schooled Applicants." PhD diss., University of Georgia.

Pugh, Allison J. 2015. *The Tumbleweed Society: Working and Caring in an Age of Insecurity*. New York: Oxford University Press.

Pyne, Jaymes. 2019. "Suspended Attitudes: Exclusion and Emotional Disengagement from School." *Sociology of Education* 92(1):59–82.

Ramey, David M. 2015. "The Social Structure of Criminalized and Medicalized School Discipline." *Sociology of Education* 88(3):181–201.

Randles, Jennifer. 2020. *Essential Dads: The Inequalities and Politics of Fathering*. Oakland: University of California Press.

Ravitch, Diane. 2010. *The Death and Life of the Great American School System: How Testing and Choice Are Undermining Education*. New York: Basic Books.

Ray, Brian D. 2009. *Home Education Reason and Research: Common Questions and Research-Based Answers about Homeschooling*. Salem, OR: National Home Education Research Institute.

———. 2010. "Academic Achievement and Demographic Traits of Homeschool Students: A Nationwide Study." *Academic Leadership* 8(1):1–32.

Ray, Victor. 2019. "A Theory of Racialized Organizations." *American Sociological Review* 84(1):26–53.

Reardon, Sean F., and Ann Owens. 2014. "60 Years after 'Brown': Trends and Consequences of School Segregation." *Annual Review of Sociology* 40:199–218.

Reich, Jennifer A. 2016. *Calling the Shots: Why Parents Reject Vaccines*. New York: New York University Press.

Renzulli, Linda A., and Lorraine Evans. 2005. "School Choice, Charter Schools, and White Flight." *Social Problems* 52(3):398–418.

Renzulli, Linda A., Heather Macpherson Parrott, and Irenee R. Beattie. 2011. "Racial Mismatch and School Type: Teacher Satisfaction and Retention in Charter and Traditional Public Schools." *Sociology of Education* 84(1):23–48.

Renzulli, Linda A., Regina E. Werum, and Anne-Kathrin Kronberg. 2020. "The Rise of Homeschooling Regulation in the Era of School Choice: Legislative and Judicial Trends, 1972–2009." *Sociological Forum* 35(2):297–322.

Reynolds, Cecil R., Russell J. Skiba, Sandra Graham, Peter Sheras, Jane Close Conoley, and Enedina Garcia-Vazquez. 2008. "Are Zero Tolerance Policies Effective in the Schools? An Evidentiary Review and Recommendations." *American Psychologist* 63(9):852–862.

Rich, Peter M., and Jennifer L. Jennings. 2015. "Choice, Information, and Constrained Options: School Transfers in a Stratified Educational System." *American Sociological Review* 80(5):1069–1098.

Riessman, Catherine Kohler. 1987. "When Gender Is Not Enough: Women Interviewing Women." *Gender & Society* 1(2):172–207.

Rios, Victor M. 2011. *Punished: Policing the Lives of Black and Latino Boys*. New York: New York University Press.

Rizzo, Salvador. 2019. "Betsy DeVos's Claim about Public Funding for Education Freedom Scholarships." *Washington Post*, April 8. www.washingtonpost.com.

Roberts, Dorothy. 1997. *Killing the Black Body: Race, Reproduction, and the Meaning of Liberty*. New York: Vintage Books.

Rocque, Michael. 2010. "Office Discipline and Student Behavior: Does Race Matter?" *American Journal of Education* 116(4):557–581.

———. 2012. "Exploring School Rampage Shootings: Research, Theory, and Policy." *Social Science Journal* 49(3):304–313.

Roda, Allison, and Amy Stuart Wells. 2013. "School Choice Policies and Racial Segregation: Where White Parents' Good Intentions and Privilege Collide." *American Journal of Education* 119(2):261–293.

Romero, Mary. 2011. *The Maid's Daughter: Living Inside and Outside the American Dream.* New York: New York University Press.

Roschelle, Anne R. 1997. *No More Kin: Exploring Race, Class, and Gender in Family Networks.* Thousand Oaks, CA: Sage.

Rose, Stephen J., and Heidi Hartmann. 2004. *Still a Man's Labor Market: The Long-Term Earnings Gap.* Washington, DC: Institute for Women's Policy Research.

Rothstein, Richard. 2015. "The Racial Achievement Gap, Segregated Schools, and Segregated Neighborhoods: A Constitutional Insult." *Race and Social Problems* 7(1):21–30.

Saldaña, Johnny. 2009. *The Coding Manual for Qualitative Researchers.* Thousand Oaks, CA: Sage.

Salem, Dorothy C. 1990. *To Better Our World: Black Women in Organized Reform, 1890–1920.* Brooklyn, NY: Carlson.

Sandberg, Sheryl. 2013. *Lean In: Women, Work, and the Will to Lead.* New York: Random House.

Sarkisian, Natalia, and Naomi Gerstel. 2004. "Kin Support among Blacks and Whites: Race and Family Organization." *American Sociological Review* 69(6):812–837.

Saunders, Mary K. 2009. "Previously Homeschooled College Freshmen: Their First Year Experiences and Persistence Rates." *Journal of College Student Retention: Research, Theory and Practice* 11(1):77–100.

Sawchuk, Stephen. 2021. "School Resource Officers (SROs), Explained." *Education Week,* November 16. www.edweek.org.

Sayer, Liana C. 2005. "Gender, Time and Inequality: Trends in Women's and Men's Paid Work, Unpaid Work and Free Time." *Social Forces* 84(1):285–303.

Sayer, Liana C., Suzanne M. Bianchi, and John P. Robinson. 2004. "Are Parents Investing Less in Children? Trends in Mothers' and Fathers' Time with Children." *American Journal of Sociology* 110(1):1–43.

Schiff, Mara. 2018. "Can Restorative Justice Disrupt the 'School-to-Prison Pipeline'?" *Contemporary Justice Review* 21(2):121–139.

Scott, Janelle T., Genevieve Siegel-Hawley, Elizabeth DeBray, Erica Frankenberg, and Kathryn McDermott. 2020. *An Agenda for Restoring Civil Rights in K-12 Federal Education Policy.* Boulder, CO: National Education Policy Center at UC Boulder.

Shapiro, Thomas M. 2017. *Toxic Inequality: How America's Wealth Gap Destroys Mobility, Deepens the Racial Divide and Threatens Our Future.* New York: Basic Books.

Sharpe, Christina. 2016. *In the Wake: On Blackness and Being.* Durham, NC: Duke University Press.

Shedd, Carla. 2015. *Unequal City: Race, Schools, and Perceptions of Injustice.* New York: Russell Sage Foundation.

Sikkink, David, and Michael O. Emerson. 2008. "School Choice and Racial Segregation in US Schools: The Role of Parents' Education." *Ethnic and Racial Studies* 31(2):267–293.

Silva, Jennifer M. 2013. *Coming Up Short: Working-Class Adulthood in an Age of Uncertainty.* New York: Oxford University Press.

Simon, Clea. 2021. "How COVID Taught America about Inequity in Education." *Harvard Gazette*, July 9. www.news.harvard.edu.

Skiba, Russell J., Robert H. Horner, Choong-Geun Chung, M. Karega Rausch, Seth L. May, and Tary Tobin. 2011. "Race Is Not Neutral: A National Investigation of African American and Latino Disproportionality in School Discipline." *School Psychology Review* 40(1):85–107.

Skiba, Russell J., Robert S. Michael, Abra Carroll Nardo, and Reece L. Peterson. 2002. "The Color of Discipline: Sources of Racial and Gender Disproportionately in School Discipline." *Urban Review* 34(4):317–342.

Smedley, Thomas C. 1992. "Socialization of Home School Children." *Home School Researcher* 8(3):9–16.

Smith, Dorothy E. 1990. *The Conceptual Practices of Power: A Feminist Sociology of Knowledge.* Toronto: University of Toronto Press.

Sojoyner, Damien M. 2013. "Black Radicals Make for Bad Citizens: Undoing the Myth of the School to Prison Pipeline." *Berkeley Review of Education* 4(2):241–263.

Solnit, Rebecca. 2022. "US Mass Shootings Will Continue until the Majority Can Overrule the Minority." *The Guardian*, May 30. www.theguardian.com/.

Sopelsa, Brooke, Tat Bellamy-Walker, and Reuters. 2022. "'Don't Say Gay' Bill: Florida Senate Passes Controversial LGBTQ School Measure." *NBC News*, March 8. www.nbcnews.com.

Sorey, Kellie, and Molly H. Duggan. 2008. "Homeschoolers Entering Community Colleges: Perceptions of Admission Officers." *Journal of College Admission* 200:22–28.

Sprague, Joey. 2005. *Feminist Methodologies for Critical Researchers: Bridging Differences.* Walnut Creek, CA: Rowman and Littlefield.

Stack, Carol. 1974. *All Our Kin: Strategies for Survival in a Black Community.* New York: Harper and Row.

Stambach, Amy, and Miriam David. 2005. "Feminist Theory and Educational Policy: How Gender Has Been 'Involved' in Family School Choice Debates." *Signs* 30(2):1633–1658.

Staples, Robert, and Leanor Boulin Johnson. 1993. *Black Families at the Crossroads: Challenges and Prospects.* San Francisco: Jossey-Bass.

Stevens, Mitchell L. 2001. *Kingdom of Children: Culture and Controversy in the Homeschooling Movement.* Princeton, NJ: Princeton University Press.

Stewart, Mahala Dyer. 2020. "Pushed or Pulled Out? The Racialization of School Choice in Black and White Mothers' (Home) Schooling Decisions for Their Children." *Sociology of Race and Ethnicity* 6(2):254–268.

Stone, Pamela. 2007. *Opting Out? Why Women Really Quit Careers and Move Home.* Berkeley: University of California Press.

Stone, Pamela, and Lisa Ackerly Hernandez. 2013. "The All-or-Nothing Workplace: Flexibility Stigma and 'Opting Out' among Professional-Managerial Women." *Journal of Social Issues* 69(2):235–256.

Strings, Sabrina. 2019. *Fearing the Black Body: The Racial Origins of Fat Phobia.* New York: New York University Press.

Stulberg, Lisa M. 2008. *Race, Schools, and Hope: African Americans and School Choice after Brown.* New York: Teachers College Press.

Suizzo, Marie-Anne, Courtney Robinson, and Erin Pahlke. 2008. "African American Mothers' Socialization Beliefs and Goals with Young Children: Themes of History, Education, and Collective Independence." *Journal of Family Issues* 29(3):287–316.

Sykes, Bryan L., Alex R. Piquero, Jason P. Gioviano, and Nicolas Pittman. 2015. "The School-to-Prison Pipeline in America, 1972–2012." *Oxford Handbooks Online Scholarly Research Reviews,* June 9. www.scholarship.miami.edu

Tatum, Beverly Daniel. 1987. *Assimilation Blues: Black Families in White Communities, Who Succeeds and Why?* New York: Basic Books.

———. 2003. *Why Are All the Black Kids Sitting Together in the Cafeteria? And Other Conversations about Race.* New York: Basic Books.

Taylor, Robert Joseph, Ivy Forsythe-Brown, Karen D. Lincoln, and Linda M. Chatters. 2017. "Extended Family Support Networks of Caribbean Black Adults in the United States." *Journal of Family Issues* 38(4):522–546.

Thébaud, Sarah. 2010. "Masculinity, Bargaining, and Breadwinning: Understanding Men's Housework in the Cultural Context of Paid Work." *Gender & Society* 24(3):330–354.

Tillet, Salamishah. 2012. *Sites of Slavery: Citizenship and Racial Democracy in the Post–Civil Rights Imagination.* Durham, NC: Duke University Press.

Togut, Torin D. 2011. "The Gestalt of the School-to-Prison Pipeline: The Duality of Overrepresentation of Minorities in Special Education and Racial Disparity in School Discipline on Minorities." *American University Journal of Gender, Social Policy and the Law* 20(1):163–181.

Triplett, Nicholas P., Ayana Allen, and Chance W. Lewis. 2014. "Zero Tolerance, School Shootings, and the Post-*Brown* Quest for Equity in Discipline Policy: An Examination of How Urban Minorities Are Punished for White Suburban Violence." *Journal of Negro Education* 83(3):352–370.

Tyson, Karolyn. 2013. "Tracking, Segregation, and the Opportunity Gap: What We Know and Why It Matters." In *Closing the Opportunity Gap: What America Must Do to Give Every Child an Even Chance*, edited by Prudence L. Carter and Kevin G. Welner, 169–180. New York: Oxford University Press.

Underhill, Megan R. 2018. "'Diversity Is Important to Me': White Parents and Exposure-to-Diversity Parenting Practices." *Sociology of Race and Ethnicity* 5(4):486–499.

US Bureau of Labor Statistics. 2020. "Employment Characteristics of Families Summary." Washington, DC: Division of Labor Force Statistics.

Utrata, Jennifer. 2015. *Women without Men: Single Mothers and Family Change in the New Russia*. Ithaca, NY: Cornell University Press.

Uttal, Lynet. 1999. "Using Kin for Child Care: Embedment in the Socioeconomic Networks of Extended Families." *Journal of Marriage and Family* 61(4):845–857.

Van DeBurg, William L. 1992. *New Day in Babylon: The Black Power Movement and American Culture, 1965–1975*. Chicago: University of Chicago Press.

Villalobos, Ana. 2014. *Motherload: Making It All Better in Insecure Times*. Oakland: University of California Press.

Vincent, Carol, and Stephen J. Ball. 2007. "'Making Up' the Middle-Class Child: Families, Activities and Class Dispositions." *Sociology* 41(6):1061–1077.

Vinovskis, Maris A. 2009. *From "A Nation at Risk" to "No Child Left Behind": National Education Goals and the Creation of Federal Education Policy*. New York: Teachers College Press.

Wadhwa, Anita. 2016. *Restorative Justice in Urban Schools: Disrupting the School-to-Prison Pipeline*. New York: Routledge.

Wallace, John M., Jr., Sara Goodkind, Cynthia M. Wallace, and Jerald G. Bachman. 2008. "Racial, Ethnic, and Gender Differences in School Discipline among U.S. High School Students: 1991–2005." *Negro Educational Review* 59(1–2):47–62.

Waterman, Stephanie J., Shelly C. Lowe, and Heather J. Shotton, eds. 2018. *Beyond Access: Indigenizing Programs for Native American Student Success*. Sterling, VA: Stylus Publishing.

Waters, Mary C. 1990. *Ethnic Options: Choosing Identities in America*. Berkeley: University of California Press.

Weinbaum, Alys Eve. 2019. *The Afterlife of Reproductive Slavery: Biocapitalism and Black Feminism's Philosophy of History*. Durham, NC: Duke University Press.

Weininger, Elliot B., Annette Lareau, and Dalton Conley. 2015. "What Money Doesn't Buy: Class Resources and Children's Participation in Organized Extracurricular Activities." *Social Forces* 94(2):479–503.

Welch, Finis, and Andrew Light. 1987. *New Evidence on School Desegregation*. Washington, DC: US Commission on Civil Rights.

Weiss, Robert S. 1994. *Learning from Strangers: The Art and Method of Qualitative Interview Studies*. New York: Free Press.

West, Candace, and Don Zimmerman. 1987. "Doing Gender." *Gender & Society* 1(2):125–151.

White, Amanda M., and Constance T. Gager. 2007. "Idle Hands and Empty Pockets? Youth Involvement in Extracurricular Activities, Social Capital, and Economic Status." *Youth & Society* 39(1):75–111.

Whitty, Geoff. 2002. *Making Sense of Education Policy: Studies in the Sociology and Politics of Education*. London: Paul Chapman Publishing.

Whitty, Geoff, Sally Power, and David Halpin. 1998. *Devolution and Choice in Education: The School, the State, and the Market*. Buckingham: Open University Press.

Wildhagen, Tina. 2009. "Why Does Cultural Capital Matter for High School Academic Performance? An Empirical Assessment of Teacher-Selection and Self-Selection Mechanisms as Explanations of the Cultural Capital Effect." *Sociological Quarterly* 50(1):173–200.

Wilkerson, Isabel. 2010. *The Warmth of Other Suns: The Epic Story of America's Great Migration*. New York: Penguin Random House.

Wilkie, Jane Riblett. 1993. "Changes in U.S. Men's Attitudes toward the Family Provider Role, 1972–1989." *Gender & Society* 7(2):261–279.

Williams, Amber D., Meeta Banerjee, Fantasy Lozada-Smith, Danny Lambouths III, and Stephanie J. Rowley. 2017. "Black Mothers' Perceptions of the Role of Race in Children's Education." *Journal of Marriage and Family* 79(4):932–946.

Williams, Heather Andrea. 2005. *Self-Taught: African American Education in Slavery and Freedom*. Chapel Hill: University of North Carolina Press.

Williams, Joan. 2000. *Unbending Gender: Why Family and Work Conflict and What to Do about It*. New York: Oxford University Press.

Wolf, Kerrin C., and Aaron Kupchik. 2017. "School Suspensions and Adverse Experiences in Adulthood." *Justice Quarterly* 34(3):407–430.

Woody, Ashley. 2020. "'They Want the Spanish but They Don't Want the Mexicans': Whiteness and Consumptive Contact in an Oregon Spanish Immersion School." *Sociology of Race and Ethnicity* 6(1):92–106.

Wooten, Melissa E. 2006. "Race and Strategic Organization." *Strategic Organization* 4(2):191–199.

Wooten, Melissa E., and Lucius Couloute. 2017. "The Production of Racial Inequality within and among Organizations." *Sociology Compass* 11(1):1–10.

Zelizer, Viviana A. 1994. *Pricing the Priceless Child: The Changing Social Value of Children*. Princeton, NJ: Princeton University Press.

———. 2011. *Economic Lives: How Culture Shapes the Economy*. Princeton, NJ: Princeton University Press.

Zimmerman, Mary K., Jacquelyn S. Litt, and Christine E. Bose. 2006. *Global Dimensions of Gender and Carework*. Stanford, CA: Stanford University Press.

INDEX

ABOUT THE AUTHOR

MAHALA DYER STEWART is Assistant Professor of Sociology at Hamilton College. She studies gender, race, and class inequalities in the context of families and schools. She has published her work in several journals and is the coeditor of *Gendered Lives, Sexual Beings: A Feminist Anthology* and *Frameworks of Inequality: An Intersectional Reader*.